St Petersburg, 1703–1825

St Petersburg, 1703–1825

Edited by

Anthony Cross
Department of Slavonic Studies
University of Cambridge

Editorial matter and selection © Anthony Cross 2003
Individual chapters © Palgrave Macmillan Ltd. 2003

All rights reserved. No reproduction, copy or transmission of this publication may be made without written permission.

No paragraph of this publication may be reproduced, copied or transmitted save with written permission or in accordance with the provisions of the Copyright, Designs and Patents Act 1988, or under the terms of any licence permitting limited copying issued by the Copyright Licensing Agency, 90 Tottenham Court Road, London W1T 4LP.

Any person who does any unauthorized act in relation to this publication may be liable to criminal prosecution and civil claims for damages.

The authors have asserted their rights to be identified as the authors of this work in accordance with the Copyright, Designs and Patents Act 1988.

First published 2003 by
PALGRAVE MACMILLAN
Houndmills, Basingstoke, Hampshire RG21 6XS and
175 Fifth Avenue, New York, N.Y. 10010
Companies and representatives throughout the world

PALGRAVE MACMILLAN is the global academic imprint of the Palgrave Macmillan division of St. Martin's Press, LLC and of Palgrave Macmillan Ltd. Macmillan® is a registered trademark in the United States, United Kingdom and other countries. Palgrave is a registered trademark in the European Union and other countries.

ISBN 1–4039–1570–9

This book is printed on paper suitable for recycling and made from fully managed and sustained forest sources.

A catalogue record for this book is available from the British Library.

Library of Congress Cataloging-in-Publication Data
St. Petersburg, 1703–1825 / edited by Anthony Cross.
    p. cm.
    Includes bibliographical references and index.
    ISBN 1–4039–1570–9
    1. Saint Petersburg (Russia) – Civilization – 18th century.
    2. Saint Petersburg (Russia) – Civilization – 19th century.
    I. Cross, Anthony Glenn.

DK557.S685 2003
947′.2108–dc21   2003048234

10 9 8 7 6 5 4 3 2 1
12 11 10 09 08 07 06 05 04 03

Printed and bound in Great Britain by
Antony Rowe Ltd, Chippenham and Eastbourne

Contents

List of Maps and Plates	vii
List of Tables	ix
Acknowledgements	x
Notes on the Contributors	xi
Introduction Anthony Cross	1
1 St Petersburg and Geographies of Modernity in Eighteenth-Century Russia Denis J.B. Shaw	6
2 St Petersburg during the Reign of Anna Ivanovna: The Forbes/Maas Chart and the Evolution of the Early Mapping of the City Michael J. Bitter	30
3 The English Embankment Anthony Cross	50
4 A Venice of the North? Italian Views of St Petersburg Maria Di Salvo	71
5 Compiling and Maintaining St Petersburg's 'Book of City Inhabitants': The 'Real' City Inhabitants George E. Munro	80
6 Governing the City: St Petersburg and Catherine II's Reforms Janet M. Hartley	99
7 Petersburg Actresses On and Off Stage (1775–1825) Wendy Rosslyn	119

8 Peter the Great's St Petersburg in the Works of
  Pavel Svin'in (1787–1839) 148
  Lindsey Hughes

9 *Vreden sever*: The Decembrists' Memories of the
  Peter-Paul Fortress 165
  Patrick O'Meara

Index 190

List of Maps and Plates

1 The Russian Academy of Sciences map of St Petersburg, created in 1737. This first official Russian map of the capital confirms the accuracy of the Forbes/Maas chart of 1734. Courtesy of the James Ford Bell Library, Minneapolis, MN.   31
2 The Forbes/Maas chart of St Petersburg and its environs. Courtesy of the Public Record Office of Northern Ireland (PRONI).   32
3 The Homann map of St Petersburg, variously dated between 1716 and 1725. The map is often used to demonstrate Domenico Trezzini's plan for the development of Vasil'evskii Island. Courtesy of Historic Urban Plans, Ithaca, NY.   37
4 J.B.A. Le Blond's plan for the reconstruction of St Petersburg, 1717. Illustration from A.W. Bunin, *Geschichte des Russischen Städtebaues bis zum 19. Jahrhundert* (Berlin, 1961), no. 110.   38
5 The map of St Petersburg accompanying F.C. Weber's *Das Veränderte Russland* (Frankfurt, 1721), which borrows extensively from the Homann map. Courtesy of the James Ford Bell Library, Minneapolis, MN.   42
6 The 'English Embankment' in the last years of Peter's reign. Detail from anonymous map of c. 1723. Courtesy of Map Collection, Yale University Library.   57
7 The 'English Embankment' on the River Neva, looking downstream from the St Isaac of Dalmatia Church and the pontoon bridge towards Galley Wharf. Drawn by Lespinasse and engraved by Cl. Fessard under the direction of Née, 1784.   60
8 The 'English Embankment', looking upstream from Galley Wharf towards the Admiralty. Drawn by Lespinasse and engraved by Fessard the Elder, 1784.   61

9   The 'English Embankment'. Detail from the map of
    St Petersburg originally prepared by John Truscott
    for the 1753 anniversary album. Engraved by
    P.F. Tardieu, 1784.   63
10 Plan of the Peter-Paul Fortress. Drawn by
    Adam Jan Sadowski.   167

List of Tables

5.1	Building materials	87
5.2	How property was acquired	89
5.3	Social origins of owners by district of town	91
5.4	How women acquired houses or land	95

Acknowledgements

Professor Bitter wishes to acknowledge the permissions to publish maps received from the Public Record Office of Northern Ireland (PRONI), the James Ford Bell Library, Minneapolis, MN, and Historic Urban Plans, Ithaca, NY.

Professor Cross wishes to acknowledge similar permission received from Yale University Library, CT.

Notes on the Contributors

Michael J. Bitter received his PhD from the University of Minnesota and is currently Assistant Professor of History at the University of Hawai'i at Hilo. He is preparing a book on the mission of George, Lord Forbes, as British Envoy to the Russian Court in 1733–34. His other work focuses on the era of Anna Ivanovna and the activities of Western Europeans in eighteenth-century Russia.

Anthony Cross is Professor of Slavonic Studies at the University of Cambridge. He is a specialist on Anglo-Russian cultural relations and on eighteenth-century Russia. Among the many books he has written and edited his *By the Banks of the Neva: Chapters from the Lives and Careers of the British in Eighteenth-Century Russia* was awarded the 1997 Antsiferov Prize as the best book by a foreign author on St Petersburg and will appear in Russian translation in 2003. He is currently working on a book entitled *Petersburg and the British: The City through the Eyes of British Writers and Artists over Three Centuries*.

Janet M. Hartley is Senior Lecturer in International History at the London School of Economics and Political Science. She has written extensively on eighteenth- and early nineteenth-century Russia and her publications include: *Guide to Documents and Manuscripts in the United Kingdom Relating to Russia and the Soviet Union* (1987); *Alexander I* (1994); *A Social History of the Russian Empire, 1659–1825* (1999); and *Charles Whitworth: Diplomat in the Age of Peter the Great* (2002). She is currently writing a book on war, state and society in Russia, 1762–1825.

Lindsey Hughes is Professor of Russian History and Director of the Centre for Russian Studies at the School of Slavonic and East European Studies, University College London. Her more recent major publications include: *Sophia Regent of Russia 1657–1704* (1990), which was awarded the AAASS Heldt Prize; (ed.), *New Perspectives on Muscovite History* (1993); *Russia in the Age of Peter the Great* (1998), which received the BASEES Nove Prize; (ed.), *Peter the Great and the West: New Perspectives* (2000); *Peter the Great: A Biography* (2002).

George E. Munro teaches at Virginia Commonwealth University in Richmond, Virginia. His research focuses on St Petersburg during the reign of Catherine II as well as on larger issues in social and economic life in late eighteenth-century Russia. Among his recent contributions are a study of food consumption in *Food in Russian History and Culture* (1997) and an examination of religious devotion in enlightenment St Petersburg (in *Moscow and Petersburg: The City in Russian Culture*, 2002).

Patrick O'Meara is Associate Professor of Russian at the University of Dublin, Trinity College. He has published a number of articles on the Decembrist Movement and is the author of *K.F. Ryleev: A Political Biography of the Decembrist Poet* (1984; Russian edition, 1989). His study of P.I. Pestel', *Russia's First Republican*, is to be published by Palgrave in 2003.

Wendy Rosslyn is Professor of Russian Literature at the University of Nottingham. Her research on Russian women in the eighteenth century includes books and articles on female poets and translators, notably *Anna Bunina (1774–1829) and the Origins of Women's Poetry in Russia* (1997) and *Feats of Agreeable Usefulness: Translations by Russian Women, 1763–1825* (2000). She is also editor of *Women and Gender in Eighteenth-Century Russia* (Ashgate, forthcoming). Her most recent research is on women's charitable work and voluntary associations in early nineteenth-century Russia.

Maria Di Salvo has taught at the universities of Genoa, Pisa and Pavia and is currently Professor of Slavic Philology at the University of Milan. She has written on the history of Slavonic linguistics, on theory of literature and on Russian literature. Her main area of interest is the history of Italo-Russian relations in the seventeenth and eighteenth centuries.

Denis J.B. Shaw is Reader in Russian Geography in the School of Geography, Earth and Environmental Sciences and Associate Member of the Centre for Russian and East European Studies, University of Birmingham. His major research interests are concerned with the historical geography of early modern Russia, the history of Russian geographical thought, and aspects of the changing geography of contemporary Russia. His principal publications include *Planning in the*

Soviet Union (London, 1981); *Landscape and Settlement in Romanov Russia, 1613–1917* (Oxford, 1990) (both with J. Pallot); and *Russia in the Modern World* (Oxford, 1999). He is co-author (with R.N. Gwynne and T. Klak) of *Alternative Capitalisms: Geographies of Emerging Regions* (London, 2003).

Introduction
Anthony Cross

Cities attract and repel in equal measure, capital cities particularly so. Capitals, like books, have their destinies and none perhaps more melancholy than St Petersburg's. Created to be the centre (in no way geographical) and showpiece of a new Russia, situated as near to the sea as despotic will rather than common sense could command, looking to the West, menacingly or welcomingly as the hour dictated, built and embellished by western or western-schooled architects and artists, Peter's city grew out of the swampy delta of the Neva, flourished, floundered and fell. Moscow, dispossessed capital of 'barbarous Muscovy', bided its time, crowned Russia's emperors and empresses, and regained its lost status by the decree of a man, whose mother had been born in a house on the English Embankment overlooking the Neva and who was also, in death, to deprive Petersburg/Petrograd of its very name. As a capital St Petersburg existed for a little over two centuries (no decree was ever promulgated giving it this status, but after the removal of the court from Moscow in 1712 it was *de facto* and so it remained until March 1918) and as a city it reaches its tercentenary in 2003.

Great cities and capitals have their mythology and for a city so relatively young, St Petersburg has a remarkably rich one. It has its founding myth; it abounds in predictions of doom and gloom, and has made many an attempt to justify Pushkin's words that Peter founded his city beneath the sea. Never sacked like many an ancient capital and never occupied by the enemy, it has nevertheless had its fabric consistently assailed by climate and undermined by jerry-building; it has been been ravaged by revolutionary events and subsequent neglect; it has survived German shelling and bombing; and has more or less weathered the assaults of Soviet planners. Even as I write, fire, the dreaded monster of the early eighteenth-century city, is reported to have raged within the Admiralty building, one of the city's great landmarks that contained within Zakharov's great spire-topped tower Korobov's original of the previous century. And this at a time when the city was emerging from the scaffolding that had surrounded for many months some of its most celebrated monuments and was about to show itself in all its glory. The city has inspired writers and artists down the decades to respond to its beauty and to its legacy – with love and with loathing – and contradictions and contrasts are part of the mysterious 'soul' with which it has been endowed. Much, to be sure, has been written, about these aspects of St Petersburg but they are not the primary concern and substance of the essays that form the present collection.

As a British-inspired tribute to the city's tercentenary, an international conference was held at Fitzwilliam College, Cambridge, at the end of August 2002. The conference, which was principally supported by the Study Group on Eighteenth-Century Russia, respected the chronological boundaries of the 'long eighteenth century' and twenty papers were read on many aspects of the city's culture, history and development within the period 1703–1825. The papers reworked for this collection represent the English-language contributions to the conference: it is a matter of regret that restrictions of time and resources made it impossible to include an equal number of papers delivered in Russian mainly, but not exclusively, by speakers from St Petersburg itself. The English-language papers are the work of established scholars in Britain, Ireland, Italy and the USA, and reflect something of the diversity of research that St Petersburg inspires beyond its boundaries. If matters of architecture and art figure less prominently than might be expected, although Russian scholars indeed spoke of sculpture collections in the Summer Garden and at Tsarskoe Selo, of landscape gardens on the estates along the Peterhof Road, of Quarenghi's project for the redevelopment of the Strelka of Vasil'evskii Island, then there are other areas which receive, by coincidence rather than design, particular emphasis in more than one of the published papers. The papers are therefore ordered in a way that reflects thematic overlap within a general chronological frame.

Denis Shaw's chapter, which provides an admirable opening to the collection, links moves towards modernity embodied in the very act of the city's founding to wider considerations of geographical space, to questions of the relationship between social and spatial change, before focusing on the introduction of European-style cartography, to be based in new institutions and benefiting from imported foreign expertise and direction. It is a wide-ranging and nuanced essay, exploring and exposing the contradictions that are inherent in almost everything posited about St Petersburg.

Cartography is the subject of Michael J. Bitter's chapter. More precisely, it is a newly discovered map or naval chart of the approaches to St Petersburg: seemingly prepared by a Dutch cartographer in Russian service for Lord Forbes, the British envoy who sailed to the Russian capital in 1734, the original chart lay unvisited, if not exactly mouldering, in a drawer in the Irish ancestral castle of the Earls of Granard, until it was unrolled by Professor Bitter, alerted by a photocopy in the Public Record Office of Northern Ireland. He sites the chart and its significance within the context of other early maps of the city on which, more often than not, what was only a planner's dream or project is found superimposed on what actually existed.

What actually happened in a very specific area of St Petersburg, the stretch of the Neva to the west of the Admiralty which became known in Catherine II's time as the English Embankment, prompted my own contribution. It seeks to show how an area which Peter designated as serving the needs of the Admiralty and of its personnel evolved into a fashionable neighbourhood and to integrate the story of the architectural development with an investigation into the appropriateness of the famous appellation.

No less a famous appellation was 'Venice of the North', vying with Amsterdam and ancient Palmyra as apt comparisons for the city Peter located within a network of rivers and wished to intersect further with canals. In a noted book by F.C. Weber, the Hanoverian resident in St Petersburg from 1714 to 1719, to which both Professor Bitter and I refer, Prince Alexander Menshikov is quoted as hoping that 'Petersburg should become another Venice, to see which Foreigners would travel thither purely out of Curiosity'. Maria Di Salvo shows that a series of Italian visitors to the city during the reigns of Anna and Catherine II were certainly drawn by curiosity but were generally hesitant to bestow such an accolade. Perhaps the most sceptical among them was the noted Venetian poet and scholar Francesco Algarotti, who nevertheless spoke of 'the great window, recently opened in the North, through which Russia looks on Europe', lines which Pushkin was to use as the epigraph to his *Bronze Horseman*.

Algarotti visited the city in 1739, but his account appeared in various languages during the reign of the great Catherine, who, as George Munro notes, is said to have remarked that she found a Russia built in wood and left it built in stone. She also sought stability and permanence for her Russia in legislation and it is the consequences for St Petersburg of her Charter to Towns of April 1785 that Professor Munro and Janet Hartley explore in their complementary papers. Professor Munro looks specifically at the requirement to compile and maintain a 'city inhabitants' book' which was to be a record of property ownership and a register of 'townsmen' within the six official categories. No copy of the completed book exists, and it is on the basis of volumes covering the first two letters of the Cyrillic alphabet which he unearthed in the archives that Professor Munro reaches interesting and persuasive conclusions. Archival research is basic to Dr Hartley's far-ranging investigation in the way the city was administered and the creation and functioning of such of its institutions as the municipal *duma* and various courts in the context of the city's distinctive social mix.

Wendy Rosslyn's detailed and fascinating excursion into the lives and loves of actresses of the Petersburg theatres begins in the second decade of Catherine's reign but the weight of evidence inevitably leads to a concentration on the reign of Alexander, when Pushkin and his fellows used the imperial theatres to parade and to applaud and pursue their favoured actresses. Perceptions of the actresses on stage dissolve into the far less known off-stage world in which the actresses, singers and dancers struggled to survive and preserve their virtue or to survive by any means, including, inevitably, prostitution, questions which Professor Rosslyn is perhaps the first among scholars of the Russian theatre to face square-on.

An excursion of the more conventional type is the subject of Lindsey Hughes' chapter. Acknowledged authority on Peter the Great and his time, she uses the eyes of an early nineteenth-century Russian author, Pavel Svin'in, to look back at the architectural legacy of the city's founder. She also considers the emergence of a new genre of Russian guidebooks to the city, written both for Russians and for foreigners (Svin'in's book was published in a bilingual edition) and reflecting an interesting stage in Russian self-awareness.

The collection is concluded with an essay sited at the extreme chronological boundary of our period but dealing with one of the most characteristic and earliest building complexes in the city – the Peter-Paul Fortress, the inevitable target of one of Svin'in's itineraries. He was interested, however, in the cathedral rather than the cells and did not reflect, for instance, on the incarceration in the fortress of the Tsarevich Aleksei Petrovich, which might have cast a shadow on his unblemished father. And volume 3 (of five) was published before the Decembrist Uprising of 14 December 1825. Walls might not speak, but the memoirs written by those who endured the long months from their arrest until July 1826 awaiting their fate in the cells of the fortress are the eloquent providers of the information that Patrick O'Meara mines so deftly. He examines all aspects of the prisoners' imprisonment that provide moments of macabre comedy but, more often, convey bleak despair and deprivation. The death on the scaffold of five Decembrists on 13 July 1826 has moved us into another era beyond 'the long eighteenth century' in the existence of Peter's city.

1
St Petersburg and Geographies of Modernity in Eighteenth-Century Russia

Denis J.B. Shaw

'Russia and Europe,' wrote W. Bruce Lincoln, 'have been firmly linked since the time of Peter the Great. And the point at which they have been joined – whether as friend or foe, cultural allies or intellectual antagonists – has always been St. Petersburg.'[1] Peter the Great's foundation of his new capital city on the shores of the Gulf of Finland has long been seen as symbolic of his desire to modernize his realm and make it into a truly European country. It has also long been seen as an important instrument in the move towards modernity.

It is difficult to think of any real parallel to Peter's momentous act in modern history although, as Robert E. Jones has reminded us, the founding of Alexandria and Constantinople in ancient times may bear some comparison.[2] But this essay seeks to broaden horizons beyond the singular act of a powerful ruler establishing a major new city in an unlikely environment, and ask whether Peter's actions may signal something quite significant about the way human societies change and adapt. More specifically, the essay attempts to consider the city's foundation and early development in the context of the opportunities and challenges posed by geographical space, linking both with the uncertainties and ambiguities which are inherent in the quest for modernity. The second half of the essay attempts to illustrate such uncertainties by briefly exploring one facet of Peter's reforms, namely his policy to introduce European mapping methods to Russia through certain institutions and key individuals who were largely clustered in St Petersburg.

In recent years social scientists, historians and historical geographers have displayed a growing interest in the ways in which social change and spatial change are interlinked and are mutually reinforcing.³ This means more than merely asserting that all social change occurs somewhere, and that social change invariably produces spatial or geographical change. Rather, it is to argue that the understanding of spatial change is vital to an understanding of social change, to an understanding of how and where societal change occurs.⁴ Robert Dodgshon, for example, argues against the assumption, reflected in much social science thinking, that human societies are in general organized to facilitate easy change.⁵ On the contrary, he avers, because human societies exist in a material world, utilize space and must adapt to the material realities which confront them, all face the problem of social inertia, an inertia which is 'geographically emplaced'.⁶ His detailed argument is complex and beyond an adequate exposition in a chapter of this length. Simply put, however, he tries to show that, as societies adapt and seek stability in an ever-challenging world, there is a tendency towards inertia at a number of levels – at the cognitive level, at the level of culture whereby things, traditions and ideas are communicated intergenerationally, at the level of institutions (rules, codes, functions), and at the socio-technical level – the physical and technical means by which society organizes and sustains itself, including its interaction with its built environment.⁷ In these circumstances there is always a tendency for social change to 'use space strategically', to seek out spaces where change can occur with the minimum of resistance. And one of the most obvious spaces where this may be the case is on society's geographical periphery.

Dodgshon and others argue that in relatively organized societies (like early modern Russia under Peter), resistance to change is likely to be greatest at society's organizing centre (in Russia's case, in the capital Moscow). The fact that Peter, desiring radical change, should decide to build a new centre on a *tabula rasa* at the periphery of his realm, far from the inertial influence of the old capital, would therefore be regarded by such scholars as entirely understandable. In various ways, they would argue, analogous processes, involving the strategic use of space, can be seen in all societies.⁸

In these terms, then, St Petersburg can be regarded, in Ogborn's phrase, as a 'space of modernity', a place where Peter's reforms could seemingly be realized.⁹ Historians have debated how far St Petersburg's role as an instrument in the reform of Russia was already formulated in Peter's mind at the moment of the city's foundation, or how far an initially pragmatic decision gradually assumed a wider significance for him. From the point of view of this essay, however, this historical debate is of less interest than the well-known fact that Peter's concern over the city's development never wavered and that he exercised the most detailed scrutiny over every aspect of its life and growth, as if it were indeed the centrepiece of his policies to transform Russia. To use the terminology of Anthony Giddens, St Petersburg was a 'locale', a place where the tsar and his closest associates were continually present, or with which they were able to maintain the closest contact. In these circumstances the exercise of surveillance, regarded by Giddens as a key to the power of the modern state, could be particularly strict.[10]

* * *

Peter's oversight over his new capital took a variety of forms. Thus, to a greater extent than anywhere else in Russia, St Petersburg was the site where, through elaborate 'police' regulation and supervision, the inhabitants could be coerced and cajoled into building and maintaining their homes in the required manner, behaving in ways deemed seemly for the residents of a modern European capital according to their rank, and properly engaging in their civic duties. The unseemly, disorderly and riotous could be removed from the city's streets, in accordance with a new accent on good order and discipline. The tsar's resolute approach was demonstrated within a few years of the city's foundation when, in November 1706, he ordered the forcible assembling of two groups of labourers, totalling 30,000 men, to work on the construction of the city the following summer. This process was repeated annually.[11] Soon Peter was ordering the forcible settlement of nobles, merchants and craftsmen in the city, somewhat ironically in view of his repeated references to the place as his 'paradise'.[12] The new settlers were required to build themselves homes in specified locations and to live there. But the tsar's wish to centre St Petersburg on remote and inaccessible Vasil'evskii Island, and to zone the city for residence according to social rank, was subsequently frustrated.[13]

Those who took up residence in St Petersburg, whether voluntarily or involuntarily, were required to conduct themselves in accordance with an increasingly elaborate code of 'police' regulations which, following European models, became ever more common across

Russia as time went on, but were applied nowhere as comprehensively as in St Petersburg. An important moment in this process occurred in 1718 with the establishment of the police administration for the city under Anton Devier, the organization which was to be responsible for law and order, hygiene and welfare in the city. Decrees on such matters as the compulsory cleaning of streets by their residents, street lighting, the maintenance of canal banks and the clearing of waterways, the billeting of troops, controls over inns and liquor stores, refuse collection, fire prevention, regulation of markets and abattoirs, and the control of beggars were in keeping with the eighteenth-century European view of what constituted proper 'police' concerns.[14] It is easy to see many of these as expressions of the desire to build up and conserve the power of the state, the health and discipline of the population as a resource of the state, and to cut out unnecessary waste.[15]

But in addition to these policies to enhance the modernity of the state, there were others which seemed designed to encourage modernity in the attitudes and outlook of the city's growing population. It may be, of course, that Peter's attempts to ensure that the residents of his new city learn to sail and to take full advantage of its riverine and maritime location by using water-borne means of transport as far as possible had more to do with his desire to build a strong navy than to turn his subjects from continentals into denizens of islands and coastal margins.[16] But his famous decree on assemblies, issued in 1718 and signed significantly enough by Devier, was designed to encourage the nobility in particular to extend their hospitality to their friends, neighbours and indeed the populace at large, thus spreading notions of decorum and polite behaviour beyond the confines of the Court.[17] Not only were such assemblies to be open to women, contrary to Muscovite norms, but the fact that pursuits like card playing, smoking, dancing and instrumental music were permitted underlined the different standards of behaviour which the tsar expected to reign in the new city compared with those characteristic of old Muscovy. Peter no doubt hoped that 'proper' standards of conduct would also be inculcated in the nobility and middling classes by means of the schools he encouraged and through such publications as *The Honourable Mirror of Youth* (*Iunosti chestnoe zertsalo*), first published in 1717. But also important was the general atmosphere promulgated by the Court and especially in the city of St Petersburg. In place of the strict religious ritual which marked the public activities of the tsar and his entourage before Peter and the annual round of fasts, festivals and solemn ceremonies which characterized the Muscovite year came a much less elaborate religious calendar greatly augmented by innumerable secular occasions designed to glorify the state, the tsar, the victories and other momentous events of the period. It was particularly in St Petersburg where the profundity of the changes which Peter introduced could be underlined.

One very obvious reason why this was so lay in the overall form and appearance of the city, perhaps a matter of greater immediate concern to Peter, as to so many other ambitious and authoritarian rulers, than the everyday behaviour of his subjects. Petersburg was the place where Renaissance and Baroque notions of urban grandeur, order and elegance could be fully realized in Russia, and where Renaissance ideas of perspective, geometrical form and symmetry could properly be applied in the city's planning and architecture, particularly through the employment of foreign architects, sculptors and other specialists. It has been pointed out that much that was apparently new in St Petersburg's architecture had its precedents in Moscow, and indeed attempts to control and regularize development, particularly with a view to fire prevention, long pre-date Peter.[18] But, as James Cracraft has correctly argued, the development of St Petersburg reflects contemporary notions of 'the ideal city' where the emphasis has moved from fortification and fire prevention towards order, regularity, legibility and rationality.[19] The ideal city of the Baroque was to be an ordered, rational city, amenable to administration and control, and freed from the quirks and absurdities of the medieval city.[20] The overall regularity and predictability of the city's plan as well as the architecture of its individual buildings would facilitate the attainment of those goals which were the guiding principles of the 'well-ordered police state'. As well as demonstrating the triumph of the notions of rationality and science which had so impressed Peter on his visits to Europe, St Petersburg's broad, straight streets and impressive architecture would add to the lustre of the regime. There was also the belief that those same straight streets and the grand architecture would somehow change Russians themselves, as though their development had previously been cramped and inhibited by Moscow's meandering lanes, cupolas and lack of sweeping vistas.

St Petersburg was the first city in Russia where anything like large-scale systematic planning was attempted and European ideas of building regulation and architectural style were applied. Building in stone wherever feasible, taking full advantage of riverine and canal frontages, planting trees and providing gardens and parkland, and endowing the city with the broad boulevards and expansive squares suitable to ceremonial display, ensured that the new city appeared like no other Russian city before it. Of course, appearance was by no means everything. Many of Peter's projects ultimately failed to come to fruition or were distorted in various ways. Moreover, the accent on appearance could not hide the severely practical concerns which underpinned the new capital's development. The presence of the Peter-Paul Fortress in the city centre together with the Admiralty, dockyard and harbour emphasized the city's military character (by no means unusual, of course, in a Baroque city). Furthermore, it was clear right from the beginning that St Petersburg was meant to be a centre of commerce.

St Petersburg's image was soon being displayed visually in the urban maps and engraved townscapes which began to proliferate as the century progressed, reflecting the new artistic vision which Russians were beginning to acquire. Early examples of this genre include the Dutch engraver Pieter Pikart's portrait of the city, made in 1704, Aleksei Zubov's panorama of 1716, and the work of the Danish architect Christoph Marselius, completed in 1725. All of these, which depict St Petersburg as a water-based city, have been analysed in some detail by Grigorii Kaganov.[21] They suggest something of the ways in which the image of the city, as well as its reality, were beginning to impinge on the Russian consciousness. St Petersburg, in other words, presented itself as a European city – new and strange no doubt to the majority of Russians who beheld it but, the tsar hoped, familiar and reassuring to the many foreigners he recruited or invited to live there, a symbol of what he wished Russia to become.

One other facet of modernity in St Petersburg that also deserves comment is the city's institutional structure. Once the victory at Poltava had been secured (1709) and the systematic settlement of the city had begun, a series of institutions began to appear which, supplementing the Court and the agencies of government and the church which now began to move from Moscow, served to underscore its increasingly secular character. Such were the educational and scientific institutions, like the famed Naval Academy (opened in 1715 when the higher classes of the Moscow School of Mathematics and Navigation moved from Moscow), the higher engineering school (which moved from Moscow in 1719), the St Petersburg medical school (1716) and facilities for the training of entrants to the civil service. The Academy of Sciences, accompanied by a Gymnasium and a university, opened after Peter's death in 1725. Allied to education and the sciences was the *Kunstkamera*, Peter's museum which also became a centre for higher learning and sprouted a library. Military hospitals made their appearance,[22] a botanical garden was organized from what had been an apothecary garden, the city gained its first typography in 1711 and began printing a newspaper (the *Vedomosti*) in the same year. This, and soon other presses, started to publish books, calendars and similar matter, part of which was of a secular kind. St Petersburg became a site for poetry, literature, theatre and music of a non-traditional type later in the century, but the first glimmerings of a secular high culture are discernible in Peter's day. The city thus provided a context in which many aspects of modernity could eventually become rooted.

Of course, many of Peter's policies in St Petersburg were paralleled in Moscow and to some degree in other cities, and this raises the question whether he could not in fact have achieved his objectives by continuing to rule from Moscow. No simple answer can be given to this question, except to note that this was a tsar to whom appearance and symbolism obviously mattered, as he assumed they also mattered to others. A tsar who had shaved off the beards of the boyars, insisted on their wearing European dress, and who reformed the calendar and clock, seemed unlikely to rest content with Moscow, whose religious and traditional orientation was visible to all and which could never be made to look European. St Petersburg's proximity to Europe, particularly to the Protestant countries of the Baltic and the north, its maritime and riverine setting, and its 'secular' appearance, meaning its relative freedom from a townscape and ethos entirely dominated by religion, gave it an atmosphere very different from that of the old capital. Moreover, given the circumstances under which the city was founded and began to develop, its society and way of life also quickly diverged from those of Moscow. The traditional hierarchical authority of the Orthodox Church, already challenged by Peter's failure to appoint a successor to the

Patriarch Adrian in 1700, was further disrupted by the move to St Petersburg, and its influence in the new city, like that of the more conservative nobility, was consequently constrained. The tsar's reforms of government, the military and the urban estates also had implications for the city's social structure and way of life. Perhaps even more important was the way in which foreigners now mingled relatively easily with Russians, particularly in St Petersburg, a process much encouraged by the city's location, its burgeoning foreign trade and by the increasing number of foreigners now being employed in the city. 'No other city in Europe boasted such a rich mixture of races and nationalities, and European visitors were amazed at the variety of languages spoken in its salons and places of business,' wrote Bruce Lincoln of the city later in the century.[23] Scholars have long pointed out how primate cities, with their admixtures and interminglings of peoples, activities and cultures, can act as potent centres for new ideas and consequent social change.[24] Add to this, in the case of Petrine St Petersburg, the continual attention or presence of an activist tsar, of his hand-picked officials, and the stimulus provided by the practical need to plan, build and defend not only a new settlement but an entire urban society, and the city's potential as a catalyst for social change is clear.

Yet it is perhaps too easy to view eighteenth-century St Petersburg as a 'space of modernity' in the simplistic sense of a platform or node from which reforms and changes cascaded down the urban hierarchy and diffused across the territory. This diffusionist view sits cosily with an approach to Russian history which emphasizes the pivotal role of the state in effecting social change in a society which is all too prone to stagnation. But social change is unlikely to occur in such a straightforward way, even in Russia. Furthermore, the concept of St Petersburg as a 'space of modernity' needs questioning. Like new cities anywhere else in the world, St Petersburg could not hide its heritage – after all, the majority of its inhabitants were Russian with Russian ways. As Nikolai Berdiaev wrote: 'Petersburg is another face of Russia than Moscow, but it is not less Russian.'[25] Moreover, even Peter the Great could not have his reforming way over every aspect of the city's life and development: not all his ambitions for the city proved practical and his injunctions were frequently resisted or frustrated. From the very beginning, the city had an 'unofficial' side, even an 'underworld'. Perhaps more than other Russian cities, its transient and shifting population must have been difficult to harness to the purposes of the 'well-ordered police state'. Behind the 'Dutch façades' facing the Neva and its tributaries, and gradually spreading along the capital's grand boulevards, lay 'the real Petersburg' consisting of 'muddy neighbourhoods, growing spontaneously, separated by swamps and stretches of forest'. 'Petersburg recalled the traditional Russian city with its trading quarters and neighbourhoods.'[26] And in such spaces the 'disordered' city could flourish, beyond the easy surveillance of the tsar and his officials, and yet essential to the life of the city they were creating.

Quite apart from the uncertainties stemming from only partial control, the city's role as Russia's new capital was also ambivalent and clearly open to challenge. As Peter's 'Paradise', the city was meant to be seen as something new, as pointing the way to a future for Russia which would be different from its past. And yet in Russia the authority of the tsar derived from hallowed tradition which was sanctified by the church. If Petersburg's role as the focus of the new were emphasized too much and the implied challenge to the spiritual foundations of the Muscovite state were taken too far, the legitimacy of the state itself might be called into question (as it was, in essence, by many Old Believers). Therefore, as Kaganov has argued: 'Removing spiritual primacy from Moscow posed one of the main cultural tasks for Peter I and his entourage.'[27] The religious status and significance of the city were secured, among other things, by the Orthodox cathedrals and churches which soon came to mark its skyline, and perhaps above all by the Alexander Nevskii Monastery situated at the eastern end of the Nevskii Prospekt, containing the sacred relics of the saint himself. Alexander Nevskii, who had been canonized in the fourteenth century, was a religious figure of enormous importance to St Petersburg in view of his associations with the region and with north-west Russia more generally. Much the same can be said of St Andrew, whose legend similarly involved northern Russia and whose cult was also revived by Peter. The many secular ceremonies which marked the city's life (and which added to rather than replaced the simplified religious calendar) were likewise usually furnished with some religious content and were often accorded religious significance. Religion, in other words, continued to have a central role in the life of Russians and in that of the state, although superstition was now frowned upon. In St Petersburg, as in Moscow, 'life without religion was inconceivable'.[28] Yet the fact that Peter's consort Catherine was crowned empress in the traditional setting of Moscow in May 1724 rather than in St Petersburg seems to suggest that the issue of the spiritual primacy of the two cities was never completely resolved in the tsar's mind.

Such ambivalences and uncertainties, I wish to suggest, were not special to Peter and his successors, not merely the consequence of Russia's peculiar problems and difficulties in pursuing the path of Europeanization, but are part of the experience of modernity itself. If the term 'modernity' means anything – and for the purposes of this essay I do not wish to go further than L.R. Lewitter when he alludes to 'a desire for improvement, a predilection for novelty', 'a historical conception of human society – the belief that its changing condition and the changing condition of mankind are the result of a process which is measured by time', and perhaps the faith that 'the world is knowable, describable and capable of improvement',[29] then it encompasses 'crises, confusions and contradictory processes and experiences',[30] giving rise to the uncertainties and perplexities which surround the term itself. This in turn suggests the possibility of a 'multiplicity of modernities', of 'fissures and contradictions' in modernities,[31] of overlapping modernities with different and yet possibly overlapping and intertwining histories and geographies. Modernity, as Miles Ogborn has written, can be seen as a 'project', though a complex and heterogeneous one. 'As a "project",' he writes, 'modernity is less a realised set of relationships, institutions and experiences than a series of claims and attempts to make and remake the future.'[32] As the eighteenth century progressed, it can be argued, St Petersburg witnessed many such claims and attempts. It is in the light of the fissured and contradictory character of modernity in the British experience that Linda Colley has asserted that 'there was more than one eighteenth-century Britain'.[33] I want to suggest similarly that there was more than one eighteenth-century St Petersburg. St Petersburg was, no doubt, a 'space of modernity' in some senses. That being so, it was a highly contested one.

One facet of modernity which Peter tried to introduce to his realm was what might be called the 'new geography' – those scientifically-oriented geographical knowledges and practices which had been gradually developing in western Europe since at least the fifteenth century but which had found only a pale reflection in Russia before his day. The practices of mathematical geography, cartography, field survey and the like, which were becoming so necessary to military strategy, navigation, practical administration, resource exploitation, transportation and many other areas,[34] interested Peter from the beginning. Already in the Turkish campaign in the latter half of the 1690s measures were being implemented to map areas of southern Russia and regions bordering on the Sea of Azov and the Black Sea in the European manner. These endeavours involved the hiring of foreign specialists and the application of mathematical techniques.[35] Mapping was to become an ongoing concern of Peter's and subsequent reigns, as were related geographical endeavours like exploration, statistical survey, the translation and publication of geographical materials, geographical education and, eventually, the writing of geographical descriptions and analyses. Peter's personal interest in geography was no doubt enhanced by his visit to Paris in 1717, during which he met and had discussions with the celebrated geographer and cartographer Guillaume Delisle. The tsar was soon commissioning expeditions to map the Caspian Sea and to explore parts of Central Asia, eastern Siberia and neighbouring regions. Before his death Peter set out to establish the Academy of Sciences, in which geography was to find a significant role among the mathematical sciences.

St Petersburg came to play an important role in these developments. As the Court and government established themselves in the city, so the prime mover for many of these initiatives located there. Peter seems to have regarded a modern geographical perspective as essential to the practice of government, as demonstrated in the General Regulation (1720) where colleges were instructed to furnish themselves with suitable maps 'depicting all borders, rivers, towns, settlements, churches, hamlets, forests and so forth'.[36] The new Senate, which moved to St Petersburg in 1713, soon began to play a major supervisory role in the project for mapping Russia, whilst the Admiralty and other government agencies concerned themselves with more specialized geographical tasks. In the area of training and the practice of field cartography, the leading role was long played by the Naval Academy, opened in St Petersburg in 1715. Here European methods of surveying and mapmaking were being introduced to Russia by foreign specialists like the famed Scottish mathematician, Henry Farquharson. But probably the most important institution for the dissemination of European geographical ideas and practices was the Academy of Sciences which opened after Peter's death in 1725.[37] The Academy provided a site where the latest scientific ideas and practices could be exchanged, argued over and developed by the (initially) completely foreign members, their adjuncts and students, with outsiders attending on specified occasions. Geography played a significant role in these deliberations, and projects for mapping and exploring Russia long occupied a considerable portion of its attention. From the mid-late 1730s, such endeavours became focused around its Geographical Department, headed after 1740 by Leonhard Euler and from 1758 by M.V. Lomonosov.

From soon after its assumption of the role of Russian capital, therefore, St Petersburg became the principal site for the development of a new form of scientifically-oriented geographical endeavour, aimed at the furtherance of the tsar's quests for internal pacification and control and external glory, and involving nothing less than a re-imagining by Russians of the country they inhabited and of its place in the world. The urgency of this task was fostered by the exigencies of the war with Sweden and the tsar's determination, using the city as his instrument, to transform Russia into a great naval and commercial power. But the concentration of foreigners in the capital, particularly in the institutions mentioned above, and the easy communication with foreigners more generally, must also have spurred a re-imagining of Russia. Thus the eighteenth century witnessed a distinct quickening in Russians' interest in Siberia, not only in the need to ensure its control and to use its resources but also in the need to understand it. The activities of exploring, mapping, describing and cataloguing Siberia quickly became a major part of the Academy of Sciences' activities, not least because of the growing awareness on the part of educated Russians and their foreign associates, many of whom lived in St Petersburg, that the eyes of the world were trained on that little-known territory. Siberia and neighbouring parts of Central Asia figured in Peter's correspondence with the philosopher G.W. von Leibniz, and also in his discussions with Guillaume Delisle.[38] In 1720, soon after his meeting with the latter, what Aleksandrovskaia has termed Russia's 'first specialised scientific expedition to yield serious scientific results' was sent to Siberia under the leadership of the Danzig physician D.-G. Messerschmidt.[39] Commissioned by the Medical Chancellery, the expedition was charged with the task of searching for medical plants as well as other notable phenomena in the plant, animal and mineral kingdoms. The opening of the Academy in 1725 was quickly followed by what became known as the First (1727–30) and Second (1733–43) Kamchatka expeditions under Vitus Bering, in aspects of which the Academy played a major role. These expeditions had the goal of exploring the far north-east of Siberia, Kamchatka and the Bering Strait, and collecting scientific data. They were regarded internationally as having a key role in filling in a major blank in the map of the known world.[40]

Expeditionary ventures, therefore, had the effect of opening the eyes and minds of elite groups in the capital to some of the realities of the remote regions which had now entered the empire, and allowed St Petersburg itself to be recognized by the eighteenth-century scientific world as a centre of science in its own right and as an organizer of new knowledge. A closely related activity was that of mapmaking. Mapping was not a new activity in eighteenth-century Russia – indeed, there is evidence that it may have begun in the fifteenth century at roughly the same time that maps were becoming more widely known and used across Europe (this alone may tell us something significant about one facet of European modernity).[41] But as time went on, a number of differences between European and Russian mapping had become apparent. One very obvious one was the lack of possibilities for printing maps in Russia – they thus remained few in number and known to relatively few people – indeed, they were largely official and usually a closely guarded secret.[42] Another difference was that, whereas Europe embraced Ptolemy's mathematical geography in its construction of maps, as exemplified in the work of Mercator, Ortelius and others, such mathematical methods were virtually unknown in Russia until almost the end of the seventeenth century. Two riders, however, require to be added. One is that mathematical methods in mapping took a long time to spread across Europe, and were by no means universally used and understood even in Peter the Great's day.[43] The other is that the Russians had evolved a perfectly adequate mode of mapping using non-mathematical methods – perfectly adequate, that is, for orientation on land, though obviously one that would not have served the marine navigational needs of the commercial lands of the West. Essentially this took the form of estimating directions and distances without sophisticated instrumentation along the lines of river and overland routes, and checking distances by questioning the local inhabitants. Similar methods had long been used in western Europe.

Peter determined to reform Russian cartographic activity by employing western specialists to teach Russians the mathematical arts of navigation, surveying, mapping and astronomy and by commissioning new maps in the European manner. One reason, as noted already, was related to the utility of maps for such activities as ship-building, navigation, military surveying and land planning. All of these fascinated the tsar and were seen as essential to Russia's military and commercial future. Another came to be the prestige which was attached to European cartographic activity in the period. Peter could not hope to emulate France, where accurate mapping based on strict mathematical methods was breaking new ground in this era. But he showed intense interest in these activities, as witnessed by his discussions with Guillaume Delisle. And he hoped to achieve recognition for Russia in the cartographic field, as suggested by his efforts to have the Caspian Sea accurately surveyed and mapped and to have the results displayed to the assembled French academicians in Paris.[44] The adoption by Russia of European-type mapping methods thus became an important symbol of the introduction of the rationality of the Scientific Revolution into Russian life.

But it was an introduction fraught with difficulty and uncertainty. The fairly elaborate pre-Petrine tradition of map making, centred on the Moscow Kremlin armoury and certain provincial centres like Tobol'sk and having close associations in certain cases with traditions of icon painting, was of limited utility. Peter was obliged to hire foreigners like Henry Farquharson, leading to the establishment of the Moscow Navigation School in 1701. The prototype for this foundation was the English Royal Mathematical School at Christ's Hospital which had been set up in 1673 to supply a growing English need for trained navigators. The higher classes of Moscow's Navigation School were transferred to St Petersburg in 1715 to become the Naval Academy (now controlled by the Admiralty). This was to be a centre for the training of naval officers, navigators, surveyors and mathematics teachers, and also participated, together with agencies of government, in mapping. After 1725 the latter activity also became the concern of the newly founded Academy of Sciences, as we have seen. Cartography in the Academy was overseen by

J.N. Delisle, brother of Guillaume, who had been appointed to the chair of astronomy, a closely aligned mathematical specialism. Delisle became in effect head of the Geographical Department on its appearance in the middle to latter part of the 1730s but then surrendered this role to Euler on account of his other interests.

Yet how to achieve the re-imagining of Russia which modernity seemed to demand was by no means straightforward. To many Russians maps must have seemed like dangerous foreign innovations, to some perhaps even the work of Antichrist, posing as they did a challenge to traditional oral, textual and iconic authority. To translate and teach abstract mathematical and scientific ideas, couched in a foreign idiom, in the absence of adequate aids like good textbooks and scientific equipment, was far from easy. Farquharson had to spend much of his time translating and preparing teaching materials, part of what was in fact a huge official and unofficial effort in assimilating foreign scientific understanding into Russian culture. The Navigation School, the Naval Academy and other institutions were plagued by problems of underfunding, poor teaching, absenteeism, disorder and infrastructural inadequacies, all of which testify to the difficulties faced by the new scientific practices.[45] The fact that Peter's reforms were introduced hastily and in 'top-down' fashion only complicated the task of absorbing them into Russian life in any straightforward fashion. The reality was obviously a good distance away from the ordered world of the tsar's imagination.

Within a few years of the opening of the Naval Academy, Peter launched what proved to be his most ambitious scientific project – that to map Russia systematically in the new, scientific manner. It was a project which was not to find fulfilment in his lifetime. Already in 1717 graduates of the Naval Academy were being sent out to various provincial locations to survey and map borders and other important features. A Senate decree of December 1720, ordered those graduates who were skilled in geodesy and geography to be sent to the provinces to map them.[46] Early in the following year the 'geodesists' received instructions, possibly composed by Peter himself or by one of his close associates, ordering that places be mapped according to their mathematically determined locations 'as shown to you in the Academy', and specifying which geographical features were to be recorded.[47] Prior to this, geodesists had already been sent out to Voronezh, Astrakhan and Moscow *gubernii*, to Siberia, and to work on the delimitation of the Swedish and Chinese borders. After the 1720 decree they were sent to other provinces.

Deficiencies in this programme soon became evident. The number of geodesists sent was quite inadequate to the task of mapping the huge territories which they had been allocated. Before the 1720 decree, for example, only four were sent to Voronezh *guberniia*, four to Astrakhan', two to work along the River Gzhat' in the western part of Moscow *guberniia*, and five to Siberia. Perhaps 35 were sent out after the 1720 decree.[48] Not surprisingly, the work took years to accomplish. In 1723, a special decree of the Senate was issued reminding governors and *voevody* to send the completed maps to the Senate and *Kamer Kollegiia*. The decree stated that so far maps had only been sent from Siberia, Azov, Nizhnii Novgorod and Kazan', and then not for all districts, and 'from others nothing has been sent and nothing known about why not'.[49] By 1725, at the time of Peter's death, maps had been received for only 30 districts (*uezdy*), or 12 per cent of the districts of the empire. They continued to arrive long afterwards.

Although the maps constituted a distinct advance on what had gone before, they were in fact a compromise between 'new' and traditional modes of mapmaking, the products of what Postnikov terms 'semi-instrumental' methods of survey.[50] Shortages of time, resources and personnel meant that a speedy and efficient method of survey had to be adopted. Postnikov makes the point that Russian survey methods at this period were heavily influenced by the use of the English 'astrolabe' (probably a circumferentor, involving checking directions by means of a compass[51]) rather than by the French approach which preferred the plane table.[52] This he believes to have been the result not only of the influence of Farquharson and his colleagues but also of the fact that the 'English' method was speedier and closer to traditional Russian methods of following river and road networks.[53] According to the 1721 and subsequent instructions issued under Peter and his immediate successors, surveying a *uezd* involved only one instrumental traverse, measuring distances by chain or rope (especially between settlements and other notable points), checking compass directions and taking sightings of visible points. Distances to settlements to the side of the main traverse might also occasionally be measured. The district border was generally surveyed in the same manner. Many distances and directions, however, were merely estimated by questioning the locals (sometimes with adjustments made to allow for exaggeration or underestimation). Limited provision was made for determining location by astronomical sightings. Although some instructions advised the taking of astronomical sightings at specified points (for example, where roads or rivers crossed *uezd* boundaries), it was unusual to do this outside the main *uezd* centre.

There is evidence to suggest that even such relatively economical methods of survey approved under Peter and his immediate successors were often only partially applied in practice, with estimates of distance and direction frequently relying more on the questionnaire method and on guesswork than on specified scientific approaches. Moreover, the geodesists and mapmakers were all too often neglectful of the detailed contents of their maps, to the annoyance of central officials who wished to use them for practical purposes. Many problems of accuracy and comprehensiveness also derived from the fact that the maps were drawn away from the field itself on the basis of the geodesists' journals and field notes rather than using the geometrically correct diagrams which would have been produced using the plane table.[54]

From the centre's point of view there were numerous issues of co-ordination and control over the geodesists in the field. What in essence was being attempted was the establishment of a form of surveillance, based on St Petersburg, over the near and distant territories of the empire which would thereby become knowable, and thus controllable, to Russia's rulers. How to ensure, however, that the geodesists fulfilled their allotted tasks adequately and efficiently, even with the training they had received and the detailed instructions and guidance regularly sent to them, was by no means easy, especially given the distances and difficult communications involved. The quality of the resulting maps was often below what had been hoped for in the centre. The task of mapping was further complicated by the fact that the methodologies which the geodesists were expected to use were in constant process of evolution. This was not merely the result of trial-and-error, but also of fundamental differences between actors in St Petersburg over what kinds of modern maps were most suitable for Russian circumstances, and who was to produce and control them.

Soon after his arrival in St Petersburg in February 1726 to take up the post of professor of astronomy at the Academy of Sciences, J.N. Delisle was given the responsibility for overseeing the Academy's contribution to the construction of Russia's first general map. Given his interests in mathematics and astronomy, Delisle interpreted this task as ensuring that Russian mapmaking follow in the steps of that of his native France, where his recently deceased elder brother Guillaume had presided over the world's most sophisticated cartography up to that time. This involved systematic mapping on a strictly mathematical basis, utilising such methods as the exact determination of geographical locations through astronomical observations, and mapping on the basis of triangulation. Delisle clearly felt that this could be achieved only by a policy of centralization through the Academy. In two memoranda written to Baron G.K. Kaiserling, the Academy's new president, in 1733, he revealed what this should mean: that Senate over-secretary I.K. Kirilov cease to be responsible for the publication of maps and transfer this responsibility to the Academy, that the Academy become the sole repository for Russia's map archives, and that it become the single agency for the advanced training, examining, supervising and disposition of the geodesists, who would in effect become the Academy's servants to be employed in any area of science it deemed necessary.[55] From 1734, when Kirilov was appointed head of the Orenburg Expedition, much of the Senate's map archive was transferred to the Academy, thus allowing serious work on the general map to begin. But progress was slow, even after the official opening of the Geographical Department in 1739. Though aided from 1735 by Euler, Delisle was sidetracked by his determination to give Russian cartography an astronomical basis by an abortive scheme of triangulation during 1737–39. Also significant was the fact that Delisle felt that cartographic activities interfered too much with his astronomical work.

Delisle's whole approach to mapping differed substantially from that of the aforementioned I.K. Kirilov. Kirilov served as Senate secretary from the early 1720s, quickly assuming responsibility for Peter the Great's mapping project and for overseeing the work of the geodesists. In 1729, under his supervision, a group of geodesists was formed in the Senate to begin preparations for creating a general map of Russia. In 1734 Kirilov was able to publish Russia's first atlas of 25 maps. Perhaps not surprisingly, this attracted considerable criticism in view of its many shortcomings. Kirilov did not share Delisle's view that what Russia needed was maps of the highest scientific provenance, which would have been amongst Europe's most advanced for the period. As a government bureaucrat, he was conscious of cost, of the practical difficulties of implementing Delisle's schemes under Russian conditions, and of Delisle's slow progress in the face of Russia's pressing need for maps. Kirilov was prepared to compromise in a way Delisle was not. Scholars have differed in their assessment of the exact relationship between the two but, to quote one commentator, it was clearly 'complex'.[56] Delisle was anxious to assert the Academy's leading role in the mapping enterprise and to ensure that Russian mapping follow the highest scientific standards. Before Kirilov's transfer to the Orenburg Expedition, Delisle complained that Kirilov was deliberately refusing to send the Academy the maps it needed. Kirilov, for his part, was keen to ensure that mapping met the needs of the government machinery, and sought to retain his leading role even after his transfer in 1734.

Kirilov died in 1737, and was succeeded by V.N. Tatishchev. Tatishchev had long had a responsibility for Russia's mapping project and proved more amenable to co-operation with the Academy and with some of Delisle's aims. He was, however, quite critical of aspects of the work and was soon proposing reforms. Tatishchev oversaw the ongoing survey and mapping of the Urals, regions in Siberia, Astrakhan and other areas, and sent the result of these labours to the Academy. In the meantime, Delisle, who was engaged in a series of controversies with his Academy colleagues, ceased to be actively concerned with cartographic work from 1740, while Euler left Russia for Berlin the following year. Oversight over the construction of Russia's first official general map or atlas thus fell into other hands. Work on the atlas was rushed for a number of reasons and finally appeared in 1745 as the 'Russian Atlas consisting of nineteen special maps – appended by a general map of this great empire'. Again, though undoubtedly a great achievement for the period and commended by no less an authority than the great French geographer J.B. d'Anville,[57] the atlas was criticized for its many shortcomings. Among the latter, the failure to incorporate the latest information, including materials from the Second Kamchatka expedition and even materials sent by Tatishchev, is especially notable. It is evident that much important material, for one reason or another, had never come into the possession of the Academy, and there were still many areas of ignorance concerning Russia's geography. Once again the quest for scientific accuracy clashed with the need for concrete, practical results.

What was really being argued about in this whole discussion about mapmaking was the nature of 'modernity' – what kinds of 'modern' maps did Russia need and what could it afford? What eventually emerged was a series of interesting compromises between 'modern' mapping methods and methods which had been in use from long before the time of Peter – selected use of instrumental measurement and the construction of maps using mathematical projections on the one hand, together with observing and surveying along the networks of rivers and other routes, the correction of distance estimates by questioning locals, and the provision of detailed textual descriptions to accompany the maps, on the other. It was precisely such compromises which cartographers had had to make in western Europe and which now constituted Russia's cartographic response to the dilemma of modernity.

What I wish to suggest, therefore, is that the city of St Petersburg provided a set of spaces within which scholars, officials and specialists could discuss and debate the new modes of mapping which had been introduced from Europe and consider their relevance to Russian needs. But the implementation of this aspect of 'modernity', in the context of St Petersburg and Russia as a whole, meant far more than applying a pre-given set of ideas and procedures to the Russian context. It meant discovering new ways of making them possible in that environment, to some degree rethinking the ideas and procedures themselves, and all in the context of the differing and conflicting values, outlooks and ambitions of people living in and beyond the city. It was in a very real sense a debate about modernity itself.

In conclusion, this essay has argued that the founding of St Petersburg was a momentous act in Peter's quest to bring modernity to Russia. But it was also an act steeped in uncertainty and compromise. Some of these uncertainties have been alluded to above: Could Peter (to say nothing of his successors) really control the life of his new city? Could the city continue to survive in its distant and hostile environment? How is the new to be introduced without sacrificing what is essential in the old? How is the new Russian capital – peripheral, unpopular, difficult of access, unfamiliar – to survive and keep in touch with the rest of Russia? What kind of modernity does Russia need? What kind can it afford? Some of these questions and debates have been highlighted above with reference to the 'new' geography and cartography being introduced in this period.

They were questions and debates which were anchored in 'new' spaces, spaces of modernity, like the Academy of Sciences, the Naval Academy and the offices of the Senate, located in the city. Other debates, other spaces, helped to comprise the medley which was eighteenth-century St Petersburg. There was indeed more than one eighteenth-century St Petersburg. Only by trying to grapple with that complexity, with the changes, experiences and identities which comprised the city, can its uncertain modernities be appreciated.

Notes

1. W.B. Lincoln, *Sunlight at Midnight: St Petersburg and the Rise of Modern Russia* (Oxford, 2001), p. 5.
2. R.E. Jones, 'Why St Petersburg?', in L. Hughes (ed.), *Peter the Great and the West: New Perspectives* (London, 2001), pp. 189–205.
3. See, for example, A. Giddens, *The Constitution of Society* (Cambridge, 1984); D. Gregory and J. Urry (eds), *Social Relations and Spatial Structure* (London, 1985); R.A. Dodgshon, *Society in Space and Time: A Geographical Perspective on Change* (Cambridge, 1998); D. Harvey, *The Condition of Postmodernity* (Oxford, 1990); D. Harvey, *Justice, Nature and the Geography of Difference* (Oxford, 1996); H. Lefebvre, *The Production of Space* (Oxford, 1991); and B. Werlen, *Society, Action and Space* (London, 1993).
4. S.S. Duncan, 'Uneven Development and the Difference that Space Makes', *Geoforum*, XX, no. 2 (1989) 131–9.
5. Dodgshon, *Society in Space and Time*, p. 51.
6. *Ibid.*, pp. 10–16.
7. *Ibid.*, pp. 1–16.
8. See, for example, Dodgshon's fascinating discussion of social and spatial change in historic China, based partly on Lattimore, *ibid.*, pp. 61–6. There are obvious affinities between the idea of social change occurring in 'marginal spaces' and the 'frontier hypothesis' of F.J. Turner. See also R. Shields, *Places on the Margin: Alternative Geographies of Modernity* (London, 1991).
9. M. Ogborn, *Spaces of Modernity: London's Geographies, 1680–1780* (New York, 1998).
10. A. Giddens, *A Contemporary Critique of Historical Materialism*, II, *The Nation State and Violence* (London, 1985), 9.
11. L. Hughes, *Russia in the Age of Peter the Great* (New Haven, 1998), p. 213.
12. *Polnoe sobranie zakonov Rossiiskoi Imperii* (hereafter *PSZ*), V, no. 2817.
13. *PSZ* V, nos. 2951, 3305, 4405, 4474.
14. *PSZ* V, nos. 3192, 3203, 3226, 3382, 3386, 3412, 3777, VI, nos. 3494, 3589, 3676, 3777, 3799, 3800, 3823, etc.
15. M. Raeff, *The Well-Ordered Police State: Social and Institutional Change through Law in the Germanies and Russia* (New Haven, 1983).

16. *PSZ* V, nos. 3139, 3191, 3238, 3387, 3396, VI, nos. 3799, 3865, 3866.
17. *PSZ* V, no. 3241.
18. Hughes, *Russia in the Age of Peter the Great*, p. 205; P.V. Sytin, *Istoriia planirovki i zastroiki Moskvy* (Moscow, 1950), pp. 83–181.
19. J. Cracraft, *The Petrine Revolution in Russian Architecture* (Chicago, 1988).
20. See, for example, L. Mumford, *The City in History* (London, 1961), pp. 395 ff; T.D. Hemming, E. Freeman and D. Meakin (eds), *The Secular City: Studies in the Enlightenment* (Exeter, 1994), especially chapters by D. Meakin, 'Topographies of the Secular City', pp. 3–11, and R. Porter, 'Enlightenment London and Urbanity', pp. 27–41; J.E. Vance, *This Scene of Man: The Role and Structure of the City in the Geography of Western Civilization* (New York, 1977), chapter 6; A.E.J. Morris, *History of Urban Form* (London, 1979); H. Roseneau, *The Ideal City: Its Architectural Evolution* (Boston, 1959); C. Mukerji, *Territorial Ambitions and the Gardens of Versailles* (Cambridge, 1997); P. Lavedan, *Histoire de l'urbanisme; Renaissance et temps modernes* (Paris, 1959); K. Krüger (ed.), *Europäische Städte im Zeitalter des Barocks* (Cologne, 1988).
21. G. Kaganov, 'As in the Ship of Peter', *Slavic Review* L, no. 4 (1991) 755–67.
22. R. Wittram, *Peter I: Czar und Kaiser* (Gottingen, 1964), p. 61.
23. Lincoln, *Sunlight at Midnight*, pp. 43–4.
24. R. Redfield and M.B. Singer, 'The Cultural Role of Cities', *Economic Development and Cultural Change*, XIII (1954) 53–73.
25. N. Berdyaev, *The Russian Idea* (London, 1947), p. 71.
26. Kaganov, 'As in the Ship of Peter', pp. 756–7.
27. *Ibid.*, p. 764.
28. Hughes, *Russia in the Age of Peter the Great*, p. 355.
29. L.R. Lewitter, 'Peter the Great and the Modern World', in Paul Dukes (ed.), *Russia and Europe* (London, 1991), pp. 92–107.
30. Ogborn, *Spaces of Modernity*, p. 12.
31. *Ibid.*, p. 11.
32. *Ibid.*, p. 28.
33. Quoted by Ogborn, *ibid.*, p. 24.
34. See, for example, Mukerji, *Territorial Ambitions*, chapter 1.
35. D.J.B. Shaw, 'Geographical Practice and its Significance in Peter the Great's Russia', *Journal of Historical Geography*, XXII, no. 2 (1996) 160–76.
36. V.F. Gnucheva, *Geograficheskii department Akademii nauk XVIII veka* (Moscow–Leningrad, 1946), p. 20.
37. In 1724, the Leipzig scholar J.-B. Mencke enquired of L. L. Blumentrost, who was to become the Academy's first president, whether the Academy would be located in St Petersburg, where few wish to be in view of the 'unhealthy air', or in Moscow. Blumentrost replied that it would be in St Petersburg where the climate was even healthier than in Moscow. A.I. Andreev, 'Osnovanie Akademii nauk v Peterburge', *Petr Velikii: sbornik statei* (Moscow–Leningrad, 1947), p. 323.
38. K.M. Baer, 'Zaslugi Petra Velikogo po chasti rasprostraneniia geograficheskikh poznanii o Rossii', *Zapiski Imperatorskogo Russkogo geograficheskogo obshchestva*, kn. III (1849), kn. IV (1850); D.M. Lebedev, *Geografiia v Rossii*

petrovskogo vremeni (Moscow–Leningrad, 1950), pp. 80–1, 111, 214–16; A. Lipski, 'The Foundation of the Russian Academy of Sciences', *Isis*, XLIV (1953) 349–54; A. Vucinich, *Science in Russian Culture: A History to 1860* (London, 1963), pp. 45 ff.
39. O.A. Aleksandrovskaia, *Stanovlenie geograficheskoi nauki v Rossii v XVIII veke* (Moscow, 1989), p. 41.
40. A.V. Efimov, *Iz istorii velikikh russkikh geograficheskikh otkrytii* (Moscow, 1971); Lebedev, *Geografiia v Rossii*, pp. 93–101; *Ekspeditsiia Beringa: sbornik dokumentov* (Moscow, 1941); L.S. Berg, *Otkrytie Kamchatki i ekspeditsii Beringa, 1725–1742* (Moscow–Leningrad, 1946); D.M. Lebedev and V.A. Esakov, *Russkie geograficheskie otkrytiia i issledovaniia s drevnikh vremen do 1917g.* (Moscow, 1971); G.D. Komkov, B.V. Levshin and L.K. Semenov, *Akademiia Nauk SSSR: kratkii istoricheskii ocherk* (Moscow, 1977), pp. 43–8.
41. P. Barber, 'Maps and Monarchs in Europe, 1550–1800', in R. Oresko, G.C. Gibbs and H.M. Scott (eds), *Royal and Republican Sovereignty in Early Modern Europe* (Cambridge, 1997), pp. 75–124; D. Buisseret (ed.), *Monarchs, Ministers and Maps: The Emergence of Cartography as a Tool of Government in Early Modern Europe* (Chicago, 1992); P.D.A. Harvey, *The History of Topographical Maps: Symbols, Pictures and Surveys* (London, 1980), pp. 156 ff.
42. Secrecy was, of course, a common characteristic of early modern European mapmaking. See Barber, 'Maps and Monarchs', pp. 83 ff; Raymond B. Craib, 'Cartography and Power in the Conquest and Creation of New Spain', *Latin American Research Review*, XXXV, no. 1 (2000) 15; J.B. Harley, 'Silences and Secrecy: the Hidden Agenda of Cartography in Early Modern Europe', *Imago Mundi*, XL (1988) 57–76.
43. Harvey, *History of Topographical Maps*, p. 156.
44. Lebedev, *Geografiia v Rossii*, p. 216; Aleksandrovskaia, *Stanovlenie geograficheskoi nauki*, pp. 29–30.
45. These issues have been described by several scholars, including W.F. Ryan, 'Navigation and the Modernisation of Petrine Russia: Teachers, Textbooks, Terminology', in R. Bartlett and J.M. Hartley (eds), *Russia in the Age of the Enlightenment: Essays for Isabel de Madariaga* (London, 1990), pp. 75–105.
46. *PSZ* VI, no. 3682.
47. Lebedev, *Geografiia v Rossii*, p. 204.
48. *Ibid.*, p. 206.
49. *Ibid.*
50. A.V. Postnikov, *Razvitie krupnomasshtabnoi kartografii v Rossii* (Moscow, 1989), p. 39.
51. W.F. Ryan, 'Scientific Instruments in Russia from the Middle Ages to Peter the Great', *Annals of Science*, XLVIII (1991) 376.
52. Postnikov, *Razvitie krupnomasshtabnoi kartografii v Rossii*, pp. 36–7.
53. Although it is often assumed that mathematical methods in mapping were quickly adopted in western Europe in the wake of the rediscovery of Ptolemy, this appears not to have been the case, particularly in large-scale

regional mapping and local surveying where popular ignorance of mathematics was a major hindrance. See Harvey, *History of Topographical Maps*, pp. 156 ff.
54. According to Postnikov, *Razvitie krupnomasshtabnoi kartografii v Rossii*, p. 43, the plane table only came into general use in Russia from the end of the eighteenth century for military survey, and for civil survey only from the 1840s.
55. Gnucheva, *Geograficheskii departament*, pp. 31–2.
56. L.A Gol'denberg, 'Ivan Kirilovich Kirilov, 1695–1737', in *Tvortsy otechestvennoi nauki: geografy* (Moscow, 1996), p. 48.
57. Gnucheva, *Geograficheskii departament*, pp. 162–78.

2
St Petersburg during the Reign of Anna Ivanovna: The Forbes/Maas Chart and the Evolution of the Early Mapping of the City

Michael J. Bitter

The year 2003 marks the 300th anniversary of the foundation of the Russian city of St Petersburg. In recent years, this northern metropolis has become familiar to western tourists and businesspeople alike. Detailed and accurate maps of the city are available from almost every large book and travel retailer, as well as on the Internet. This contemporary level of accessibility of maps and charts showing St Petersburg's landmarks, general design and surroundings differs markedly from the situation during the city's early history.

When St Petersburg celebrated its thirtieth anniversary, more than two and a half centuries ago, very few accurate maps of the new Russian capital existed. Several of the widely publicized urban plans available in the early 1730s projected the city's future growth and construction, rather than representing the reality of the city's extent at the time.[1] The factual information included on these maps was based on the surveying, sounding and mapping work done initially by order of Peter the Great. As R.E. Jones points out, when Peter first gained access to the Baltic Sea at the mouth of the Neva River, he 'largely repeated what he had already done at Azov'.[2] That is, he ordered surveys and soundings of the region and its waterways. These findings provided the essential geographical information upon which the earliest maps of the future Russian capital were based.

Although this original surveying activity provided cartographers with an accurate foundation, the early representation of the growth and development of the city itself was another matter. An official, accurate map of St Petersburg was not published until after 1737, when the Russian Academy of Sciences produced its own plan, depicting the capital as it stood in that year (Figure 1).[3] Consequently, in the years before 1737, truly accurate depictions of the city were difficult to obtain, and relatively few of them have survived. One of these rare accurate depictions of the city has weathered the 250 years between its creation and its 'rediscovery' for scholarship in Castle Forbes, the residence of the Earls of Granard. Castle Forbes is located in County Longford, in the Republic of Ireland, far from the borders of Russia. This hand-coloured chart, kept for centuries in the Earls' private apartments, depicts not only the Russian capital, but also surrounding points of interest along the Gulf of Finland, including the island port of Kronstadt and the imperial summer residences located on the southern coast (Figure 2).[4] The chart was almost certainly created for George, Lord Forbes, the Third

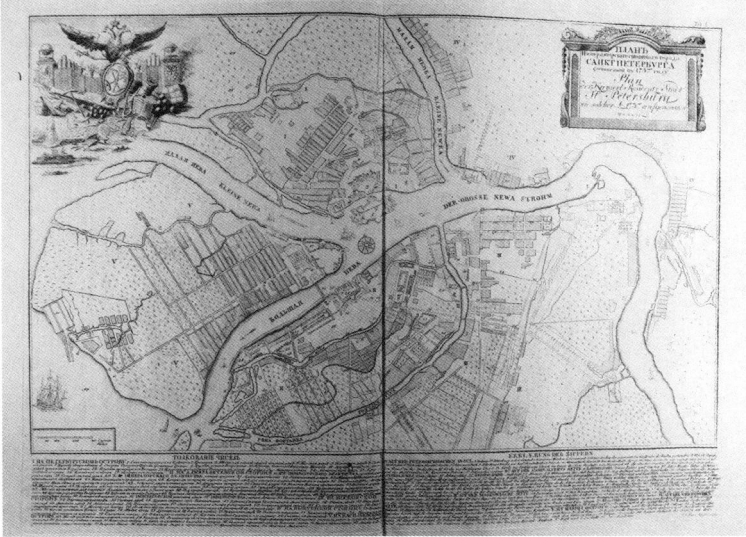

Figure 1 The Russian Academy of Sciences map of St Petersburg, created in 1737. This first official Russian map of the capital confirms the accuracy of the Forbes/Maas chart of 1734. Courtesy of the James Ford Bell Library, Minneapolis, MN.

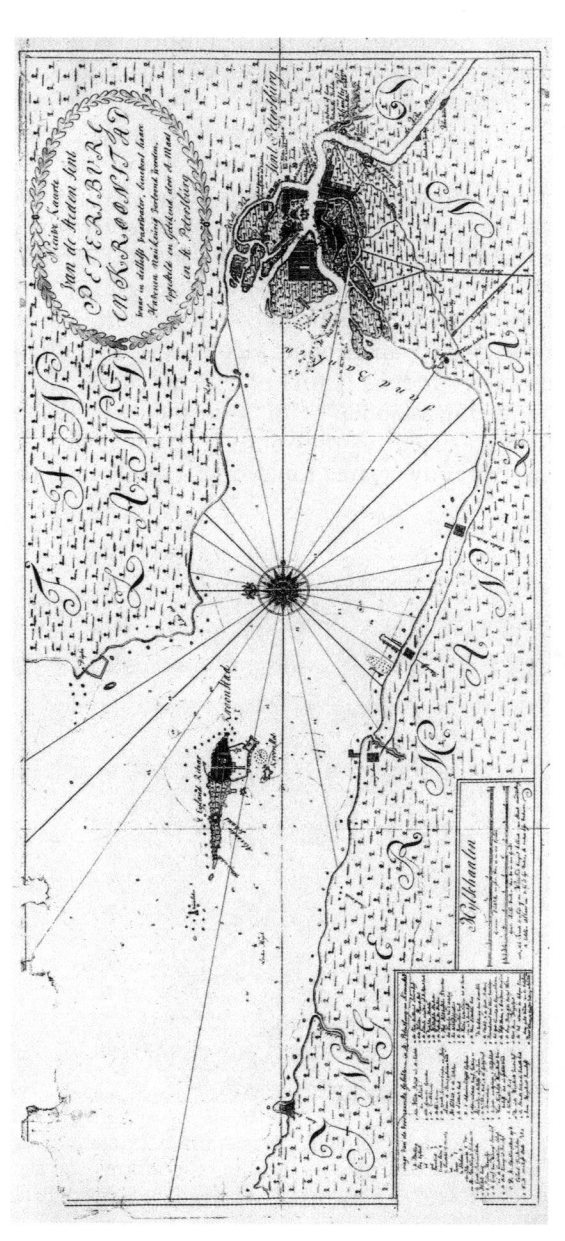

Figure 2 The Forbes/Maas chart of St Petersburg and its environs. Courtesy of the Public Record Office of Northern Ireland (PRONI).

Earl of Granard, during the course of his mission to Russia in the 1730s, and appears to be unique in several details. As an historical artefact, it provides a valuable portrait of St Petersburg during the early life of the city, a time from which very few accurate descriptions have survived. The story of how this chart of the Russian capital and its surroundings came to rest in central Ireland is intimately connected with the history of Anglo-Russian diplomatic and commercial relations.

The Forbes/Maas chart of St Petersburg was created in the Russian capital in 1734 by Abraham Maas. A Dutch cartographer, Maas entered Russian service during the reign of Peter the Great, as did so many other western Europeans.[5] He specialized in creating maps and charts of the eastern portion of the Gulf of Finland. Like the Forbes/Maas chart, some other plans drawn by Maas include detailed depth measurements of the sea lanes between Kronstadt and St Petersburg, a feature that is absent from most contemporary published maps of the city and its surroundings. This and several other characteristic features of the chart are understandable only within its unique historical context.

In contrast to the limited amount of information available regarding the chart's creator, Abraham Maas, the life and activities of its first owner are well documented. He was George, Lord Forbes, who, in the same year that he obtained the chart, became the Third Earl of Granard. Lord Forbes acquired this plan in St Petersburg, where he lived for a year as Great Britain's Envoy Extraordinary and Minister Plenipotentiary to the court of the Empress Anna Ivanovna (ruled 1730–40). While there, he regularly met with the most influential advisers to the tsaritsa, including Andrei Osterman, head of the Russian foreign ministry, and Ernst Johann Biron, Anna's infamous favourite. Lord Forbes's relationship with these men guided the course of Anglo-Russian relations during his year of residence in the Russian capital.

Forbes's mission to Russia was an important and productive one. The British King, George II, sent him to the Russian court with instructions to negotiate a new, more advantageous commercial treaty on behalf of the English merchants trading with Russia through the Baltic and White Seas. The naval supplies that Britain purchased from Russia – hemp, sailcloth, masts, tar and pitch – were vitally important to the operation of the British fleet, making them, in turn, essential to the establishment and preservation of Britain's maritime hegemony. Yet, during the final years of Peter the Great's reign, Russian expansion along the coasts of the Baltic Sea strained relations between the Russian tsar and the first Hanoverian king of England, George I. This diplomatic animosity made it increasingly difficult for English merchants trading in Russia to maintain their historically privileged position within the Russian market. By the late 1720s, Prussian merchants had successfully captured lucrative contracts, formerly held by the English, for the supply of woollen cloth used to make Russian army uniforms. Due to the immense size of its land army, Russia purchased this 'soldiers' cloth', as it was called, in great quantity. It was one of the few commodities manufactured in England that could be sold to Russia in such volume, and at such a significant profit, as to have an impact on the balance of trade between the two nations. Britain's insatiable appetite for naval supplies combined with energetic Prussian competition to produce a significant trade imbalance between London and St Petersburg. British merchants purchased far more in Russia than they could sell and were forced, therefore, to pay for their purchases with gold and silver. As a result of this trade deficit, London merchants sent to Russia £225,000 annually. A deficit of this proportion, and the loss of specie that it entailed, was diametrically opposed to the precepts of eighteenth-century mercantilism.

With Forbes's mission, the British sought to regain and strengthen their commercial position at the court of St Petersburg. As a consequence of his distinguished naval career, Lord Forbes had many friends in high office and was well known to George II, whom he had served on special missions to other European courts in the past. The envoy's elevated social standing and proximity to the king were designed to impress upon the tsaritsa the respect and sincerity of the British monarch for the Russian ruler. Leaders in London believed that this demonstration of political and personal goodwill would assure their Russian counterparts' willingness to negotiate a trade treaty favourable to British interests. However, the Russian court was interested not only in a commercial agreement, but also in a defensive alliance. This was a level of commitment to the Russian court that the British were unwilling to undertake. The resulting delicacy of Lord Forbes's negotiations required that he lengthen his period of residence in St Petersburg, allowing him an opportunity to indulge his natural curiosity by observing the Russian court, the common people, and their new imperial capital. Among the tangible results of his extended residence in St Petersburg were a brief written account of Russia, as well as the acquisition of the chart of the city and its surroundings described here.

With the conclusion of the Anglo-Russian Commercial Treaty of 1734, the mission of Lord Forbes to Russia proved to be a stunning success. The commercial agreement was signed within several months of Forbes's recall from St Petersburg, securing the overwhelmingly advantageous trade concessions that the Envoy had negotiated during the course of his stay in the Russian capital. With this treaty, the British merchants recovered their dominant position in the Russian market. One authority has credited the Commercial Treaty with ushering in a 'golden age' of the English Russia Company's 'power and influence' in St Petersburg.[6] The Treaty accomplished virtually all of London's goals by significantly strengthening the position of English merchants in Russia, while at the same time avoiding any entangling, defensive alliance with the tsaritsa.

In the same year that Forbes returned to Great Britain, he inherited the earldom from his father and, by 1740, had retired from public office to his family's estates in Ireland. The Third Earl of Granard kept the personal documents relating to his mission and the notes he had made while in St Petersburg among the family's private papers. For well over 250 years, these materials remained in Castle Forbes, unavailable to scholars.[7]

The inaccessibility of the Forbes papers meant that an early, detailed and accurate chart of the former Russian capital and its environs has escaped scholarly investigation until now. The chart has been stored, rolled in the drawer of a bureau located in the private office of the Earls of Granard. In the early 1990s, it was catalogued and photocopied under the direction of the Public Record Office of Northern Ireland in Belfast.[8] Both the original and the photocopy were used for the purposes of this description.

In general, few truly accurate maps were drawn of the city of St Petersburg during its first decades of existence. One of these early plans was created by the Swiss/Italian architect Domenico Trezzini. Trezzini came to Russia in 1703 from his position at the court of Denmark and spent the next thirty years of his life contributing to the style and layout of the new Russian capital. Most authorities agree that he 'was the most important of the architects who worked for Peter I', an assessment based, among other things, on 'his influence on the overall shape of the nascent city'.[9] Trezzini died in St Petersburg in 1734, the year the Forbes/Maas chart depicting many of his creations was made.[10]

One of Trezzini's first major assignments was to rebuild the Peter-Paul fortress in stone, a task with which he was occupied for several decades. Peter the Great envisaged his new capital surrounded by water, on the model of Amsterdam. With this in mind, the tsar planned the centre of St Petersburg on Vasil'evskii Island. Trezzini was the first architect to create a city plan reflecting Peter's island-centred vision.[11] Any copy of Trezzini's original plan, first printed in 1716, is very difficult to obtain, but the Russian architectural historian, I.A. Egorov, suggests that the Swiss architect's design for the city centre on Vasil'evskii Island was very much like that portrayed on the 1716 Homann map of Petersburg (Figure 3).[12] In fact, one of the best works on Trezzini, that by I. Lisaevich, mistakenly identifies a photographic reproduction of the Homann map as a plan of the city by Trezzini himself.[13] In his publication describing the architecture and design of the city, Egorov has very little of a positive nature to say concerning Trezzini's early plans. Using the Homann map to illustrate Trezzini's intentions, he refers to them as 'expressionless and mediocre'.[14]

Though very few of his earliest original drawings of an urban plan survive, Trezzini was responsible for the design and construction of several of the capital's most prominent public buildings. Some of these structures still stand within the Peter and Paul fortress, and on the easternmost tip of Vasil'evskii Island, known as the Strelka ('little arrow-head'). Originally, the Strelka was to be the administrative centre of the city, as the location of the Twelve Colleges building, now St Petersburg University, attests. Although Peter the Great decreed the relocation of many of Petersburg's residents from the area near the Admiralty to Vasil'evskii Island, the subsequent growth of the city defied his original plan of making this Island its centre. Nevertheless, as long as Peter lived, Vasil'evskii Island remained the central focus of the city.

In 1716, Peter met the French architect Jean Baptiste Alexandre Le Blond while visiting France.[15] Le Blond 'is generally considered the ablest of the architects to have worked under Peter I'.[16] He was a pupil of the famous French architect Le Nôtre, designer of

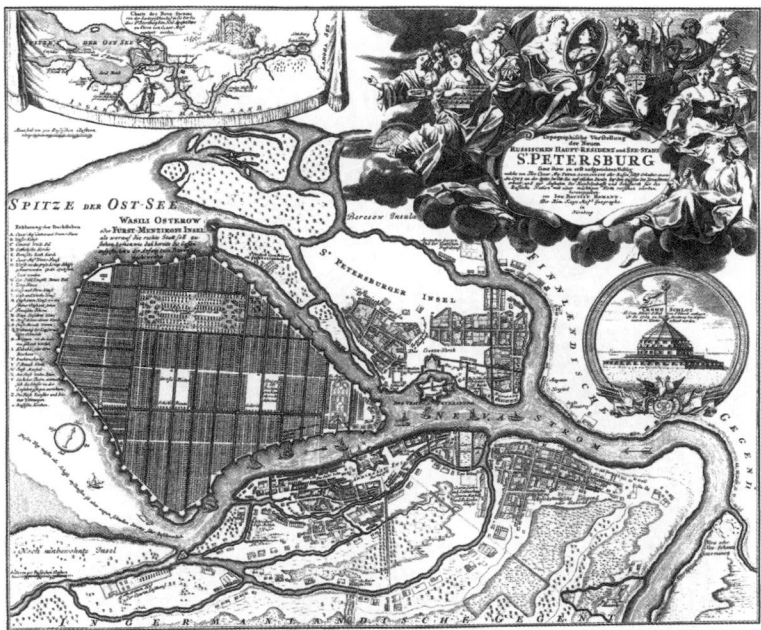

Figure 3 The Homann map of St Petersburg, variously dated between 1716 and 1725. The map is often used to demonstrate Domenico Trezzini's plan for the development of Vasil'evskii Island. Courtesy of Historic Urban Plans, Ithaca, NY.

Versailles, and Peter was so impressed with his talent that he prohibited any subsequent construction in Petersburg without Le Blond's approval. From the time he arrived in the Russian capital until his death in 1719, Le Blond was in charge of all construction in and around the city. At the tsar's request, and with Domenico Trezzini's help, he created a unified urban plan for the development of St Petersburg (Figure 4).[17] Like all of the earliest plans by Trezzini, and others, Le Blond's ambitious design was an 'ideal' proposal for the construction of the city, rather than a record of what had been accomplished.[18] Printed in 1717, it is, perhaps, the most famous and widely published of these early proposals. Unlike Trezzini's extremely scarce and far more modest proposal, which was created in 1715 and

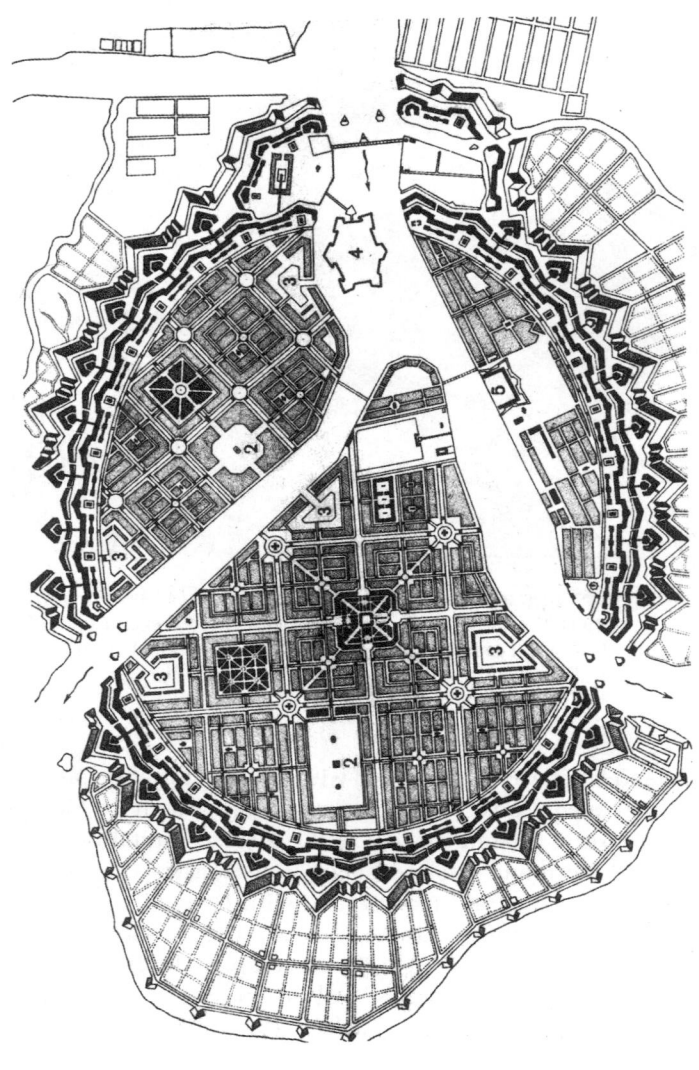

Figure 4 J.B.A. Le Blond's plan for the reconstruction of St Petersburg, 1717. Illustration from A.W. Bunin, *Geschichte des Russischen Städtebaues bis zum 19. Jahrhundert* (Berlin, 1961), no. 110.

approved and printed in 1716, the design of Peter's new director of urban construction is found in virtually all publications concerned with the early history of St Petersburg. In accordance with Peter I's wishes, Le Blond's plan also centred the city on Vasil'evskii Island, where the tsar's palace would be built. It included an elaborate ring of defensive battlements that surrounded this central city. James Cracraft suggests that the grandiose nature of Le Blond's plan 'would have been far beyond the technical and financial resources at Peter's command'.[19] Egorov believes that it was technically far superior to Trezzini's modest plan, which he describes as 'vastly inferior to Leblond's design'.[20] Despite the apparent aesthetic superiority of Le Blond's city plan, it was, of course, no more likely to be realized than Trezzini's, or any others, as the 'natural' growth of the capital gradually moved the centre of the city towards the Admiralty, or southern, bank of the Neva River.

The early urban designs of the plans by Le Blond, Trezzini, and others are evident in the most widely publicized maps that followed. A variety of factors including the swampy, low-lying nature of the soil on the proposed central (Vasil'evskii) island, mistakes during construction, and the defeat of Sweden in the Great Northern War (1700–21) rendered certain key elements of these early plans impossible or unnecessary. Still, the idea of a completely developed, urban and fortified centre of the city on Vasil'evskii Island, to the north-west of the modern city centre, remained a feature in the work of most later cartographers. According to Egorov and Cracraft, it was Trezzini's original 1715 plan for the city centre, as represented on the Homann map of 1716 (with later editions), that influenced both the subsequent development of Vasil'evskii Island, as well as a majority of western representations of the Russian capital throughout the eighteenth century.[21] This characteristic element of the early urban plans of St Petersburg tended to obscure the reality of the city's growth.

As they were designed to do, the early urban proposals set a precedent for combining the representation of existing structures found in the new capital with a whole variety of projected, but not yet realized, developments. For example, Le Blond's 1717 plan of St Petersburg includes accurate representations of the Admiralty and the Peter-Paul fortress, yet the avenues, palaces and gardens located on the aforementioned Vasil'evskii Island are almost entirely fictional. This combination of real and projected construction depicted on the same plan tends to obscure the actual extent and configuration of the city in any given year. It is possible that the perpetuation of this obfuscation of the size and shape of the new capital might have been encouraged by Peter the Great and his successors at a time when Russian leaders increasingly sought not only European acceptance, but an ever greater acknowledgement of their role in European political decision-making.

During the eighteenth century, the absence of documentary evidence provided by more modern technology meant that a city's size and shape were recorded and publicized almost exclusively through maps. The influence or outright control of a monarch over cartographers and their work translated into the ability to control the public, and, therefore, the international, perception of the extent and grandeur of a given city. Considering the desire of Peter the Great and his successors to secure and perpetuate Russia's prominence among the European courts, it is not difficult to understand why the earliest original projections of a large and well-planned capital would serve as the models for several widely published maps of the city.

Le Blond, Trezzini and the other earliest city planners should be excused for combining real and imagined elements on the same plan, since Peter expressly commissioned them to design the layout of the future capital. Their drawings are, by nature, diagrams of forthcoming construction, taking into account existing structures and serving as foundational plans for the future.

The next generation of cartographers and authors, who produced the earliest representations of St Petersburg for publication, had no such commission. Their goal was to portray the city as it stood, yet several of them seem to have relied too heavily on first generation projections created by Trezzini, Le Blond and the others. They, too, depict the city with both real and imagined elements, leaving an impression with the viewer that the capital was much more developed than was actually the case. Two maps of the city that were widely distributed in the 1720s, demonstrate this tendency and seem to be closely linked to the earliest plans in this respect. A thorough comparison, in this instance as well as others, highlights the relative accuracy of the Forbes/Maas chart, as well as its place in the evolution of the cartography of the capital.

A German map of St Petersburg created by Johann Baptiste Homann in Nuremburg became one of the most recognizable representations of the city in western Europe towards the end of the first quarter of the eighteenth century (Figure 3). The map is not dated and, although it appeared in a popular Homann atlas in the 1730s, it was probably created several years before this publication.[22] Some historians and cartographers believe this map dates from 1718, or possibly earlier. Homann, who died in 1724, was employed by Peter the Great to make many maps that were based on Russian originals, since the German mapmaker never travelled to Russia. There is, in fact, much to indicate that the Homann map of the Russian capital was significantly influenced by early plans such as Trezzini's and Le Blond's. As mentioned above, scholars who study Domenico Trezzini and his work, such as Lisaevich and Egorov, often use this Homann map to fill the gap in the cartographic record of his plans for Vasil'evskii Island and its development as the centre of St Petersburg.

The degree of development of Vasil'evskii Island on the Homann map, here also identified as 'Fürst-Menzikofs Insel', seems to suggest a stronger relationship to these earlier plans than to the reality of the capital's urban growth. A note included on the map itself acknowledges the fact that the island '*should* be the location of the true city with the streets already marked out and building started'.[23] The level of development of Vasil'evskii Island depicted on the Homann map demonstrates continuity with earlier plans as well as with those that followed, especially those associated with Friedrich Christian Weber's account of Russia discussed below. An inset view of the fortress of 'Cronslot' is included on the Homann map. This feature is also a part of the maps contained in Weber's later publications.

The map of St Petersburg that accompanied Friedrich Christian Weber's account of Russia, *Das veränderte Russland...*, first published in 1721, represents Vasil'evskii Island as both encircled with fortifications and completely developed, with a regular grid of streets and blocks of residential buildings (Figure 5).[24] Near the centre is a large, landscaped park identified as a 'tree and pleasure garden for the enjoyment of all people'.[25] The Weber map is remarkably similar to the Homann map in this and many other respects. In the year of this map's publication, both the buildings and the park did not yet exist. In fact, due to the shift of the city's centre from Vasil'evskii Island to

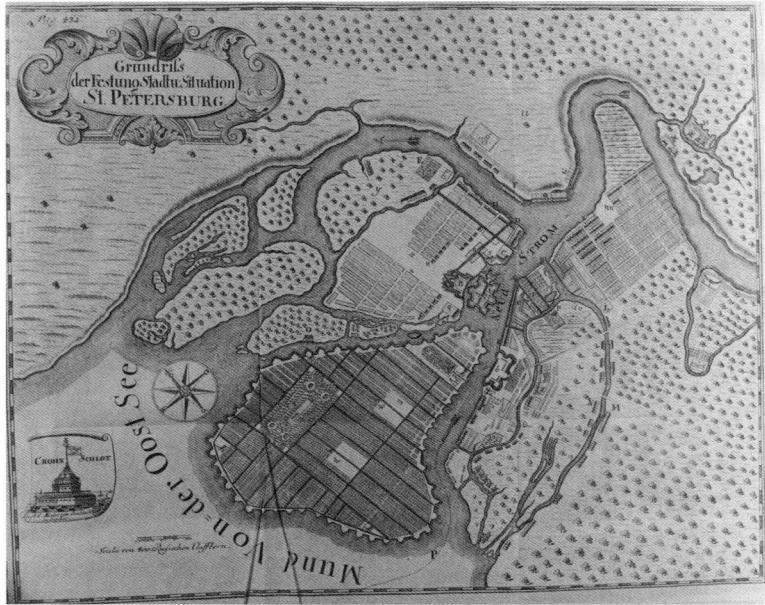

Figure 5 The map of St Petersburg accompanying F.C. Weber's *Das veränderte Russland* (Frankfurt, 1721), which borrows extensively from the Homann map. Courtesy of the James Ford Bell Library, Minneapolis, MN.

the area that was then known as Admiralty Island, the anticipated formal garden and palace ensemble was never built. Although these features are clearly shown on the map, an explanatory note in the text of Weber's book acknowledges that the drawing is a projection of the future by pointing out that the streets of the island were laid out and the construction had already started,[26] and that, eventually, the whole island would be populated and fortified with a line of breastworks.[27] The wording here is remarkably similar to that found on the Homann map and the reference to future fortification may betray a familiarity and connection with Le Blond's grandiose design of 1717.

The Forbes/Maas chart as well as the later Russian Academy of Sciences plan differ markedly from the Homann and Weber maps of an earlier period. Of special interest is the fact that these later plans show the city as *less* developed than those produced 15–20 years earlier. Both the Forbes/Maas chart and the Academy map show Vasil'evskii Island as largely undeveloped, with regular streets covering only about one-third of its area, and buildings even less. Of particular significance is the depiction on the Forbes/Maas and Academy plans of a 'galley harbour'[28] located on the gulf, or western, side of the island. This harbour is ignored in earlier maps, despite the fact that they show this particular section of the city to be completely developed. By comparison with the Forbes/Maas and Academy plans, the Weber map also exaggerates the extent of completed construction in the eastern section of the city, north of the Alexander Nevskii Monastery. Here, the earlier map depicts a solid block of buildings, with a grid of regular streets, stretching from the Fontanka river (near the Summer Palace) eastward, or up river, to the bank of the Neva before it bends toward the city. The later plans show only a limited number of structures clustered around the Fontanka, with large forested areas reaching toward the eastern Neva. The Forbes chart identifies the region as the 'het Tierhof', with only scattered structures located along the bank of the river.

In other regions of the city, the Weber and Homann maps are remarkably similar to both the Forbes/Maas and the Academy plans. It comes as no surprise that the most notable sites in the centre of the city are accurately portrayed on all of the maps. The earliest edifices of the capital, such as the Peter-Paul fortress, the Admiralty, the Cronwerk and Prince Menshikov's palace, appear with little variation. Even less famous, yet still important structures are equally as universal in their representation. Among these are the new slaughterhouse (a point of interest on all of the maps), the Tartar suburb and the great market on Petersburg Island, as well as the Apothecary garden to the north, on what the earlier maps refer to as Beresow Island. The Forbes/Maas and Academy plans consider this area to be the northern part of Petersburg Island, rather than an entirely separate island. The variation in the description and placement of these most recognizable symbols of the city is slight.

The Forbes/Maas chart is larger than most contemporary maps of the capital, measuring 138 cm (4.53 ft) horizontally by 60 cm (1.97 ft) vertically. In storage for two and one half centuries, it was rolled from right to left. As a consequence, the left (outside) portion of the map has been damaged. This damage consists of missing fragments of the map in the upper and lower left corners. The loss of the upper portion, apparently representing a small area of the Baltic Sea, seems to have only a slight impact on the research value of the document. The missing fragment in the lower left corner of the map is far more serious, since it includes roughly 16 per cent of the legend identifying significant buildings and locations within the heart of the city. Through a simultaneous examination of several maps of St Petersburg from the period, a number of these missing items have been reliably identified.[29] They consist mainly of points of interest in the section of the city that lie to the north of the Peter-Paul Fortress, usually identified on contemporary maps as Petersburg Island.

The Forbes/Maas chart seems to be unique in several ways. It combines the detail, while actually exceeding the accuracy, of almost all contemporary published maps of the capital city with the broad geographical scope of a naval chart representing the Gulf of Finland. In this respect, it is accurately titled *Nieuwe Kaarte van de Steden Sint Petersburg en Kroonstad waar in desselbts vaarwater, benevens haare Havenen naukeurig vertoond werden, opgesteld en Getekend door A:Maas in St. Petersburg*.[30] As the previous discussion regarding Vasil'evskii Island indicates, the detailed information regarding the city is more accurate than that found on almost any map of St Petersburg published before 1734. In addition, the geographical features depicted in the Gulf would have made this chart a valuable navigational tool for the region. The chart depicts an area stretching from the settlement on the left bank of the Neva river in the east, as it bends towards the city, identified here as *Schans ter Nÿen*, to a point far to the west of the island of Kronstadt. The most westward terrestrial point identified is the *Krasne Gorki* (Krasnye gorki?), beyond the *Liebidie Reka* (Lebiazhia River?). The territory to the north of the capital, including *Lisini Nos*, is labelled Finland, and that encompassing the southern coast of the gulf is labelled *Ingermanland*. Identified within these boundaries are the notable sites of the city of St Petersburg itself, the port of *Kroonstad* (Kronstadt) on the island of *Ritzar* (Kotlin), and the rural imperial residences of *Strelna muse* (Strel'na), *Peterhoff* (Peterhof), and *Oranjenboom* (Oranienbaum). Very few, if any, published contemporary plans combine such geographic scope with so accurate and detailed a view of the central city and its prominent buildings.

The Forbes/Maas chart is a geographical document uniquely tied to the mission of Britain's Envoy Extraordinary in 1733–34. The broad scope of the chart seems to represent Lord Forbes's interests and activities, particularly as they were related to events in the spring of 1734. During the course of his mission, he had visited the summer residences of the tsaritsa, including Peterhof and Oranienbaum, on several occasions. In the spring of 1734, at the time that he was recalled to London, Forbes was preparing to spend the summer with the Russian court at Peterhof. Each summer, the court moved to the seaside residence during the month of July. Due to the lack of accommodations near the tsaritsa's summer residence, Forbes was fitting out a yacht on which he intended to live during this seasonal visit. This arrangement for accommodation at the summer residence was not as unusual as it may initially appear, considering the fact that Forbes was a career naval officer. He planned to solve his problem of accommodation as he attended the Russian Court in a way that appealed to his love of the sea. As the second son of the Earl of Granard, he had entered naval service at an early age. By the time he sailed to Russia as George II's envoy, he was 56 years old and could reflect on a distinguished naval career. In fact, shortly after his return to London from St Petersburg, he became an admiral of the fleet. The chart he obtained in 1734 may have been acquired specifically for his planned summer 'residence' on the Gulf of Finland. The details of stone reefs, sand banks and depths of sea lanes included on the chart would have been exceedingly valuable for navigating the waters between the capital and Peterhof. Landmarks of the city and the surrounding countryside are clearly marked on the plan. In addition to these very practical pieces of information, the chart seems to reflect Forbes's naval interests in a variety of other ways.

Unlike most of the city maps that were published within a few years of 1734, the Forbes/Maas chart includes a detailed description of the port of Kronstadt. Various harbours of the port are identified, as well as several buildings and fortifications on the island that were connected with shipbuilding and the navy. These details would have been of enormous interest to a naval officer like Forbes. He had visited the island briefly upon his arrival in 1733, when the man-of-war carrying him to Russia had anchored off the port, but no evidence exists of any further visits. The information on the chart may have represented the most intimate knowledge of the port Lord Forbes was likely to obtain. In addition to the plan of Kronstadt and various landmarks, the depths of the waterways between the port and the capital are recorded. Again, this was an important detail that certainly would have appealed to a naval officer and provided very practical and valuable information for a summer of cruising on the Gulf. Few known plans of St Petersburg in this period contain these detailed elements.

Lord Forbes returned from his mission to the Russian court with a very practical and accurate plan of the capital and its surrounding waterways. He obviously obtained it for his personal use, as a sort of useful souvenir, keeping it with his papers at Castle Forbes. Unlike the chart, his official correspondence remained at the Northern Department (the future Foreign Office) in London. The Forbes/Maas chart of St Petersburg represents a significant step in the evolution of the mapping of the city. In general, its accuracy supersedes that of earlier published plans and anticipates the creation of the Academy of Sciences map of the capital three years later.

Notes

1. This is a valid criticism of several early maps of the city, including those available to the educated public of the early eighteenth century, such as that which accompanied F.C. Weber's *Das veränderte Russland* (Frankfurt, 1721) (Figure 5), as well as one of the most widely distributed and copied maps by Johann Baptiste Homann (Figure 3).
2. R.E. Jones, 'Why St. Petersburg?', in L. Hughes (ed.), *Peter the Great and the West: New Perspectives* (London, 2001), p. 194.
3. A reproduction and brief discussion of this Academy map can be found in Alexei Postnikov, *Russia in Maps: A History of the Geographical Study and Cartography of the Country* (Moscow, 1996), pp. 42, 49. Though Postnikov states that this map 'details the entire city in five sections, and depicts town buildings as they stood in 1737', the publication date of the map reproduced is given as 1741. The author of the present article has studied an original of this Academy map found in the collection of the James Ford Bell Library at the University of Minnesota in Minneapolis, Minnesota. This original is part of a collection of Russian maps assembled by the First Earl of Malmesbury. It is catalogued as: Russian maps/ by various cartographers; collected by Lord Malmesbury, British ambassador to the court of Catherine the Great. [S.I.: s.n.], 1728–83, 2 vols.

4. This chart, as well as the private papers of the Third Earl of Granard which explain its origins, have been microfilmed. These copies are located in the Public Record Office of Northern Ireland (PRONI) in Belfast.
5. Little biographical information regarding Maas is available from any source, but recent discussions with Dr Edwin Okhuizen, an Amsterdam map historian researching Dutch cartographers in the service of Peter the Great, have provided several important details. Dr Okhuizen is the foremost authority on Maas. He has completed a dissertation on Dutch cartographers in the service of Peter the Great, and is planning a detailed study of Maas and his plans of the eastern portion of the Gulf of Finland. According to Dr Okhuizen, Maas appears to have been a prolific and detail-oriented cartographer.
6. Anthony Cross, *By the Banks of the Neva* (Cambridge, 1997), p. 46.
7. Several scholars knew of the existence of the Forbes papers through the cataloguing efforts of the Royal Commission on Manuscripts. See the *Second Report of the Royal Commission on Historical Manuscripts* (London, 1874), p. 216. Although Lord Forbes's correspondence is described in this volume, the 1734 chart of St Petersburg is not mentioned. For a scholarly reference to the Forbes materials prior to their more recent cataloguing and copying by the Public Record Office in Belfast, see Betty Kemp, 'Sir Francis Dashwood's Diary of his Visit to St. Petersburg in 1733', *Slavonic and East European Review*, XXXVIII (1959) 194–222. Dashwood travelled to St Petersburg as a passenger on the ship carrying Lord Forbes to his post in May/June 1733.
8. The copy is catalogued among the Forbes papers in the Public Record Office of Northern Ireland (PRONI), Forbes Documents T3765/F/1.
9. James Cracraft, *The Petrine Revolution in Russian Architecture* (Chicago, 1988), p. 160.
10. From 27 November 1994 to 6 February 1995, the Museo Cantonale d'Arte in Lugano, Switzerland, presented an exhibition entitled 'Domenico Trezzini e la costruzione di San Pietroburgo'. A catalogue of this exhibition, with the same title, was published in Florence in 1994. It is one of the most recent publications dedicated to the life and work of Trezzini in Russia.
11. Cracraft states, 'It was Trezzini and his assistants who first laid out the streets and squares of Vasilevskii Island, projected to be the city's central district...' (Cracraft, *Petrine Revolution*, p. 156).
12. I.A. Egorov, *The Architectural Planning of St. Petersburg* (Athens, Ohio, 1969), p. 21. Egorov here uses the Homann map (Figure 3) to illustrate Trezzini's plan. He identifies the Homann map as 'An etching made by I.B. Homann in 1716, showing Trezzini's planning project for Vasil'evski Island'.
13. I. Lisaevich, *Pervyi arkhitektor Peterburga* (Leningrad, 1971), p. 57.
14. Egorov, *Architectural Planning*, p. 25.
15. Although he died in 1719, Le Blond was responsible for much of the early planning of the new capital city as well as the summer residences of Peterhof and Strel'na. Peter I appears to have valued Le Blond's

contributions to the design and construction of the city. The French architect received an annual salary of 5,000 roubles for his work, five times the salary of his predecessor and colleague Dominico Trezzini.
16. Cracraft, *Petrine Revolution*, p. 158.
17. *Ibid.*
18. For a thorough discussion of the creation and timing of these early plans of St Petersburg, see T.A. Bazarova's article, 'Plany petrovskogo Peterburga', in Iu. N. Bespiatykh (ed.), *Fenomen Peterburga* (Saint Petersburg, 2000), pp. 314–26.
19. Cracraft, *Petrine Revolution*, p. 159.
20. Egorov, *Architectural Planning*, p. 25.
21. *Ibid.*, p. 23; and Cracraft, *Petrine Revolution*, p. 159.
22. J.B. Homann, *Grosser atlas uber die gantze Welt wie diese sowel...* (Nuremberg, 1731), Plate 131.
23. Translation from the German text of the map. This is precisely the wording used in the later 'Weber' plans of the city, supporting the theory of an additional close link between the Homann and Weber maps. See below.
24. F.C. Weber, *Das veränderte Russland: in welchem die jetzige verfassung des geist- und weltlichem regiments...in einem biss 1720 gehenden journal vorgestellt werden, mit einer accuraten land-carte und kupferstichen versehe* (Frankfurt, 1721).
25. *Ibid.*, p. 432.
26. In the legend to the map included in Weber's work, under 'm.' he writes, 'Auf dieser Insul, Wasili-Osterow genannt, soll die rechted Stadt zu stehen kommen, und sind die Gassen schon ausgesteckt, auch bereits ein Anfang zu bauen gemacht' (see above).
27. My translation from the original German found on p. 464 in Weber's description of the city. The first published English translation of this work, *The Present State of Russia...* printed in 1723, includes a plan of the city based even more identifiably on the earlier Homann map. In fact, the cartouche found in the upper right of this map is nearly an exact mirror image of that found on the original Homann map. The explanatory notes mentioned above are also included in English translation on the 1723 English version of the Weber text. They are accurate translations from the German Homann originals.
28. The Forbes chart uses the phrase 'de Galey Haven' and the Academy map 'Galeeren Hafen'. It is, of course, possible that this harbour was constructed between 1725 and 1734, though during much of this period the northern city was ignored by the Russian Court, which tended to favour Moscow, especially from 1727 to 1731. Other sources date the construction of the harbour between 1715 and 1720. Today, the waterway that corresponds to this 'harbour' is located just to the southeast of the Pribaltiiskaia Hotel.
29. The maps found to be most valuable for the purposes of this reconstruction were the 1737 Academy map of St Petersburg, as well as that found in F.C. Weber's German account of Russia dating from 1721.

30. This brief title and description, including the year 1734, is found in a cartouche located in the upper right corner of the document. I am indebted to Dr Edwin Okhuizen for the following translation: 'New map of the towns of St Petersburg and Kronstadt, which accurately shows [presents] that waterway [channel] next to her harbours, composed and drawn by A. Maas in St Petersburg.'

3
The English Embankment
Anthony Cross

For the student of the history of St Petersburg and of Anglo-Russian relations no subject might seem more self-recommending than the English Embankment (*Angliiskaia naberezhnaia*), eloquently named and strategically placed in the heart of the city and on the left bank of the Neva in full flow for the Gulf of Finland. Let us, like Pushkin and his friend Onegin in the poet's famous drawing, lean on the granite parapet of the Neva embankment and gaze across the river, but from Vasil'evskii Island, near the Academy of Arts, towards the Admiralty Side and the Bronze Horseman, which stands in what is now Decembrists' Square (*ploshchad' Dekabristov*), but was first Isaakievskaia, then Petrovskaia, then Senatskaia, and let our eyes move right past the rounded corner of Carlo Rossi's Senate, which was only built in 1829–32 and which today houses the Russian State Historical Archive (RGIA). What we see today is, of course, somewhat different from what Pushkin and his contemporaries saw, but not unrecognizably so. True, the golden dome of St Isaacs gleams for us as it did not for him and the Lt Shmidt Bridge, even in its first incarnations as the Blagoveshchenskii and the Nikolaevskii, did not yet span the river, but the line of buildings on the opposite embankment, despite many late nineteenth-century adjustments and changes, produces a more or less similar impression of flow and harmony. Distance indeed lends enchantment to the view and too close an acquaintance today with many of the buildings brings a sense of melancholy at what was and at what has still to be done, noble tercentenary efforts notwithstanding. It is, however, the English Embankment within the historical parameters set for the conference which is the subject of this essay, the first century and a quarter of its 300-year existence.

Of course, the English Embankment as such had not existed for a century and a quarter, certainly not under that name and certainly not as a recognizable thoroughfare. There had been a river bank as long as there had been a river and despite Pushkin's emphasizing the unpopulated nature of the lands that Peter the Great surveyed in 1703, there had been a Finnish homestead where the Admiralty was to be established, and yet another near what is now Work Square (*ploshchad' Truda*), approximately mid-point along the embankment. Peter was not one to scorn sites which experience (if not his own) had shown to have advantages (just as he had the Summer Garden laid out where the Swedish major Konau had earlier had an estate). Nevertheless, the Neva delta was generally a most unlikely and unpropitious place for a capital city and the western area of what became known as the Admiralty Island (*Admiralteiskii ostrov*) or (First) Admiralty District was marshy and covered in scrub and subject to frequent inundation, but thereby no different from many other places on the left bank and on the islands.[1]

The Admiralty was to stand in the middle of what was, indeed, also an island, formed to the south by the meandering River M'ia or Moika. To the east of the Admiralty along what became Dvortsovaia or Palace Embankment down to the Summer Garden and beyond residences, including the first modest Winter Palaces, were to be built for the high and mighty, but to the west everything was intended to be subservient to the needs and demands of shipbuilding. The necessity of making the Admiralty not simply a vast shipyard but also a fortress, bristling with cannon and complementing the firepower of the Peter-Paul Fortress across the river, was, however, soon recognized and it was as part of these defences that a wide and open area, a glacis, was created on the land-side of the Admiralty. Beyond this space, to the south towards the Moika and to the west, there grew up numerous settlements (*slobody*) of workers engaged in all aspects of shipbuilding, soldiers and sailors and a warren of unplanned and unregulated alleys and wooden houses. Names such as Morskie, Pushkarskaia, Priadil'naia and Kuznetskaia point clearly to their origins and, not unexpectedly, some were subsequently preserved in street names (e.g. Bol'shaia and Malaia Morskaia, Pushkarskaia, now Pochtamtskaia). The Shnevenskaia *sloboda*, situated near the present-day Work Square, differed from others in that it bore the name of the commanding officer of a company of naval infantry, Shnevenets, who may, among other duties, have been responsible for the gun batteries established along the shore line that was to be the English Embankment. It was also there that in 1706 Peter ordered the establishment of a prison (*katorzhnyi dom*) for recalcitrant admiralty workers and officials, among whom a number were to be forced to row in chains in the galleys which were built in the galley wharf (*galernyi dvor*, later *verf'*), situated at the western end of Admiralty Island since 1711.

The whole area between the two wharves was originally known as New Holland (*Novaia Gollandiia*), perhaps in memory of Peter's sojourn in Dutch shipyards rather than for a concentration of Dutch craftsmen and specialists; later the name was given specifically to the island formed by the Moika and two new canals (the Galernyi Canal, dug in 1717, and the Kriukov Canal, in 1719), where for a brief period Peter had a small summer house and formal garden, and the entrance to which from the Moika eventually became Vallin de la Mothe's imposing arch (only completed in 1779). A whole system of canals was created, of which the most important was the Admiralteiskii, completed in 1720. This canal was also known as Priadil'nyi, indicating the location of the huge and vital rope-walk (*priadil'nyi* or *kanatnyi dvor*), which began to produce cordage in 1721 and is described in detail by the Holsteiner Bergholz.[2] The Admiralteiskii Canal connected to the east with the wide moat and inner canal of the Admiralty itself. The canals allowed supplies of timber and masts and cordage to be moved quickly and efficiently (as well, of course, as aiding drainage). The Kriukov (apparently named after the contractor) and Galernyi Canals joined the Neva to the Moika, the former bisecting what was to become the English Embankment and the latter forming its western boundary. Although the Galernyi still exists under its present name of the Novo-Admiralteiskii, the part of the Kriukov canal which ran from the Admiralteiskii canal to the Neva was filled in in 1842 when construction work was started on the Blagoveshchenskii Bridge. In that year the same fate befell the Admiralteiskii canal from its point of intersection with the Kriukov to the east where it emerged on Senate Square and the resultant road became the Konnogvardeiskii or Horseguards Boulevard.

By the time the various canals were dug, the first significant development had begun on the future English Embankment and its inner parallel street, Galernaia. The great early twentieth-century historian of St Petersburg, P.N. Stolpianskii, liked to cite what took place as evidence that 'Petersburg was built without any strict, thought-out plan'[3] and to emphasize that Peter, who was originally firmly opposed to the building of private dwellings in this general area, was virtually outflanked by the city's governor Prince Aleksandr Menshikov. At all events, Menshikov was intent on developing the large plot he had secured opposite his palace on Vasil'evskii Island and in 1715–16 there were built the so-called *kniazheskie mazanki*,[4] a long and high daub building with tiled roof, which provided lodgings for foreign workmen, and alongside a tavern or *kabak* which proved, quite unexpectedly, of course, popular and well used. To the east Menshikov's plot looked towards the wooden Church of St Isaac of Dalmatia, which had been built where the Bronze Horseman would be sited decades later and which would be replaced by a stone church designed by Mattarnovi and begun in 1719. To the west the French architect Le Blond set up soon after his arrival in 1716 a series of specialist workshops. By the end of 1715 the first regulation on the dimensions and heights of houses was issued and followed by the first register of plots 'from the Avsteriia [a corruption of *osteria* and referring to the Menshikov building] downstream'.[5] Other plots were distributed among Peter's favourites, not surprisingly including the English shipbuilders Richard Cozens and Joseph Nye, who worked in the Admiralty yards. The development of the embankment was affected by numerous specific and general decrees in these years, not least those which demanded building in accordance with the standard houses designed by Trezzini and Le Blond and in stone or *mazankovyi*, observance of a single building line, the *krasnaia liniia*, and of a unified 'horizon'. There was intensive building in the area after 1719, although Peter's exasperation, not to call it something more, at his subjects' inability or unwillingness to build in accordance with his edicts or, indeed, to inhabit their houses, is clearly felt in repeat edicts. In 1721 the permission to have a common wall between adjacent houses emphasized the unity of façades, establishing what became a significant feature: that there should be no gateways from the embankment itself, only from the rear of the properties from what became Galernaia Street. Peter was, however, particularly concerned about the mushrooming of private wooden homes in this back area, which would become the right side of

Galernaia: on the left side were the warehouses and other official buildings serving the ropewalk and facing the canal. In connection with the building of the ropewalk, there had been issued an *ukaz* in June 1720 'not to build in St Petersburg near the ropewalk and other buildings belonging to the Admiralty' and in 1723 Peter personally inspected the area and ordered the dismantling of buildings (*mazankovye* in fact) belonging to Menshikov and others.[6]

The state of the actual embankment itself was a continuing cause for concern. Owners were obliged to secure the bank with rows of piles and earth tightly packed behind fascines and faced on the riverside by a wall of planks, painted black and white. Each property was obliged to have a landing stage, reached by twin flights of stairs. The constant flooding, however, caused havoc, particularly the high inundation of 1721, after which it was ordered that the roadway should be paved in stone and that suitable underground drains be constructed from the houses to the river. Ordering was one thing; fulfilling was another. One of Menshikov's last decrees as governor in April 1727 referred to the urgent need to repave the embankment.[7]

Foreign accounts of St Petersburg provide interesting glimpses of the western area of Admiralty Island during Peter's reign. Friedrich Christian Weber, who was the Hanoverian Resident in the Russian capital between 1714 and 1719, published in 1721 his *Das veränderte Russland*, which appeared in English two years later. The detailed description of St Petersburg he included as an appendix to his account was essentially an updating of an anonymous German account of 1718, now attributed to a certain Geerkens:[8]

> South-west of the Admiralty-yard stands the Admiralty Church whither the Court goes to divine Service. It is of Wood and but small, for which reason it is to be taken down, and another to be built on the large Place. Next to it stands Prince Menzicoff's Inn, a long Building of Carpenters-work, covered with Pantiles. But as it is not yet fitted up for the Reception of Strangers, there live in it at present some German and French Manufacturers and Artificers, particularly the Handicraftsmen who came from Dantzick in the Year 1716, for whom the Czar pays House-rent to Prince Menzicoff. Behind this Building is the Rope yard which furnishes the Fleet with Ropes and other Necessaries. Next to it live the Coppersmiths and lower down on the Water-side is the great

Admiralty Forge in which there are thirty odd Furnaces. ... Somewhat lower is the Slaughter-house which furnishes this part of the Town with Meat in abundance; further down along the Water stands a great *Ambare* or Store-house, near which they build Gallies, between twenty and thirty every Year.[9]

The French traveller Aubry de la Motraye visited the Russian capital a year after Peter's death and from his description it is clear that a considerable amount of building had taken place towards the end of his reign along the river-bank from the Admiralty to the Galley Wharf:

> On the S.W. of this Yard, is a fine Church built of Brick, or which seemed to promise so when I saw it, for it was not then finished: and they proceeded as slowly in this, as in the other Works begun before the Death of Peter the First. On the same Side along the Neva, almost as far as Catherine-Hoff, there is a great Number of Palaces of Brick and Stone, which belong to the Nobility, and Sea and Land-Officers; ... Near the new Church in Admiralty-Island stands Prince Menzikoff's Inn, a long building of Timber; which has no manner of Magnificence about it, but consists of a great Number of low Rooms, with other Conveniences, for the Entertainment of Strangers. Behind these Palaces in Admiralty-Island stands the Rope-Yard, about 800 steps long. There is but one broad well-paved Street, between the Courts or little Gardens belonging to these Palaces, and this long Building. On the same side with the Rope-Yard, upon the bank of the little Canal, which forms the Admiralty-Island, stands the Forge of the Admiralty, in which are 32 Furnaces. Further down at the Extremity of the Island, upon the Bank of the River Neva, is the Admiralty of Galleys situated where the little Canal communicates by a little Branch with the River, and refunds the Water it borrowed from below the Imperial Summer-Palace, by two larger Branches, one about 200 Paces below this Admiralty, and the other about 300 Paces lower; so that it forms as the same Time a little Island with it.[10]

It is, however, a recently discovered and published drawing of the left bank of the Neva from the Foundry in the east to the Gulf of Finland that provides a unique, bird's eye view of the Admiralty area.

Probably the work of a Dutchman working in the shipyards, the drawing nevertheless is captioned in English (of a sort). It is entitled 'The E.S. Prospective of St. Peterboug [sic] up the Goulff of Fienlad [sic] with Part of the River Neva', and has been tentatively dated between 1721 and 1724.[11] It shows to the west of the Admiralty the as yet unfinished Church of St Isaac and between it and the Kriukov Canal along the embankment some five large mansions, four with their own landing stages, and one smaller house. To the right of the canal stands another large mansion. The embankment is then seen to bend forward before a further straight section, on which stand some seven or eight houses presenting a single façade, continues as far as the Galernyi Canal. Behind this section of the embankment up the River Moika can be four further streets with considerable numbers of houses; on the eastern section there is one row of houses shown between the embankment and the ropewalk (Figure 6).

Menshikov's very personal interest in the area of the embankment where he had his property led to the establishing of the first pontoon bridge across the Neva also in 1727, a structure which Peter would hardly have countenanced but which was a convenient link between Menshikov's palace on Vasil'evskii Island and the Admiralty Side. However, Menshikov's fall from power in the autumn of that year was followed not only by the dismantling of the bridge but also by the removal of the court to Moscow. The subsequent neglect of the capital was only halted by Anna's accession and her return to St Petersburg at the beginning of 1732.

Among the empress's first acts was the restoration 'without delay' of the Isaakievskii Bridge (so-called because of its proximity to the Church of St Isaac of Dalmatia) and she turned her attention to the adjoining embankment, issuing a decree 'on the building of houses and the strengthening of the banks of the River Neva by those persons who had received plots in St Petersburg located below the Admiralty' (10 June 1732).[12] She was insistent that those who had been granted plots along the embankment should build stone houses on them. In their number was Richard Cozens who said that Peter I had promised to have a house built for him but had died when only the foundation had been laid and he (Cozens) had no funds to continue with the building; the plot was taken away from Cozens and he was transferred to the Archangel shipyards. Two years later it was given to Peter I's cousin Aleksandr L'vovich Naryshkin, and it was he

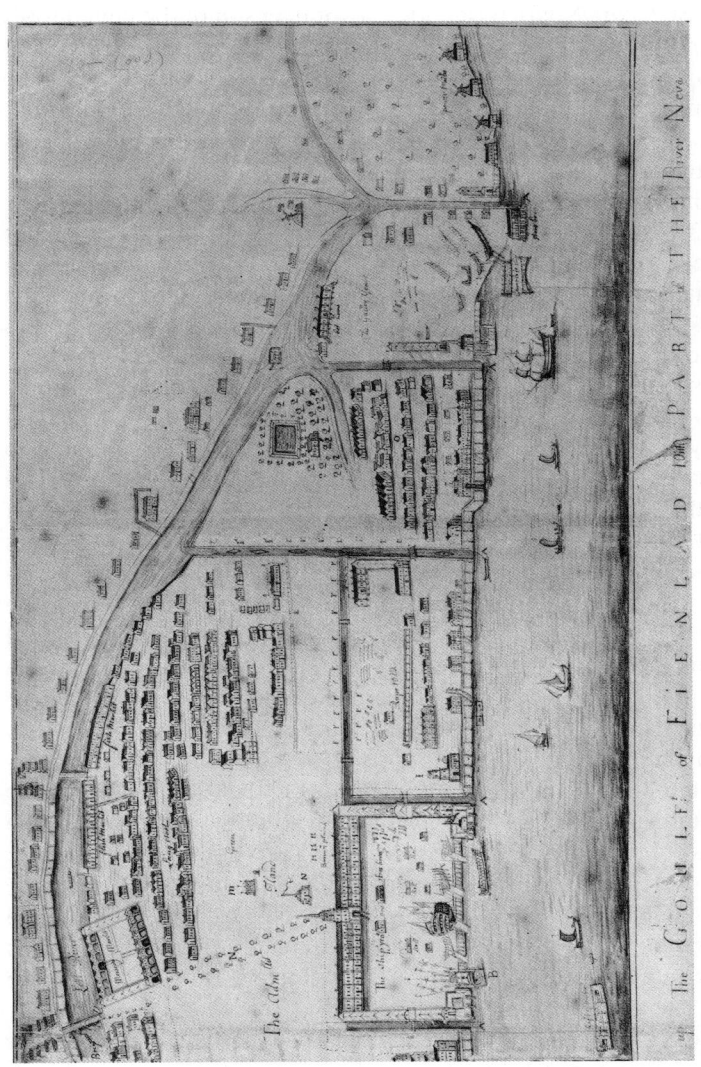

Figure 6 The 'English Embankment' in the last years of Peter's reign. Detail from anonymous map of c. 1723. Courtesy of Map Collection, Yale University Library.

who built the first stone house facing the river. Not only Cozens but others dragged their feet, reluctant to commit themselves to life by the Neva. Nikita Nikitich Demidov, a younger son of the famed Urals industrialist, provides another example: unwilling both to live and develop the plot his father had received under Peter, very near to Menshikov's plot, he was threatened with arrest and eventually built on another site he was made to accept at the very end of the embankment by the Galernyi Canal (no. 74).

In the interim between Anna's threats and the building of the impressive line of stone houses which at last defined the embankment there occurred the events that were crucial to its future development and character. In 1736 and twice again in 1737 fires raged through the Admiralty area, conveniently destroying hundreds of wooden houses and presenting a golden opportunity for fundamental redevelopment. It was subsequent to this that the flowing line of two- and three-storey houses was essentially achieved, unbroken except between nos. 20 and 22 (Nye's house), where there was created an alley through to Galernaia and known nowadays as pereulok Leonova, but earlier as Zamiatin and, later and briefly, Grafskii perulok,[13] and between nos. 40 and 42, where the Kriukov Canal entered the Neva. Anna's Commission for the Orderly Development of St Petersburg, established in June 1737 and perhaps mainly noted for introducing the system of 'the three prongs' (Nevskii Prospekt, Gorokhovaia Street and the future Voznesenskii Prospekt), essentially extended this principle to five prongs with a developed Galernaia Street/English Embankment counterbalancing Millionnaia Street/Palace Embankment. The English Embankment became the home of some of the leading Russian aristocratic families. From the 1730s, alongside the Chancellor Count A.I. Osterman, who had been given and who substantially rebuilt the disgraced Menshikov's property, we find the names of Cherkasskii, Trubetskoi, Naryshkin, Golitsyn, Eropkin, Iusupov, Lobanov, Polianskii, Buturlin and Kurakin, with only Nye seeming to introduce a foreign note; and beyond the Kriukov Canal, further names such as Viazemskii, Khovanskii, Golovkin, Sheremetev, Dolgorukii and, of course, the aforementioned Demidov.

There is a rare engraving by the little-known artist Ottomar Elliger from a drawing by Christoph Marselius of the embankment downstream from the pontoon bridge and St Isaac's, dating from the late 1730s, which shows gaps still existing between the mansions and thereby differs considerably from the scene as depicted in engravings from drawings by Mikhail Makhaev and published in the famous album marking the fiftieth anniversary of the city in 1753.[14] The two plates in the album which are of direct interest to us are entitled 'The Prospect Down the Neva from the Nevskii Bridge between the Isaac Church and the Cadet Corps', engraved by Iakov Vasil'ev, and 'The Prospect Up the Neva to the East between Galley Wharf and the 13th Line of Vasil'evskii Island', engraved by Ivan Eliakov. They were widely copied abroad, by Charles Lespinasse, for instance, for the folio album accompanying Le Clerc's *Histoire physique, morale, civile et politique de la Russie moderne*, published in Paris in 1783–84, and thus offering to Europe as contemporary views of buildings which had by then much changed. The first engraving, taken from slightly more downstream than Elliger's, shows a much more continuous façade allegedly achieved within a decade or so (Figure 7). Apart from a different style of belltower on the Isaac Church, the most immediately striking difference is the enormous transformation of the Osterman mansion into the imposing ornate Baroque palace of A.P. Bestuzhev-Riumin, who gained possession in 1744, only to lose it in 1763 when it became the home of the Senate. The second engraving shows the English Embankment from the other end by the Galley Wharf and starting with Demidov's house (no. 74 by the modern numbering) (Figure 8). Ten houses along is the two-storeyed mansion of Count Sheremetev, which had been empty for a number of years and was purchased in 1753 by Baron Jacob Wolff, the British Minister Resident, as the future English Church. Revamped and internally much altered, it opened for divine service in March 1754. Forty years later there appeared in *Gentleman's Magazine* a unique engraving purporting to show the church, 'a regular structure of Italian architecture'.[15]

The large plan of the city which accompanied the jubilee album was the work of the Petersburg-born Englishman John Truscott of the Academy's Geographical Department. Like almost all earlier existing plans, it combines reality and fantasy: as was said of the Van Zigheim plan prepared for the 1737 commission, 'it was not only a topographical map of the city but to a certain degree a planning tool as well',[16] and, in this case, was intended to produce a very positive reaction to its 'completeness' from the foreign courts to which it was liberally distributed. With respect to the embankment, however, it shows the the façades of the houses presented a united front to the

Figure 7 The 'English Embankment' on the River Neva, looking downstream from the St Isaac of Dalmatia Church and the pontoon bridge towards Galley Wharf. Drawn by Lespinasse and engraved by Cl. Fessard under the direction of Née, 1784.

Figure 8 The 'English Embankment', looking upstream from Galley Wharf towards the Admiralty. Drawn by Lespinasse and engraved by Fessard the Elder, 1784.

embankment and extended to Galernaia with outbuildings and wings that form inner courts with carriage entrance (Figure 9).

The reign of Catherine brought fundamental changes and improvements to many parts of the city, but perhaps the most important for its future as the elegant thoroughfare it became was the cladding of the English Embankment in granite over the years 1767–88 as conceived by Iurii Fel'ten and for the first time the upkeep of the embankment itself became the responsibility of the government rather than of the individual house-owners. From Petrine days owners were encouraged to have their own landing stages but the number was now reduced to five small and one large granite piers, creating their own rhythmic breaks in the granite parapet: the largest near the Galernyi or Novo-Admiralteiskii Canal was called the Konnyi, since it was precisely there that horses brought to the city from England and elsewhere were unloaded. In 1788 the existing bridge across the Kriukov Canal was replaced by an elegant high bascule bridge with columns, designed by Ivan Starov. It was described in a contemporary source as 'a beautiful drawbridge... which has a plain column of granite at each of its four corners, two fathom and a half in height and four feet in diameter, resting on a base of four cubic feet. The pillars and their bases are hollowed out for containing the machinery by which the draw-bridge is wound up and down as by clock-work.'[17] From the 1770s there was considerable rebuilding of many of the mansions of Anna's era, reflecting in many cases the new classical tastes of Catherine.

All these features have been caught for us in the coloured engravings and paintings of the Swedish artist Benjamin Paterssen.[18] The great sweep of the English Embankment, some 1.25 kilometres in length, is the subject of three coloured prints published in 1799 and dedicated to Paul I. The three sections of the embankment are depicted from their corresponding viewpoints on Vasil'evskii Island, where the foreground is enlivened by everyday scenes (*bytovye stsenki*), almost as valuable for their social content as the background across the river, for architectural history. The engravings thus present a frontal view, as opposed to the sweep up or down stream, as favoured by Makhaev, in which the Neva is dominant, although Paterssen himself adopts this viewpoint in his watercolour of 1801 which presents us with a close-up of the Senate, as reconstructed by Starov (?) in the 1780s from the existing Bestuzhev-Riumin mansion,

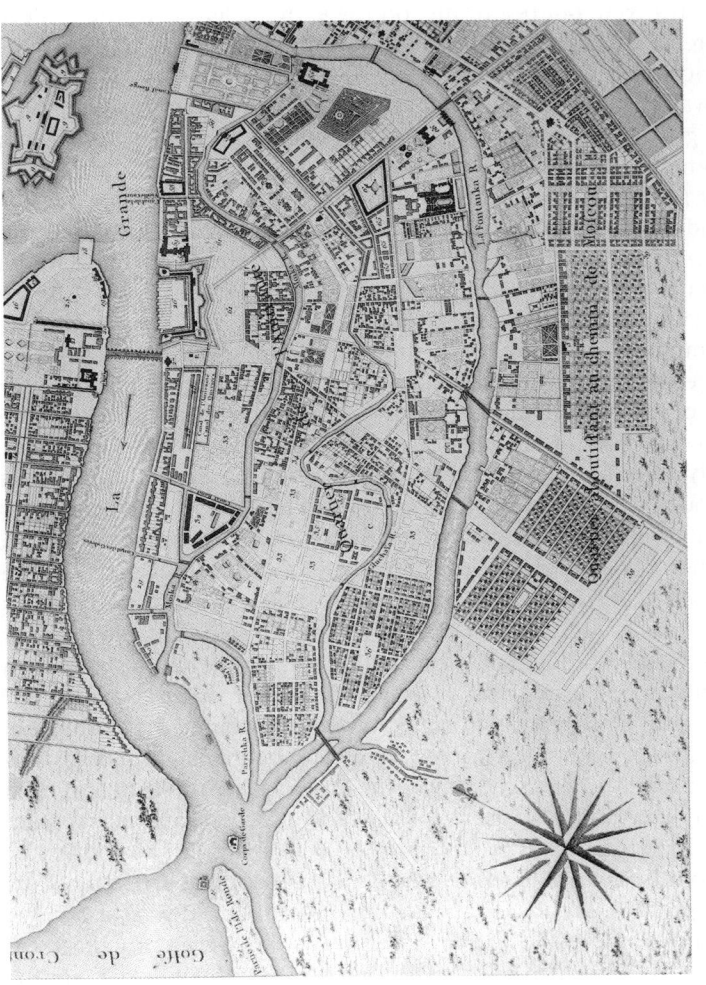

Figure 9 The 'English Embankment'. Detail from the map of St Petersburg originally prepared by John Truscott for the 1753 anniversary album. Engraved by P.F. Tardieu, 1784.

and a river crowded with shipping. A fifth work of interest is Paterssen's oil painting from the beginning of the nineteenth century, virtually reproducing the view in the second part of the earlier triptych, but beginning, on the extreme left, with the College of Foreign Affairs (no. 32), which was one of the early commissions of Giacomo Quarenghi.

It was to this building that the young Alexander Pushkin came after graduating from the Tsarskoe Selo lyceum in 1817, when Quarenghi's presence on the English Embankment had been reinformed just two years earlier when his long-approved plans for the rebuilding of the English Church were finally realized. Pushkin is not known to have visited the English Church, although in the 1830s he had a flat on Galernaia, very near to the church's entrance. A house he did visit frequently in the few years before his exile was even more a triumphant expression of the high classicism of Alexander I's reign. On the site of Menshikov's *kniazheskie mazanki*, starting at the very dawn of the embankment's history, next to the Senate building, the transformations of which down the eighteenth century we have already traced and which, of course, was to be further and finally reshaped by Carlo Rossi, stood a house belonging in mid-century to the police-chief V.F. Saltykov and later to Count Stroganov, for whom Voronikhin rebuilt it in the 1790s (and as such seen clearly on the Paterssen watercolour of the Senate). In 1800 it became the property of the Lavals, Aleksandra Grigor'evna, the daughter of the talented G.V. Kozitskii, Catherine II's 'literary assistant', and her husband Ivan Stepanovich or Jean Laval, a former instructor in the Naval Cadet Corps, ennobled by Paul. In 1806 they commissioned the architect of the Bourse, Thomas de Thomon, to create the mansion that has survived virtually unchanged. It was the house in which Pushkin recited his ode 'Freedom' ('Vol'nost'', 1819) and it occupies a special place in the topography of the Decembrists' Petersburg. It and the Senate formed the entrance to the English Embankment and are emblematic of the prestigious thoroughfare it truly became in Alexander's reign. A second example of the 'imperial front' assumed by many houses at this period is provided by what is now the Museum of the City in the Soviet Period (in 1963 the pre-Soviet exhibition was removed to the Peter and Paul Fortress). It is, of course, the Rumiantsev Mansion (no. 44), the façade of which was created in 1825 by the architect V.A. Glinka, when the owner Nikolai Petrovich Rumiantsev resolved to turn his home into a museum. The twelve-columned portico concealed the house in which Rumiantsev had lived since 1802 and where gathered noted scholars and writers; but before he sold the house to Rumiantsev, there had lived there for some thirteen years the English merchant Thomas Warre.[19]

And so to the question of the Englishness of the English Embankment. What's in a name? An embankment is an embankment by any other name, although in this case it is the change in the qualifying epithet that is at issue (while recognizing, of course, that in Russian *naberezhnaia* is a substantivized adjective!). The embankment or non-embankment, indeed, seems first to have been called Beregovaia, then became Nizhniaia (to distinguish it from Verzhniaia (i.e. Dvortsovaia)), then Galernaia, and only Aglinskaia/Angliiskaia from the first years of the nineteenth century. It is certainly only on nineteenth-century maps that it bears this name. It was, however, widely known as the English Line or Quay during Catherine's reign, as witnessed not least by Archdeacon Coxe, who wrote in 1779 of 'the English line, so-called because the whole row is principally occupied by English merchants'.[20] Confirmation of his assertion is easily found in the columns of the *St Petersburg News* (*Sanktpeterburgskie vedomosti*), where the advertisements and lists of departees provide valuable evidence of the precise whereabouts of such institutions as the English inn and the English shops and of the addresses where people, and not only the British, of course, were living permanently or temporarily. Throughout the last decades of the eighteenth century it was almost without exception that *Galernyi dvor* was used to designate houses along the embankment, but an exception I did find in October 1790, where the sale of one of the houses is announced as follows: 'On the English Embankment (*Po Aglinskoi naberezhnoi*) there is for sale the house at no. 246, located between the houses of the British Consul Mr Cayley and the English merchant Mr Raikes'.[21]

As we have seen, Cozens and Nye were the first Englishmen to own plots, and in the latter case, a house, on the embankment and, given their profession, it was understandable. At approximately the same period Henry Hodgkin, a prominent merchant and member of the notorious British Monastery, had an adjacent plot (no. 8) with warehouses and sheds and a wooden house. It was only during Anna's reign, however, that the English began to appear in numbers as a result of two seemingly unrelated events: the great fires of 1736 and

1737 led the intensive building of mainly three-storey brick buildings along the embankment and in 1735 there was promulgated an imperial *ukaz* which exempted the resident British from the heavy burden of billeting soldiers, as agreed in the previous year's Anglo-Russian Commercial Treaty. The Russian owners of many of the houses were therefore more than ready to rent them, or parts of them, precisely to members of the British Factory (although Jonas Hanway, who was resident in the 1740s, suggests the Russian authorities attempted at times to ignore the privilege).[22] In the 1740s and 1750s we find merchants such as Henry Sanders, William Vigor and William Riches and the watchmaker Joseph Smith; in the 1730s the British Resident Claudius Rondeau lived in I.I. Buturlin's house (no. 34) and his successor Jacob Wolff lived opposite the house where Nye had lived by Zamiatin pereulok.[23] A decree of 1759 allowed merchants to purchase properties, but Wolff, as we have seen, had already bought in his own name in 1753 the future English Church.

Catherine's reign saw a rush to buy along the English Embankment and over the next decades many of the leading merchants acquired impressive homes. A far from comprehensive count would suggest at least 32 British subjects owned houses there in the last four decades of the century, not, of course, all simultaneously and, in several cases, successively possessing the same house.[24] Thus no. 40, which Alexander Baxter, the future Russian Consul-General in London, bought in 1761 from Count Khovanskii and sold in 1763 to Henry Klausing, who sold it later to Thomas Bonar; or no. 62, which belonged to William Glen in the 1760s, before he sold it to Dr Matthew Halliday, from whom it was apparently acquired by the Russian government in 1790 and given to Admiral Greig's widow, Sara.[25] There was perhaps a not unexpected clustering of British-owned properties around the English Church, the focal point of the community, and in fact, virtually every house to the west of the Kriukov Canal, nos. 38–74, was at some during Catherine's reign owned by a British subject. In addition to names already mentioned, there figure leading merchants such as William Porter, Baron Richard Sutherland, Timothy Raikes, Godfrey Thornton and John Cayley, British Consul-General and Agent of the Russia Company,[26] as well as the eminent Dr John Rogerson, Catherine's body physician, who had moved in 1789 from the two-storey house (no. 18) he had occupied from 1776 to no. 60 by the church.

The Englishness of the English Embankment was paralleled, indeed, given depth by the Englishness of Galernaia Street. Not only did the embankment houses have entrances into their courtyards from the street, but frequently had independent buildings. James Brodgen, a guest of the Cayleys in 1787–88, describes his house as 'situated in the English Line, which is joined to a Lane they call the *back line* by a long yard, at the bottom of which is a small house over the gateway', in which he was to stay.[27] Galernaia was a very animated street with shops and tradesmen, a coffee house, an English inn, and access to the church's Subscription Library.[28]

The situation was, however, gradually to change. In his translation of Heinrich Storch's *Gemälde von St.-Petersburg* (Riga, 1793–94), which appeared some seven years after the German original, the Rev. William Tooke made a number of interesting additions, mainly referring to the British community, which he knew so well from personal experience. He thus writes about 'the English stationary in St. Petersburg':

> The Galeerenhof, one of the finest districts of the city, was formerly almost entirely occupied by the English, and it was therefore commonly called the English Line. At the same time that these noble mansions are suitable to the honour in which their inhabitants were held, their situation on the quay of the Neva, renders the situation of the English here the most enviable of any capital in Europe. They have since been supplanted by the principal russian noblemen, and some german merchants have got in.[29]

The situation presents an ironic parallel to the fate of the English Club, which had been set up to cater for the needs of the British community but which, as the British were ousted, became increasingly a Russian space. The English Embankment, finally so called in the reign of Alexander, lost the British owners which led to its name and it became the fashionable location for leading Russian families. It was in the 1820s that the English Embankment was given wide granite pavements and it became in the following reign the fashionable venue for early summer promenades by the upper classes, far from the bustle – and filth – of Nevksii.[30]

Certain British families continued to live on the English Embankment – the Cayleys, for instance until the late 1870s – and there were, indeed, a few, a very few, British, who subsequently bought properties. The plaques which are found on many of the houses today usually commemorate late nineteenth-century–early twentieth-century individual, occasionally institutional, ownerships of the mansions, since this was a period of massive reconstruction which left almost none of the existing eighteenth-century buildings with original features. Two plaques do in fact designate British ownership. No. 38, the house that wraps around the corner to face Work Square, belonged for most of the second half of the nineteenth century to Alexander Clark, owner of Clark & Co., grain and flax exporters, and all signs are lost of the big estate with two separate houses, pond and gardens that had existed during Catherine's reign. British merchants had lived there then, and so had Denis Fonvizin, who wrote there his masterpiece *The Minor* (*Nedorosl'*). The second plaque is more directly connected with our period, for it is on the house of Dr James Wylie, the personal physician of Paul I and Alexander I, the last house on the embankment, which we have already encountered as belonging to Nikita Demidov and his descendants from whom Wylie bought it in 1804. It escaped rebuilding later in the century and remains very much as Wylie left it. He occupied only one small flat in the huge building, facing the canal rather than the river; purely anecdotally, in one of the flats he let, Maria Blank, the mother of Lenin, was born in 1835. Then, of course, there remains the English Church, reconstructed for the last time in 1876 by the architect D.K. Boltenhagen, when the top-storey windows were lost, although its present sorry fate is be a shop offering cut-price souvenirs rather than the saving of our souls. It is only a pity that the British Consulate did not purchase one of the buildings; instead, the Dutch fly their flag over no. 12, where William Glen once lived. At least, the name of the embankment, known in the Soviet period as the Embankment of the Red Fleet, lives on, restored for the visit of Queen Elizabeth II in 1994.

Notes

1. The following were the principal secondary sources consulted in the writing of this essay: P.N. Petrov, *Istoriia Sankt-Peterburga s osnovaniia goroda, do vvedeniia v deistvie vybornogo gorodskogo upravleniia, po uchrezhdeniiam i guberniiam 1703–1782* (St Petersburg, 1884); M.I. Pyliaev, *Staryi Peterburg*, 2nd edn (Spb., 1889); P.N. Stolpianskii, *Kak voznik, osnovalsia*

i ros Sanktpiterburkh (Petrograd, 1918); P.N. Stolpianskii, *Staryi Peterburg: Dvorets Truda* (Petrograd, 1923); I.A. Egorov, *The Architectural Planning of St. Petersburg* (Athens, Ohio, 1969); O.N. Zakharov, *Arkhitekturnye panoramy nevskikh beregov* (Leningrad, 1984); S.P. Zavarikhin, *Iavlenie Sankt-Piter-Burkha* (Spb., 1996); T.A. Solov'eva, *K prichalam Angliiskoi naberezhnoi* (Spb., 1998); A.M. Platunov, *Tak stroilsia Peterburg*, 2nd edn (Spb., 2000).
2. *Dnevnik kamer-iunker F.V. Berkhgol'tsa*, III (Moscow, 1903), 45.
3. Stolpianskii, *Staryi Peterburg: Dvorets Truda*, p. 5.
4. Peter the Great advocated the construction of *mazanki* as cheap, rapid and relatively fire-resistant. The British ambassador in St Petersburg Charles Whitworth described them 'of lath work, timber and plaister after the old fashion in England' (*Sbornik Imperatorskogo Russkogo Istoricheskogo Obshchestva*, LXI (Spb., 1888) 206), and the translator of Weber's *Das veränderte Russland* as 'Carpenters-work' (*The Present State of Russia*, I (London, 1723) *passim*).
5. Stolpianstii, *Staryi Peterburg: Dvorets Truda*, p. 18.
6. *Ibid.*, p. 17.
7. See Petrov, *Istoriia Sankt-Peterburga*, pp. 145, 248.
8. See Iu. N. Bespiatykh, *Peterburg Petra I v inostrannykh opisaniiakh* (Leningrad, 1991), pp. 4–12.
9. *The Present State of Russia*, I, 312–13.
10. *The Voyages and Travels of A. De La Motraye, in Several Provinces and Places of the Kingdoms and Dukedoms of Prussia, Russia, Poland &c.*, III (London, 1732), 165–6.
11. Larissa Salmina-Haskell, 'An Unknown Drawing of St Petersburg During the Reign of Peter the Great', *Oxford Slavonic Papers*, NS XXIX (1996) 1–7. The original map is preserved in the Map Room of the Sterling Library of Yale University, Ms. 352 AN. L.547. 1720.
12. Stolpianskii, *Staryi Peterburg: Dvorets Truda*, p. 19.
13. So named after Aleksei Ivanovich Zamiatin, who owned the plot after Nye. It briefly came into the possession of Count Aleksei Orlov in 1765, hence the name 'Grafskii', before reverting to its former name.
14. See G.N. Komelova, *Vidy Peterburga i ego okrestnostei serediny XVIII veka: Graviury po risunkam M. Makhaeva* (Leningrad, 1968). See also more generally, Larissa Salmina-Haskell, *Panoramic Views of St. Petersburg 1716–1835* (Oxford, 1993).
15. *Gentleman's Magazine*, LXVI, pt I (1796) 373, reproduced in my *By the Banks of the Neva: Chapters from the Lives and Careers of the British in Eighteenth-Century Russia* (Cambridge, 1997), p. 91.
16. Egorov, *Architectural Planning*, p. 31.
17. *The Picture of Petersburg. From the German of Henry Storch* (London, 1801), pp. 22–3.
18. See G. Komelova, G. Printseva and I. Kotel'nikova, *Peterburg v proizvedeniiakh Patersena* (Moscow, 1978).
19. See the recent study by T.A. Solov'eva, *Rumiantsevskii dom* (Spb., 2002).
20. William Coxe, *Travels into Poland, Russia, Sweden, and Denmark*, 5th edn, II (London, 1802), 104.

21. *Sanktpeterburgskie vedomosti*, no. 80 (8 October 1790) 1321.
22. Jonas Hanway, *An Historical Account of the British Trade over the Caspian Sea:with a Journal of Travels from London through Russia into Persia: and back again through Russia, Germany and Holland*, I (London, 1754), 376.
23. It was, incidentally, in 'Wulf's house' (no. 20) that Dr Thomas Dimsdale lived when he returned to St Petersburg in 1781 to inoculate the Grand Dukes Alexander and Constantine.
24. Based principally but not exclusively on the information contained in Solov'eva, *K prichalam* and an unpublished essay graciously given to me some years ago by the noted historian of Petersburg streets, Larisa Broitman.
25. The Treasury bought the three-storeyed house for 30,000 roubles in February 1790 and it remained in the Greigs' possession for the next twenty years: Viktor Antonov, 'Admiral Greig's Tomb', *Study Group on Eighteenth-Century Russia Newsletter*, no. 12 (1984) 29.
26. On the life style of such as the Cayleys and Raikes, see my *By the Banks of the Neva*, pp. 84–8.
27. James Cracraft, 'James Brogden in Russia, 1787–1788', *Slavonic and East European Review*, XLVII (1969) 227–8.
28. In more detail, see my *By the Banks of the Neva*, pp. 26–8.
29. *The Picture of Petersburg*, p. 575.
30. See Stolpianskii, *Staryi Peterburg: Dvorets Truda*, pp. 21–2, quoting an article which appeared in *Severnaia pchela* in 1840.

4
A Venice of the North? Italian Views of St Petersburg

Maria Di Salvo

The aim of this essay is not to analyse everything that was written by Italian visitors to St Petersburg in the eighteenth century, but rather to discuss certain attitudes which reflect a way of looking at and understanding the city. In most cases the evolution of Italian observations is similar to that of other Europeans who visited the 'new capital'; however, it is possible to single out certain unique features. I think most people of my generation have at some time or other come across the cliché 'Venice of the North': Amsterdam was the 'Venice of the North', as indeed was Stockholm, as well, of course, as St Petersburg. Any European town built on islands seemed to claim a right to this definition; but, as the parallel was usually not developed further, and did not bring a deeper understanding of the character of these towns, it remained simply a convenient phrase for schooltexts and guidebooks.

Of the three towns mentioned, only the youngest, St Petersburg, seems to have looked for a lasting association with Venice in its search for an identity. If, as Lotman and Uspenskii show,[1] Rome provided an ideological background for the foundation of the new capital and the building of its main places of worship, Venice appealed to men of letters and artists and thus contributed in different ways to shape the cultural myth of the town. In Peter's reign, it offered the model of a seafaring people at ease on the sea; later, the common element was afforded by water itself, which is one of the main components of the 'Petersburg text'; and, especially in the twentieth century, the two cities have been associated by an increasing atmosphere of decaying beauty.

In general, the fact that St Petersburg was built by Italian architects (although some of them, like Trezzini or Rusca, originated from the Italian-speaking part of Switzerland) suggests the assumption that contemporary Italian visitors ought to have felt more at home there than anywhere else in Russia, and one would expect from them expressions of recognition of a familiar urban landscape. As we shall see, this was not the case, and there were other aspects of the capital which tended to attract their attention. Obviously, as often happens, Italians were more likely to note peculiarities than stress similarities, but this is not always a satisfactory explanation of their attitude, which was, at best, one of aloof admiration.

I am not aware of any early Italian descriptions of St Petersburg. Giambattista Venuti, who arrived in Russia in 1727 with the Duke de Liria and soon moved to Moscow in order to follow the coronation of Peter II, paid only a passing tribute to the beauty of the town in a letter to his family, and the long report he claims to have sent is probably lost. Nor should we expect praise of the charms of the city from the *Lettres moscovites* (1735) by Francesco Locatelli, who was imprisoned there for almost two years, and whose aim in writing his pamphlet was to warn foreigners of the danger represented by Russia and to persuade them not to offer their services to the Russian state. A neutral approach to St Petersburg was impossible throughout the first half of the eighteenth century, as it was only too natural for anybody who knew the circumstances of its foundation to associate it with Peter's plans and to test whether Russia had entirely overcome its barbarous past: in Lotman's words, the town has been an object of study from its very birth.

This is certainly true of *Letters from Russia* (*Viaggi di Russia*), a little book that Francesco Algarotti published in 1760 and soon became very popular and was translated into many European languages. Algarotti had visited Russia in the summer of 1739, when he had accompanied Charles Calvert, 5th Lord Baltimore, to represent George II at the wedding of Anna Leopol'dovna to the Prince of Brunswick. It is highly probable that the author was inspired to resume the story of his journey at twenty years' distance by his correspondence with Voltaire, who at this time was working on his *Histoire de l'empire de Russie sous Pierre le Grand*. Voltaire's book began to circulate almost at the same time as Algarotti's, but the latter did not fully share the philosopher's admiration for Peter, as his stay in St Petersburg and his reflections on the state of the country had convinced him of the arbitrariness of the tsar's choices and of their limited impact on Russian life.

A Venetian, significantly he avoids any parallel between St Petersburg and his home town: he writes in detail and with admiration about the Russian army, praises the beauty of the ships in Kronstadt, but is very critical, for instance, of Peter's establishing the Admiralty in the capital, as the big ships built in town need to be carried at high cost to Kronstadt, and for many months of the year are trapped in ice in the shallow Gulf of Finland. It would have been more rational, he suggests, to build wharfs in the more reliable Reval, but Peter liked big ships and wanted to see them built near his residence: thus the lot of the Russian fleet was determined by the whim of a despot.

The question of despotism is constantly raised by the consequences of Peter's reforms and on this point Algarotti is even more outspoken in the brief and as yet unpublished notebook, currently housed in the British Library, which is the diary of his journey.[2] If he chose in the book to speak in general and to avoid details that might be already outdated, in the diary we find more direct and undiplomatic comments. 'The Tsar Peter,' he writes, 'had in mind to build Petersburg as a Dutch town, as can be seen, among other things, from the canals he built there with the only aim, one could say, of building bridges across them; but the right way would have been to give freedom to the people, who would make the canals themselves, had it become necessary.'[3] Even in this context, though, Algarotti does not suggest any association with Venice.

When reading the description of the main buildings of St Petersburg, one should not forget that Algarotti, who favoured classicism, was decidedly hostile to the baroque; so he is critical of the Winter Palace, newly built by Rastrelli, which he describes as 'half Italian and half French, or rather in the modern and silly Italian style, like most of the buildings in town';[4] but, significantly, when Algarotti reworked his notes for publication, he declared that the leading architectural style in the town was a mixture of Italian, French and Dutch, with Dutch prevailing over the others.

The site of the capital, he writes, is one of the most delightful in the world:

> if the ground were a little higher and less marshy, if the plans had not been changed so many times, if a Palladio had been the

architect and the building materials had been of a better quality and better assembled and, furthermore, if it were inhabited by people who try to live there pleasantly and comfortably, St Petersburg would be surely one the finest towns in the world.[5]

Criticism of the poor quality of buildings is very common in Italian descriptions, as well as an appreciation of the view from the river, which apparently contrasted with the shabby and chaotic appearance of the rest of the town.

The impression with which the reader is left by Algarotti's notes is a sense of passivity hovering over the town, of emptiness and uncouthness; something is lacking, and it is those living, trading, working people who ought to implement the tsar's plans and realize his vision. Once again, the cause is despotism, with its sudden and unpredictable giving and withdrawal of favour that hindered even the aristocracy from taking the initiative. The lack of enterprise in Russia was particularly unacceptable to Algarotti, who was an ardent supporter of trade and an admirer of England; and this is why, in order to invigorate the Russian economy by bringing money into the country, he makes an original (and very modern) proposal: 'as Petersburg at present arouses such interest throughout the world, many foreigners, especially English, would certainly wish to visit it, if they were comfortably accommodated, well received by the Court and attracted by magnificent and pompous shows, that cannot be seen anywhere else.'[6] So he suggests staging troop parades, naval battles and combat with wild animals, like those that were popular in Ancient Rome.

The contrast between, on the one hand, the scale and magnificence of the city and, on the other, beauty and good taste, remained a frequent object of comment and continued to be so when Catherine II made major changes to the face of the city. The accession of the new empress aroused curiosity in Italy, as it did throughout Europe, and raised almost as many questions as Peter's reforms. In 1770 Vittorio Alfieri, the poet and playwright, visited the country he had heard praised by the Russians who had studied with him in Turin. His heart was full of expectation, but, as he wrote later in his autobiography, 'no sooner had I reached this Asiatic encampment of wooden huts than Rome, Genoa, Venice, and Florence rose to my recollection; and I could not refrain from laughing'.[7] He strongly disliked the place and those barbarians disguised in European attire and had no desire to see more. His repulsion, as he explained, stemmed from his deep hatred of tyranny and from the fact that he thought St Petersburg to be under greater military rule than Berlin and found the people suffering under utter servitude. Alfieri's absolute (and early) dislike of Catherine is best explained by his antityrannical beliefs and pre-Romantic individualism. The abbé Giovanni Battista Casti's reasons were perhaps rather less noble. After serving as court poet from 1777 to 1779 as well as writing librettos and panegyrics lauding the Empress, he composed a satirical poem about Catherine called *The Tartar Poem* (*Il Poema tartaro*), which was published for the first time in 1786. It was particularly offensive to the Empress because it revived the association of Russia with Tartary which had been so common in pre-Petrine times. Nevertheless Casti, who might have been working out a grudge he had against the Royal Court, also wrote in a letter about St Petersburg being 'rich in fine canals, well constructed, not entirely in good taste but always magnificent'.[8]

In Algarotti's diary we find strikingly similar observations and criticisms, as indeed we do with other Italians who wrote about it. The prevalence of an aesthetic approach probably reflects the characteristics of Italian immigration as well as the professional interests of those who, throughout the eighteenth century, sought their fortune at the Russian Court. Many of them were actors, musicians and architects who were to spend much of their life in St Petersburg. Their professional activities, so far from their homeland, were ill suited to the keeping of diaries and similar records. Their archives – if they ever existed – were often destroyed after their death or ended up scattered across Europe. Their testimonies are fragmentary, often cautious for fear of postal censorship and hence unspecific or lacking detail. Only occasionally, as is the case with the architect Giacomo Quarenghi, do we come upon a genuine correspondence;[9] however, it deals largely with technical questions and lacks information about affairs of state and people in high places.

A letter written in 1780, not long after his arrival in Russia, contains the first and most spontaneous of Quarenghi's feelings about St Petersburg. After commenting – as everyone did – on the size of the city with its many enormous buildings, he observed, in a manner reminiscent of Algarotti, that 'many buildings are certainly not in the Palladian style.... Our Italians can hardly claim to have brought good taste as they did in France under Francis I and in other foreign countries in better days. French and German taste have prevailed and continue to do so here although they don't enjoy much success, given the supremacy nowadays of a simple and pure style: a fact which pleases me greatly.'[10] A little over ten years later, Pietro Gonzaga wrote to Francesco Fontanesi, who was a candidate to replace him as court theatre scene-painter:

> The city is large and beautiful. Building work carries on apace despite the many wars, and buildings emerge like mushrooms. The canals which cross the city are a source of wonder; their banks, made of fine granite and fine stones, have solid iron railings for the safety and beauty of the streets which run alongside them. The main districts are not uniformly built, but planned with tasteful asymmetry and they form junctions of differing dimensions. Many buildings are in fine taste and among the best are those of our Quarenghi. There are lovely country-houses, gardens in the English style which are very popular here, greenhouses for pleasure and for commerce, thanks to which we always have fruit and vegetables at little expense. There are also wines of every quality and price and if you know how to administer your affairs, life is not expensive. The beauty of the women, I might add, is another of the pleasures of St Petersburg.[11]

The city was thus acquiring its own physiognomy. It was no longer the haphazard result of unplanned reconstruction and different influences but, especially along the riverfront and the Winter Palace, a planned whole which might have seemed a little military to Alfieri (long before Custine). Coherent governmental activity was becoming increasingly evident in St Petersburg. With regard to this, there is what I consider to be the most interesting (although somewhat fragmentary) description of the city written by an Italian. I published it some years ago from a manuscript belonging to the Biblioteca Corsini in Rome and, as it only exists in Italian, it is probably unknown to many people.[12] Its author remains unidentified, but was obviously a member of the diplomatic mission of the future Cardinal Archetti, who was sent in 1783–84 to discuss with Catherine the situation and rights of those Catholic White Russians who had become subject to the Russian Empire after the first partition of Poland. In his report he not only sketched with great precision the map of the town, but also described in detail a number of new buildings under construction, recording the vast amounts of money assigned by the Empress for the development of the city. This writer was critical of both individual buildings and architectural details, although he also described the ice hills on the River Neva, the sleighs and the amusements, including clubs and theatres, the cost of tickets and the money earned by singers and dancers. Dress is profusely dealt with, and much attention is given to its social differentiation; we are also informed of public transport, lighting and the role of the police. The anonymous author is obviously interested in the social and administrative organization of the capital and the impression his report conveys is of a town swarming with people, colourfully dressed and rushing about on duty: a picture that anticipates the scene commonly depicted in nineteenth-century literature.

The emergence of a westernized elite and the development of new forms of sociability are the most relevant feature in the reports of the second half of the century: St Petersburg was becoming a more familiar place, where visitors were not continuously drawn to reflect on whether Russians were still barbarous or not and were ready to observe their life more sympathetically. Giacomo Casanova, who was there in 1765, recalled in his late *Memoirs* (written between 1789 and 1798) not only the buildings and parades he had attended, but also his conversations and amusements with Russians; like Casti (but unlike earlier visitors), he gave their names and portrayed them as full personalities. Many of his criticisms are reminiscent of those of his compatriot Algarotti; however, the latter had obtained his information from other foreigners, whilst Casanova spent most of his time in Russian company, taking part in masked balls and card-playing evenings, and socializing.

St Petersburg was on the way to becoming a city in which foreigners felt at home, where they found that certain aspects of life were familiar to them. As P. Gonzaga wrote in the above-mentioned letter, 'one lives as well as one does in all other countries'. Reading through the pages written by Casanova, one finds – as one does in some of Casti's letters – a feeling of normal life as the author moves among different places and people. The cosmopolitan adventurer is as much at his ease in Petersburg as he is in Venice, but is nevertheless reluctant to draw comparisons between the two cities. The splendour and solemnity of the monuments of St Petersburg rather suggest a parallel with Rome, as Archetti wrote: 'I believe one can call Petersburg the Rome of the North. It is eight years since I saw the sights of the true Rome and many of those I see here in Petersburg are amazing indeed.'[13]

The reports of Italian travellers, which I have tried briefly to set down, reflect two particular aspects. The first is the growth of the town, which takes on peculiar features that cannot be compared to any pre-existing reality; from this point of view the parallel with Venice appears increasingly to be a literary device and not the result of actual perception. It sets out to place the new city in a European context in much the same way as Sumarokov was to become 'the Russian Racine', or Lomonosov 'the Russian Pindar'.

The second and no less important aspect is the attitude of the travellers themselves, who, in the second half of the century, were keener to include Russia (and St Petersburg as its most European town) in their cultural package not as a magnificent, but still silent pageant that needed to find a suitable content (as had been the case for Algarotti), but as a window on a world that was worth exploring more closely.

Notes

1. 'Otzvuki kontseptsii "Moskva – tretii Rim" v ideologii Petra Pervogo (K probleme srednevekovoi traditsii v kul'ture barokko)' [1982], in Iu. M. Lotman, *Izbrannye stat'i*, III (Tallinn, 1993), 201–12.
2. British Library, Add. Mss. 17482, *Giornale del viaggio da Londra a Petersbourg*. Antonio Franceschetti has written a number of articles about the journal; see for instance, in English, his 'From the Travel Journal to the *Viaggi di Russia* of Algarotti', in *The Enlightenment in a Western Mediterranean Context* (Missasauga, Benben, 1984), pp. 97–103. See also S. Rotta, 'Russia 1739: Il filosofo sedentario e il filosofo viaggiatore', in M.L. Dodero and M.C. Bragone (eds), *Tra Russia e Italia, nel Settecento* (Bergamo, 2002), pp. 33–78.
3. *Giornale del viaggio*, f. 54v.
4. *Ibid.*, f. 23v.
5. *Ibid.*, f. 23.
6. *Ibid.*, f. 56v.
7. V. Alfieri, *Vita scritta da esso*, English text quoted from V. Alfieri, *Memoirs* (London, New York and Toronto, 1961), p. 102.
8. Only one letter from St Petersburg (31 May 1776, to J. Kaunitz) seems to have survived: see G.B. Casti, *Epistolario*, ed. by A. Fallico (Viterbo, 1984),

pp. 95–101; but many other letters refer to the city and to Russia. From these we get the impression that Casti had a considerable circle of acquaintances in the capital and knew many intrigues going on in the social world.
9. V. Zanella (ed.), *G. Quarenghi. Architetto a Pietroburgo* (Venezia, 1988).
10. *Ibid.*, p. 44 (letter to P.A. Serassi).
11. Letter by P. Gonzaga from St Petersburg, 26 December (Old Style) 1792, in *Notizie biografiche in continuazione della Biblioteca Modonese di Girolamo Tiraboschi*, I (Modena, 1833, reprint Bologna, 1972), 477–8.
12. M. Di Salvo, 'Scene di vita pietroburghese colte da un visitatore italiano (1783–1784)', *Europa Orientalis*, XVI/1 (1997) 151–78.
13. Letter by Archetti of 30 June/11 July 1783: M.J. Rouët de Journel, *Nonciatures de Russie d'après les documents authentiques*, I. *Nonciature d'Archetti* (Città del Vaticano, 1952), p. 93.

5
Compiling and Maintaining St Petersburg's 'Book of City Inhabitants': The 'Real' City Inhabitants

George E. Munro

As one of the provisions of the Charter to the Towns (promulgated 21 April 1785), Catherine the Great called for each town in the empire to 'compile and maintain' a Book of City Inhabitants (*Kniga gorodskikh obyvatelei*). This book was to have several uses. According to the Charter itself, it was to be compiled 'so that each citizen's acquisitions may be transferred from father to son, to grandson, to great-grandson, and to their posterity'.[1] The book was therefore upon its simplest reading to be a legal document used to establish the right to ownership, in particular the ownership of immovable property.

Just as Catherine envisaged the Charter to the Towns as the equivalent for townsmen to the nobles' Charter to the Nobility issued the same day – which also happened to be her birthday – she intended for the Book of City Inhabitants to play an analogous role for townsmen to the Office of Heraldry for the nobility. A person was officially recognized as 'well-born' or noble by meeting at least one of the 22 criteria set forth in the Charter to the Nobility.[2] Similarly, one was legally recognized as a townsman only by meeting the requirements for registering in one of six officially recognized categories.

The rights and privileges granted by the Charter to the urban estate pertained only to the six categories: (1) those who owned house or land, who were termed 'genuine' or 'real town inhabitants'; (2) those registered in merchant guilds; (3) those inscribed in craft organizations; (4) resident merchants from other towns or countries; (5) 'eminent' citizens, defined by wealth or educational attainment;

and (6) petty townsmen, the so-called *posad* people.[3] There were carefully defined proofs of status for each of the categories. No one could be inscribed in the book without offering proof of status, and no one not inscribed in the book was to be considered a 'citizen' in the narrow definition of the term, someone with the status of belonging to, or having his identity in, the city.

Finally, the Book of City Inhabitants was intended to comprise the official list of names of those people subject to public service under Catherine's reorganized system of urban administration. Only registered citizens were eligible to serve in elected positions in the city council or the six-voice council,[4] as judges in various courts, or as elders in corporate bodies for merchants and craftsmen.

Of the Charter's 178 articles, 26 (just under 15 per cent) dealt directly with the Book of City Inhabitants. Its compilation and maintenance were at the heart of the Charter. Much of the information the book was supposed to contain was already kept by the city police, but those data had to be expanded and reorganized into a new format.

The information to be included for every registered citizen was spelled out in the text of the Charter and also – to ensure that it could not be missed – provided in tabular form. Seven articles of information were asked of each registrant:

1. whether married, and to whom;
2. the number of children if any, their names, and their gender;
3. if unmarried, whether never married or widowed;
4. in whose name real property in town (defined as house, other structure, or plot of land) was registered, how it was acquired (whether built, inherited, purchased or received in dowry), and its location;
5. whether the registrant lived in town or elsewhere;
6. type of economic activity engaged in; and
7. a summary of townsman's duties or other responsibilities one had carried out.[5]

Noble families listed in the heraldry book of the nobility were also supposed to be included in the Book of City Inhabitants, but they were not required to provide any further information for the Book of City Inhabitants than given name, family name, rank (if there was one) and the address of the immovable property that was owned.

Nobles owning property or buildings could thus participate in city government as well as in institutions peculiar to their own legal estate. As will be seen, peasants could also become 'citizens' through owning urban immovable property.[6]

This chapter attempts to reconstruct, from partial evidence brought together for the compilation of the Book of City Inhabitants, a picture of home and property ownership in late eighteenth-century St Petersburg. In some ways, the evidence from this particular source confirms what we know about housing in St Petersburg from other sources. In other ways, however, the evidence here presented challenges what we think we know. The evidence makes it clear that houses, shops and property were owned by people from a wide range of social backgrounds. Houses were acquired in a variety of ways. Women participated fully in ownership. A number of individuals, primarily merchants, had already become owners of multiple dwellings. On occasion an owner spread ownership among members of his family, placing the titles of houses and shops in the hands of wives and children, including underaged daughters. In short, we learn a great deal to flesh out our knowledge of the social history of St Petersburg in the latter part of Catherine's reign.

Most importantly, the evidence contained in the materials pertaining to the compilation of the Book of City Inhabitants demonstrates that the form of urban government introduced by Catherine in 1785 could potentially have undercut the very structure of Russian society. Granting voice in city government to property owners cut across fixed legal and social boundaries within Russian society that defined the hierarchy of legal status pertaining to estate, ethnos and gender.

According to the Charter to the Towns, responsibility for gathering the data about home and property owners, alphabetizing it, putting it into standardized form and producing a formal copy of a Book of City Inhabitants was placed upon elected elders and deputies who were to be chosen every three years. Not surprisingly, the task proved onerous and time-consuming for men who were also trying to make a living. Those chosen for the duty found it difficult to carry it out and sought in various ways to evade or postpone it. In St Petersburg, elections to various new city offices created by the Charter to the Towns were held in the summer and early autumn of 1785. The six-voice council was supposed to oversee the book's compilation.

One merchant (*kupets*) was elected from each of the ten administrative districts of the city to do the actual work.[7] By early spring 1786, however, little had been accomplished. The city's mayor ('city head', *gorodskoi glava*), Semen Kalashnikov, sent the six-voice council a curt notice on 20 March 1786 that the book should be compiled 'immediately', reminding the council that it did not have to gather all the information itself, but had the authority to request necessary information from other governmental offices. In fact, the city magistracy had already compiled most of the information needed for the last five categories of city inhabitants. The only fresh data to be assembled had to do with owners of immovable property, a wholly new category.[8] Much of this information had been assembled during the winter just passed, at least for the first two letters of the alphabet.

Over the next three months, through late June 1786, communications passed back and forth between the mayor, the six-voice council, the city magistracy, the St Petersburg police and the delegates responsible for doing the work in an effort to bring the task to completion. It turned out, however, that the magistracy records were in complete disarray and required a lot of work to sort out. More significantly, the delegates representing two districts of the city, Leontii Kapitonov from Second Admiralty and Vasilei Ustinov from Vyborg Side, had never taken up their duties. It was finally ascertained that Kapitonov was no longer registered as a merchant and therefore considered himself ineligible to serve on the committee compiling the book. He had been registered as a merchant for the year 1785, but in November of that year, because of a decrease in the amount of his capital, he had fallen back into the petty townsman category in his registration for 1786. Ustinov, it turned out, had business interests in the nearby city and naval base of Kronstadt and spent most of his time there. It was not even clear that he was receiving the various communications addressed to him.

If two of the ten deputies were so difficult to locate and put to work on the project of compiling the Book of City Inhabitants, can it be assumed that the ten deputies chosen for the task were men on the margins and that more substantial merchants avoided service? Of the ten men (eleven counting Kapitonov's replacement), only one is numbered as a home owner in the materials on which this study is based (surnames starting with letters 'A' and 'B'). This was Vasilei Alekseev, a St Petersburg merchant who had come to the city from being a merchant in Eletsk. He was 50 years old and married to a woman who had been widowed by another St Petersburg merchant. The couple had two small children, a one-year-old son and a three-year-old daughter. Alekseev represented the First Admiralty, where he owned a stone house that he had purchased. As one of only two merchant homeowners in First Admiralty district, Alekseev was a substantial merchant if not one of the wealthiest in town. His election as deputy tends to argue against the notion that the service was reserved for those men of lesser wealth who were unable to avoid it.

In mid-June 1786, Mayor Kalashnikov ran out of patience with the lack of progress on the part of Alekseev and the other merchant delegates compiling the Book of City Inhabitants. To a request from the deputies to give them more time, Kalashnikov responded sharply on 17 June, accusing them angrily of not having taken their work seriously and reminding them that not one section of the book had yet been completed. Therefore, he ordered them to report for duty on the book's compilation every working day from eight o'clock in the morning until two o'clock in the afternoon and then again from four until eight in the evening until the book was completed. To ensure that they complied with this ten-hour-day schedule, they had to clock in daily with one of the secretaries at the city council. For the men selected to compile the book, this order represented a disaster for their businesses, which were left essentially without anyone to conduct them. Belatedly recognizing this, the mayor relented within two weeks, ordering half of the deputies to work on the Book of City Inhabitants in the mornings and half in the afternoons.

Meanwhile, the city magistracy refused to provide its records for the men to use as a basis for the Book of City Inhabitants, stating that lists held by the various guilds could be used for that purpose instead.[9] Eventually, the magistracy was forced to modify its oppositional stance, at least in part. In November 1787, the first department of the city magistracy released to the six-voice council, for the use of the deputies compiling the Book of City Inhabitants, a list of the 119 new registrants in the St Petersburg merchant guilds during that year.[10] Other than names, however, the list provided none of the specific information that was supposed to be included in the Book of City Inhabitants.

How did the ten men selected for the onerous chore of compiling the Book of City Inhabitants set about their work? Parts of drafts of the compilation survive in the St Petersburg city archive. The present study is based on the draft copy, or workbook, containing the surnames starting with the letters 'A' and 'B' in the Cyrillic alphabet.[11] The internal evidence of the manuscript suggests that this was the second redaction of the list of property owners. The first count was dated 6 November 1785, the so-called 'black' copy. The copy here examined, dated 5 January 1786, was labelled as the second, 'white' copy.

It is assumed that these two letters, 'A' and 'B', provide a typical cross-section of owners of immovable property in late eighteenth-century St Petersburg. Of the 28 letters in the Russian alphabet with which surnames commonly start, the letter 'B' is one of the more common, the letter 'A' less so. Together they comprise perhaps 7 per cent of Russian surnames.[12] Most of the names on the manuscript are Russian, but by no means all. The well-known physician Baron Georg Thomas von Asch[13] is included, as are the French goldsmith Jean Ador,[14] the German merchant Fedor Amburger,[15] the English merchant Thomas Bonar, the Dutch merchant Login Boehtlingk[16] and the English clockmaker John Bottom (Ivan Botom),[17] just to name a few of the more prominent among the many foreigners, mostly merchants and tradesmen, whose names appear on the lists. The entries for nobles are the simplest of all, in accordance with the instructions cited above for listing the well-born in the Book of City Inhabitants: only their names and the address and type of house are noted.

The sampling in the workbook contains between 480 and 500 names. If they can be taken to represent 7 per cent, or a fourteenth part, of the owners of immovable property in the city, then there may have been almost 7,000 property owners in the city at the beginning of 1786. Assuming that the city's population numbered from 185,000 to 200,000 at the time, depending on the season of year, then one in every 26–29 people in the city was a property owner.

As workbooks, the surviving bound volumes are filled with strikeovers, rewordings and eliminated entries.[18] The organizing principle was not alphabetical but geographical. Entries follow a rough order by address, generally starting with the first quarter (*kvartal*) of each of the ten administrative districts of the city and progressing through the others. Occasionally, names initially omitted were inserted later, crowded into the top or bottom margins. The strikeovers and rewordings were often made as part of an effort to establish uniformity in the wording of each of the seven specific items of information called for. The notebooks therefore show attempts to reduce the answers to questions to a standardized form. The initial differences in the ways questions were answered may have resulted from their having been recorded by different scribes, but in at least some cases the lack of uniformity seems to be a result of recording the verbatim statements of the people answering the questions. For example, first drafts frequently seem to show pride of ownership, especially in cases of owners of smaller houses ('I live in the house that I built with my own hands'), which in the revised copy is reduced to a far more bland statement ('Lives in a house built by him'). Who were these owners of immovable property? The vast majority of those listed owned houses, yet ten people registering in this category declared ownership not of houses but of shops, usually in a merchants' yard (*gostinyi dvor*). Only two of those ten were men. Kozma Kozmin Borisov, a 41-year-old merchant, owned a shop in the Stone[19] Merchants' Yard on Garden Street that he had purchased from merchant Ivan Denisov; Borisov reported that he lived in a house belonging to his wife Katerina Mikhailova, a house she had bought in Third Admiralty district. Il'ia Emelianov Barmin also owned a shop in the Stone Merchants' Yard, inherited from his father, and two wooden shops he had bought himself. His father had been one of St Petersburg's wealthiest merchants before his death and had also willed a stone shop to his wife and the family's stone house to another son, Dmitrii. In most of the remaining eight cases where women were declared to be owners of shops only, their husband or father owned the house where they lived. Female ownership in such cases was probably less genuine than a matter of accounting.

Registrants in the first, so-called 'real' category of the Book of City Inhabitants might be in possession of houses, shops or land. In the evidence examined, only 20 people of more than 480 reported owning a piece of immovable property, either an empty lot or a garden plot, with no structures built on it. In the majority of cases this was surely a temporary situation. According to the plans adopted in the 1760s to manage and direct the city's growth, vacant lots could be given to private individuals by the main police administration, but with the expectation that construction would begin within a five-year period. Failing that, the land could be reclaimed by the police and assigned to someone else. In a number of cases found here, the home owner cited the gift of land from the police as the origin of ownership.

Table 5.1   Building materials

	Houses				Shops		
	Stone	Wood	Unknown	Lot	Stone	Wood	Unknown
First Admiralty	32		1		1		
Second Admiralty	13	28	3		3	3	
Third Admiralty	27	34	5	3	27	6	2
Foundry	6	31	6				
Moscow	9	29	11	3	2	4	
Rozhestvenskaia	1	35	1	2			3
Carriage	21	19	1	6		2	3
Vasil'evskii Island	7	38	13	7	1	3	1
Petersburg Side		46	9	5		7	11
Vyborg Side	1	23	21	4			
TOTALS	117	283	71	30	34	25	20
			[471]				[79]

Catherine the Great is supposed to have said in one of her *bons mots* that she found Russia built of wood and left it built of stone. This comment should have applied to St Petersburg if any place in the empire. The evidence from the mid-1780s, more than two-thirds of the way through her reign, suggests otherwise (see Table 5.1). The only part of town built wholly of stone was First Admiralty, circumscribed by the Moika and Neva rivers. In eight of the districts of the city the ratio of stone to wooden houses was not even close to 1:1. In only one other district besides First Admiralty were the majority of houses in our sampling built of stone, and barely so. This was Carriage district, hardly the locus of wealth and influence in the city. What explains the preponderance of stone houses there?

Carriage district, lying in the southeastern part of the city, had grown up as the suburb settlement for men responsible for the post and post-horses, and particularly for carrying the post to Moscow. Carriage district was built haphazardly, consisting of typical Russian peasant log houses, each erected around its central stove and, consonant with the employment of its inhabitants, blacksmithies and leatherworking shops. In the course of two or three years starting in 1773 a series of devastating fires in the Moscow Postal Suburb – its traditional name – burned down a significant number of houses and stables. As a result the city's planning commission, which had largely completed its work on St Petersburg by the end of the 1760s and turned to planning other towns, set to work to learn how such fires might be averted in the future. As in many small neighbourhoods at the city's periphery, the commission found, houses were built too closely together. There was no regular street pattern, but houses and outbuildings were thrown together indiscriminately and totally without plan. The commission proposed that each house have its own yard, that more space be left between houses, and that more streets traverse the neighbourhood. Streets were to be laid in grid pattern; houses, built of brick, were individually to occupy small plots of land so that all of the houses were freestanding. The plan involved total eradication of the old community's physical identity and creation of a new 'subdivision'. The neighbourhood would continue to house the same people, but in finer and more durable structures. Construction began immediately and by 1782 nearly 170 houses had been built at a cost to the Treasury of just over 90,000 roubles.[20] Most of the houses were built as duplexes, to house two households, clearly seen in the number of property owners who registered as possessing a 'half-house' (*poludomik*); virtually all of them declared that under the new provisions of the Charter to the Towns they were now, in 1785, registered among the St Petersburg petty townsmen, having transferred registration there from the category of post-men. A few had the means even to register as merchants.

The new, neatly arrayed brick houses in Carriage district were built for its inhabitants at the cost of the state treasury. The government provided initial assistance to other property owners too. It has already been noted that the main police chancellery granted building lots starting in the 1760s to those willing and able to build on them. This provision applied specifically to large tracts of land in desirable locations and presumably to people of some means. Provisions were also made for people at the lower end of the economic scale, the archly termed 'base people' for whom Peter the Great himself had proposed architectural styles and house sizes earlier in the century. At least 18 home owners in Rozhestvenskaia district, all of them employed by or connected to the Office of Construction of Her Majesty's Houses and Gardens, indicated that they had built their houses on land owned or granted to them by the chancellery office (Table 5.2). The figure would be even higher if widows of former employees who had inherited their house from

Table 5.2 How property was acquired

Dist	Inher	Dowr	Purch	Deed	Debt	Built by self; land from								
						Unkn	Purch	Treas	Police	Hosp	H&G	Mona	Other	Unkn
1ADM	8		18	1					1					6
2ADM	11		20	5			1		2				1	3
3ADM	9		36	5		3			4				1	16
Found.	9		24	5					2		1		1	2
Mosc.	10		19	2		1	4		6				1	7
Rozh	1	2	2			4					15	10	3	4
Carr.	1		1			1		18				5	1	18
V.O.	12		26	1		1	1		2				1	13
SPb	11		18	18	6	1		1					4	6
Vyb	2		19			2		2		16				6
TOTALS	74	2	183	37	6	13	6	21	17	16	16	15	13	81

Total cases included here: 500
Number of cases in which land was given to owners: 64
Number of cases in which houses were built for owners: 21 (total 85)

their late husbands were added to the list. Employees of the naval and military hospital on Vyborg Side, which building still serves as a research hospital today, built their houses on land granted them by the hospital; at least 15 and as many as 20 from our sample 'built on land from the government's hospital', many of them adding, 'by permission of the command'.

Employees of the Alexander Nevskii Monastery living in Rozhestvenskaia district built their houses on monastery land; their number included monastery servitors, a diocesan cook, a night watchman at the monastery and a deacon.

These examples of workers in the post system, construction workers, health-care employees, and monastery employees provide evidence to substantiate the detailed contemporary descriptions of St Petersburg by such observers as Johann Gottlieb Georgi.[21] Various districts of the city received their character and definition from the people who lived in them (Table 5.3). Titled nobility – in this case, princes, counts and barons – clustered near to the winter and summer palaces. Non-titled nobility holding civilian ranks in the Table of Ranks and their military counterparts were spread somewhat more widely throughout town, clustering in Foundry (where the artillery-casting works were located) and on Vasil'evskii Island. Craftsmen and artisans owned houses in moderate numbers throughout the city.

Most numerous of all were the merchants, spread throughout the city in considerable numbers everywhere except in Rozhestvenskaia. The greatest concentrations of merchants were in Third Admiralty, where the Stone Merchants' Yard and Apraksin Yard, a centre of wholesale trade, attracted all sorts of wholesale and retail commerce. Vasil'evskii Island and Moscow district were the other two administrative sections of town where merchant real estate owners outnumbered those of any other social entity.

As imperial capital, St Petersburg drew to itself large numbers of people unique to a capital city, a fact reflected in home ownership. High-level functionaries in the civil administration and officers in military service were among the groups most represented numerically among home owners, with 11.5 and 10.8 per cent respectively. Their houses tended to be among the most expensive as measured by location and building materials. When the much less pretentious houses of lower ranking civil and military officialdom are added to them, such as civil servants below the Table of Ranks, those serving

Table 5.3 Social origins of owners by district of town

Group	1 Admir	2 Admir	3 Admir	Foundry	Moscow	Rozhest	Carriage	Vasil Is	Pet Side	Vyb Side
Titled nobility	5	1	1		3					1
Court Servitor		2	2	3	1	1				1
Civil Table of Ranks	9	4	3	10	7	2	3	11	6	
Civil below Table of Ranks		2	1	1	2			7	11	3
Gentry			2							
Lower court employee			2	6	8	21	2			
Army officer	2	10	1	11	4	1		10	8	6
Army soldier				2					5	13
Admiralty employee	1		20		1					12
Clergy		5				10	5		4	1
Merchant	6	7	29	3	16	1	14	18	9	5
Petty townsman							21	1	3	
Craftsman/artisan	5	8	3	3	2		3	6	8	2
Other/unknown	4	4	5	2	5	1	3	3	5	5
Peasant/serf						1	1	1		
TOTALS	32	43	68	41	49	38	52	57	59	49
[Female]	6	12	23	17	16	6	13	19	16	3

the imperial court in various capacities, and active or retired soldiers and sailors, the total share of home owners deriving their incomes directly from the imperial administration climbs to nearly 52 per cent ($N = 254$). The ubiquitous merchants made up the largest single group of home owners, however, with 22.1 per cent of privately owned houses in their hands. Also significant in number, the fourth largest group of home owners, were craftsmen and artisans, representing 8.2 per cent. A number of the people in both categories were indirectly dependent on the government, court and military for their livelihoods, to be sure.

A few merchant families were beginning to consolidate large holdings of real estate. A good example is Ivan Andreev Apaishchikov, aged 56 in 1785, married to the daughter of another St Petersburg merchant, 18 years his junior. They had one son, aged six, and four daughters ranging in age from 15 to infancy. (As in other sources, sons are always listed first no matter where they came chronologically, then daughters.) Apaishchikov owned property in all three Admiralty districts, Moscow district and Petersburg Side, a total of four houses, ten shops and two places for storing wares. In Second Admiralty he had bought a wooden house with some masonry construction from the widow of a foreign merchant named Stegelman. In Third Admiralty he had bought a stone house with a wooden addition at auction. A second stone house in Third Admiralty was registered in his wife's name. Under its listing, she stated that the house had been built by her on a lot granted by the main police. In the previous listing of his wooden house bought at auction, Apaishchikov testified that this latter house had been built by his own capital on land given to his wife. The same was true of the wooden house in Moscow district registered in his wife's name: she stated it was built by her on land given by the police; he said it was built by his own capital on land that formerly was a vacant lot, subsequently registered in his wife's name.

Apaishchikov had either built or bought all four houses he owned. Not so for all of his shops. A stone shop in the Great Merchants' Yard he had inherited from his father; likewise two wooden shops and a barn in markets on Petersburg Side. Five additional shops in the Great Merchants' Yard he had initially rented as wooden shops from the Commerce College, which administered the Merchants' Yard. When the college permitted merchants willing to pay for it to rebuild their shops in stone in exchange for ownership of them, Apaishchikov had taken advantage of the deal. Those shops were registered not in his own name, but in those of his 15- and 14-year-old daughters. Finally, Apaishchikov had bought two shops and a storage shed on Petersburg Side from other St Petersburg merchants.

Other merchants may not have accumulated quite as much property as Ivan Andreev Apaishchikov, but were doing quite well. Grigorei Anisimov Abrosimov owned five houses on Vasil'evskii Island (one inherited, two purchased, two acquired 'by deed', which presumably also meant by purchase) and two shops in the Stone Merchants' Yard in Third Admiralty. Aleksandr Petrov Berezin owned two houses, seven stone shops and three wooden ones. The extended Barmin family, St Petersburg merchants, owned a number of houses and shops.

Merchants often were clearly products of social mobility. Successful merchants from small towns like Olonets, Novaia Ladoga or Kaluga, just to give examples, moved their residence and registration to St Petersburg. Peasants could become merchants. Nine of the home owners in this sample – almost 2 per cent – identified themselves as merchants who had registered as such from the economic peasantry. Fedor Ivanov syn Avtanomov, St Petersburg merchant, aged 45, from the economic peasantry, had purchased a stone house in Foundry district and a wooden one with connected stone shops in Third Admiralty. Vasilei Grigoriev Bragin, St Petersburg merchant, aged 32, had purchased two wooden houses on Vasil'evskii Island and two stone shops, one in Second Admiralty and the other on Vasil'evskii.

Three other merchants divulged the information simply that they had come from the peasantry. But most interesting were the serfs who had become property owners in St Petersburg. Fedor Stepanov Baklanov, formerly a manorial serf, aged 30, registered in the St Petersburg merchants in 1769 (when he was only 14 years old!), was married to the daughter of a St Petersburg merchant, had a son and four daughters, and owned a rambling wooden house in Moscow district covering two lots. Matvei Alekseev, aged 60, a serf of Count Volodimer Grigorievich Orlov, who continued to pay quitrent to cover his obligations to his master and whose wife and two sons in their mid-twenties still lived on the estate in the countryside, owned a wooden house on Vasil'evskii Island near Smolenskoe cemetery, right on the small stream called Black Brook. Ivan Alekseev, a peasant of Mr Aleksandr Vasilievich Khomuninnikov, owned a small house on land given him by the Office for Building Her Majesty's Lands and Gardens.

Everyone registered in the Book of City Inhabitants was eligible to sit in the urban corporation and participate in elections to city offices. Was there any significance in the fact that a handful of serfs could potentially hold seats on the city council? Would these men actually have exercised their right to participate in city government? Did Catherine even suspect that there were serf property owners in the capital city of the empire? It would be interesting to find a case somewhere in the archives where the issue of dual status had to be dealt with. Would the courts have decided that a serf registered in town in the highest classification of urban dweller, as a 'real' city inhabitant, was after all still only a serf? Or would urban status have trumped serfdom?

If peasants represented a tiny percentage of property owners, women did not. Assuming that the evidence of letters 'A' and 'B' is indicative of the situation throughout the alphabet, women controlled slightly more than one quarter of all the privately-owned real estate in St Petersburg (Table 5.4). Michelle Marrese and others have been reminding us recently of the role that women played as estate owners in Russia.[22] Almost half of the women owning real property in St Petersburg claimed to have purchased their house or houses. As was seen with the Apaishchikov family, however, it is difficult to know whether in fact the woman in question was in complete control of her finances or whether the purchase was made in her name by her husband or some other male relative. More than a quarter of the women who had property acquired it through inheritance, most often from the death of a husband. In one case a woman indicated that she had half inherited the house – from her mother – and half purchased it. Unfortunately we do not know from whom – perhaps from a sibling? The answers that women gave to this question vary so widely that one suspects the answers were written in their very words. Twelve women claimed to have built their homes themselves. Once again, the case of the Apaishchikovs warns us to be cautious, but one is tempted to see these women as active agents seeking to control their own destinies.

By their own testimony a number of women made their living from renting out parts or all of their houses as apartments, shops or

Table 5.4 How women acquired houses or land

Inherited (4)		37
From husband (widow)	18	
From husband jointly with children	7	
From father	3	
From parents	1	
After son's death	1	
A share from father	2	
Given in dowry, now hers again as widow	1	
Half inherited from mother, half purchased	1	1
Purchased (50)		61
By deed	8	
At auction	1	
By promissory note	1	
By mortgage with son	1	
Built by her (1)		12
On land from		
Church of Nativity of the Virgin	1	
Main police	3	
Administration of HIM Lands & Gardens	1	
Monastery land	3	
Inherited land	1	
Allotted land	1	
Empty lot	1	
Built by husband on purchased lot	1	1
Built by treasury (all widows)	3	3
No information (2)		12
Widow	8	
Princess of Holstein, Ekaterina Petrovna Bariatinskaia	1	
Wife of Col. Petr Beketov	1	
TOTALS		127

both. In Second Admiralty Maria Semenova Antipeva, the 40-year-old widow of a journeyman engraver in naval service supported herself and her five children ranging in age from 3 to 18 from the wooden house she and the children had inherited from her husband. In the same part of town Stepanida Andreeva, the widow of a master joiner, likewise reported that she 'has her subsistence from the house'. Yet again in Second Admiralty, Avdotia Afonaseva, the widow of a naval navigator, 'is nourished from the house'. Many other examples could be shown of this way for women to support themselves independently in St Petersburg by providing needed services in rented space for housing and commercial establishments.

Very few houses were jointly owned. St Petersburg was such a new city and most construction was so recent in the 1780s that the complications of home ownership caused by contested inheritance and competing claims of purchase and deeds to plots of land and structures had not had time yet to develop. There were a few potential cases for dispute, however. In Foundry district a stone house that had belonged to a major in the artillery, Pengov, went after his death to his widow. She sold part of the house to a lieutenant Sharishov. Upon her death the part of the house she owned went to her two brothers, the collegiate assessor Fedor Fedorov Birgerov and the artillery lieutenant-colonel Bogdan Fedorov Birgerov. One begins to sense the need for a lawyer to sort things out. Notaries were beginning to come into use at this time in defining legal rights in cases dealing with contested letters of credit, in which area the law was becoming more precisely defined.[23] Only after the Book of City Inhabitants was compiled would there be a basis for the development of specialists interpreting the laws on the ownership of immovable property in cities.

So, how did it go with Mayor Kalashnikov and the elected deputies to compile the Book of City Inhabitants? Mayor Kalashnikov met with no greater success in 1788 than he had in 1786 and 1787 in his efforts to get the book finished. There was considerable wrangling back and forth between the city magistracy and the six-voice council, on behalf of the deputies compiling the book, over the quality and completeness of the data provided by the magistracy. The disputes might have been rendered unnecessary had the deputies undertaken a house-by-house, building-by-building census of each district of town. The circumstances under which people lived made that approach extremely difficult for all classifications except home owners. By the end of 1788 it was clear that the task would have to carry over beyond the new elections to the city council as the terms of the first deputies elected under the 1785 Charter expired.

Some parts of the book were completed, however. When the proper data could be accumulated quickly, it was. For example, the list of merchants in First Admiralty district was compiled before the end of 1785. This was the very core of the city, the territory bounded by the Moika Canal and the Neva, encompassing the Winter Palace and the Admiralty. It was characterized less by commerce than by the grand palaces of the wealthy and powerful; the entire length of Million Street lay within the district. Only 50 merchants were registered there in 1785.

The Book of City Inhabitants remained uncompleted at the end of the three-year term of office of the first officials elected under the terms of the Charter to the Towns. Despite its intended significance for the internal working of the system of urban government Catherine instituted in 1785, it apparently was never completed. No copy, at least, has been found in the city's archives. Not until the annual 'address books' began to appear in the early nineteenth century would a list of the city's home owners be compiled and maintained.

Notes

1. David Griffiths and George E. Munro (trans and eds), *Catherine II's Charters of 1785 to the Nobility and the Towns* (Bakersfield, CA, 1991), 'Charter on the Rights and Benefits for the Towns of the Russian Empire', article 53, p. 28. All citations from the Charter are drawn from this translation, which reproduces the Russian text on facing pages. (The Charter originally appeared in *Polnoe sobranie zakonov rossiiskoi imperii s 1649 goda*, Collection 1, 45 vols. (St Petersburg, 1830), XXII, No. 16.187.)
2. *Ibid.*, 'Charter on the Rights, Freedoms and Privileges of the Well-Born Russian Nobility', article 92, pp. 15–21.
3. *Ibid.*, 'Charter on the Rights and Benefits for the Towns of the Russian Empire', articles 63–8, pp. 30–1.
4. The city council was made up of multiple representatives of the six recognized categories of population based either on geographical divisions (wards or 'quarters') or specialization. Thus each craft guild had a representative. The six-voice council was the smaller executive body in which each of the six categories had one representative and one vote.
5. *Ibid.*, articles 58–9, pp. 29–30.
6. *Ibid.*, article 58, note, p. 29.
7. The ten districts were: First Admiralty, Second Admiralty, Third Admiralty, Foundry, Moscow, Rozhestvenskaia [in some sources Rozhdestvenskaia], Carriage, Vasil'evskii Island, Petersburg Side, and Vyborg Side. The ten men elected to carry out the duty were Vasilei Alekseev, Andrei Strunnikov (replaced Leontii Kapitonov in 1786), Dmitrii Shorokhov, Ivan Dereviagin, Trofim Danilov, Ivan Venediktov, Ivan Chilikin, Vlad Dubrovin, Iakov Kunkin and Vasilii Ustinov.
8. Tsentral'nyi gosudarstvennyi istoricheskii arkhiv Sankt-Peterburga [hereafter TsGIA SPb], *fond* 781, *opis'* 2, *delo* 9, *listy* 1–2.
9. *Ibid., list* 16.
10. *Ibid., listy* 51–6. The list contained 181 names because in some cases (39 of 119) the names of multiple family members were included in a single

registration. Other data included the day and month of registration, the former registered status of the registrant, and where, and the amount of capital declared (the basis for taxation).

11. TsGIA SPb, *fond* 781, *opis'* 4, *delo* 107.
12. The list of Russian surnames compiled by Morton Benson [Morton Benson (comp.), *Dictionary of Russian Personal Names*, 2nd edn revised (Philadelphia, 1969)] indicates that only the letters 'K' and 'S' outstrip 'B'. My estimate of 7 per cent is subjective, based on perusal of name indexes in a wide variety of books, estimates made by Russian friends, and a summary survey of telephone books.
13. Georg Thomas von Asch (1729–1807) was the third son of the head of St Petersburg's post office, originally from Breslau. Following his medical education at Tübingen and Göttingen, Georg Thomas made a career as a doctor in the Russian army. For more on him see John T. Alexander, *Bubonic Plague in Early Modern Russia: Public Health & Urban Disaster* (Baltimore, 1980).
14. The stone house at No. 145 in First Admiralty was registered to 'Ivan Ador, son of the late goldsmith Ivan Ador, aged 3 [*sic*] years'. Catherine's renowned jeweller, the Genevan Jean Pierre Ador, had died on 12 July 1784. His son Jean was born on 12 June 1782, making him three years old at the end of 1785.
15. Friedrich Amburger [Fedor Karlovich], entry No. 4,743 in the Amburger-Archiv: http://www.lrz-muenchen.de/%7Eoeihist/abfrage.htm.
16. Various family members are listed in the Amburger-Archiv. See previous note.
17. Briefly mentioned in Anthony Cross, *By the Banks of the Neva. Chapters from the Lives and Careers of the British in Eighteenth-Century Russia* (Cambridge, 1997), p. 231.
18. Even so, two names starting with other letters (Ivan Varfolomei and Safonia Timofeeva Trofimova) escaped deletion.
19. The term 'stone' usually means 'masonry' or 'brick', rather than 'built of rock'. A stone structure was generally much more expensive to build than a wooden one.
20. Rossiiskii gosudarstvennyi istoricheskii arkhiv, *fond* 1329, *opis'* 2, *delo* 104, No. 38, *listy* 111–14; Rossiiskii gosudarstvennyi arkhiv drevnikh aktov, *fond* 16, *delo* 516, *list* 2.
21. Johann Gottlieb Georgi, *Opisanie rossiisko-imperatorskago stolichnago goroda Sankt-Peterburga i dostopamiatnostei v okrestnostiakh onogo* (3 vols. in 1; St Petersburg, 1794).
22. Michelle Lamarche Marrese, *A Woman's Kingdom: Noblewomen and the Control of Property in Russia, 1700–1861* (Ithaca and London, 2002).
23. See Philipp Heinrich Dilthey, *Nachal'nyia osnovaniia veksel'nago prava, a osoblivo rossiiskago, kupno i shvedskago, s pribavleniem raznykh rossiiskikh uzakonenii, k tomu prinadlezhashchikh, dlia upotrebleniia v Moskovskom iuridicheskom fakul'tete, po udobneishemu sposobu razpolozhenniia. 5. izd., vnov' popravlennoe i umnozhennoe* (Moscow, 1794).

6
Governing the City: St Petersburg and Catherine II's Reforms

Janet M. Hartley

St Petersburg was unique. As far as administration is concerned, it was the unique composition of the population of the city which was most significant. The most obvious point of distinctiveness of St Petersburg compared with other Russian towns was the presence of the following: the court and courtiers; large numbers of bureaucrats, officials and clerical staff who were employed in the offices of state; the wealthiest nobles and their serf retinues; army and naval officers resident in the city between campaigns or employed in ministries; foreigners in many professions; the scholars, scientists and artists associated with the academies; a small number of very wealthy merchants. Contemporary statistical information on city population in late eighteenth-century Russia has to be treated with caution but it at least demonstrates something of the oddity of St Petersburg. In 1801 it has been estimated that the 'townspeople' of the city (the merchants and the artisans, the *meshchane*) numbered some 38,000 persons, but they were collectively outnumbered by 13,200 members of the nobility, 26,100 servants, 39,100 soldiers and officers and over 50,000 peasants.[1] In addition, the *transience* of the population of the city was also distinctive, not only in the number of wealthy nobles who retired for the summer months to their country estates, and in the movement of foreign and Russian merchants back and forth from the city but also the army of transient peasants and workers who supplied a city without a natural economic hinterland with foodstuffs, hand-made goods and labour. The city housed some of the most wealthy inhabitants of the empire and at the same time some of the most impoverished and needy within its boundaries.

Catherine, of course, penned her legislation for the reordering of the administration of the Russian empire in St Petersburg. To an extent, her legislation for Russia *is* legislation for St Petersburg, the city with which she was most familiar. Indeed, George Munro has pointed out that the Charter to the Towns of 1785 was preceded five years earlier by a draft project for the municipal government of St Petersburg entitled 'Concerning the City of St Petersburg', which is almost identical to the first 28 articles of the Charter.[2] In fact, Catherine's legislation was supposed to be applicable to all towns in the Russian empire (unlike that of her successor Nicholas I who passed legislation specifically for St Petersburg), as was her legislation for courts, fiscal and welfare institutions in her Statute on Provincial Administration of 1775, her Police Statute of 1782 and her Statute on National Education of 1786.[3] But there are elements of her legislation which seem to be influenced by the distinctive social composition of St Petersburg and issues affecting it.

The most obvious influence of the social composition of St Petersburg on legislation can be found in the Charter to the Towns.[4] The Charter divided urban society into six categories: (1) 'real citizens', who owned houses or property in the towns; (2) merchants, registered into three guilds according to the amount of declared capital (third guild for those with registered capital of 1,000–5,000 roubles, second guild for those with capital of 5,000–10,000 roubles, and first guild for those with capital of 10,000–50,000 roubles); (3) artisans (*meshchane*) registered in craft guilds (*tsekhi*); (4) foreign nationals and merchants from other towns; (5) 'eminent' citizens, comprising those with capital of over 50,000 roubles, bankers, shipowners, wholesale traders, townspeople who had served in the urban courts established in 1775, artists and academics; (6) members of the *posad*, that is, people who lived and worked in the town but lacked the skill or capital to register as artisans or merchants.

It was only in St Petersburg and Moscow that these categories could be realistically filled by the inhabitants of the town. The category of 'eminent citizens' seems to have been defined with the unusual economic and cultural composition of the city in mind. In 1786 those classified as 'eminent citizens' in St Petersburg included one banker, three academics, seven artists and fourteen 'capitalists' (that is persons with declared capital of over 50,000 roubles).[5] As far as the foreigners were concerned, Storch calculated that there were

17,660 Germans, 3,720 Finns, 2,290 Frenchmen, 1,860 Swedes, 930 Englishmen, 50 Dutchmen and a number of Poles, Spaniards, Italians and Portuguese in the city.[6] Foreign nationals were relatively rare in other Russian towns, or at least, *western* foreign nationals were – although the merchant communities of Russian southern cities were dominated by Greeks and Armenians. In Khar'kov, for example, which was quite an important economic centre, no one qualified to register as an eminent citizen and there were no foreigners or merchants from other towns (or at least none registered formally in the Khar'kov urban society).[7] Furthermore, in most Russian towns there were few merchants with sufficient capital to register in the first guild. In Iaroslavl', for example, in 1800, only seven merchants were registered in the first guild, 122 in the second guild and 3,966 in the third guild.[8]

The presence of large numbers of nobles, officials, servants and soldiers, foreigners, and of at least a few 'eminent citizens', made St Petersburg distinct not only from other towns in Russia (with the exception of Moscow), but also made it quite different from the small, district, towns in the St Petersburg *guberniia* which Catherine's administrative reforms also served, where there were considerable numbers of peasants but few officials, foreigners and no 'eminent' citizens, and where most 'townspeople' were artisans. In the district town of Shlissel'burg in the St Petersburg *guberniia*, it was reported in 1780 that 'there were no merchants in the town'.[9] In the St Petersburg *guberniia* in 1786, merchants were registered in all three guilds only in the city of St Petersburg itself; in the districts they could be found in the second guild in only two towns and in the third guild only in four towns.[10] In the same year it was reported that representatives for urban institutions from the categories of eminent citizens, foreigners and merchants from other towns could be found only in the city of St Petersburg itself, and not in the district towns of the *guberniia*.[11]

The definition of the urban community was a significant weakness in the Charter. Its failure to correspond to the reality of the majority of Russian towns meant that the composition of the new urban institutions, which were based on representation from these six urban categories, could not in practice meet the requirements of the legislation. The Charter established general town councils or *duma*s in all towns formed of representatives of all the newly defined six categories of townspeople but this elected members of a higher *duma* – the six-councillor *duma* – which was supposed to comprise one representative from all six categories. Outside St Petersburg and Moscow, however, the six-councillor *duma*s often had to operate with fewer than its complement of six members because the six categories could not be filled. In this respect, the example of St Petersburg, which seem to drive the definition of social categories, served to weaken the whole structure of municipal legislation after 1785.

Even within St Petersburg, the legislation led to an uneven representation of social groups. The poorly framed legislation concerning the composition of the general town *duma*s was partly to blame. In principle all handicrafts could be represented by one member, house-owners and *posad* members could represent each administrative section, or *chast'*, of the town (and there were ten such sections or *chasti* in the city of St Petersburg), each foreign national group could have a representative, each of the categories of 'eminent' citizens could also be represented – but the merchants could only be represented by a maximum of three members, one for each of the three merchant guilds. In the St Petersburg general town *duma*, therefore, in theory the merchants could have been outnumbered by every other group. In practice, the evidence suggests that this did not happen. Membership of all categories fluctuated and sometimes included more than three merchants and fewer representatives from other groups than the legislation permitted.[12] This allowed the general town *duma* to function, but only by bypassing the strict requirements of the legislation and allowing representation better to reflect the economic forces of the city.

Furthermore, some aspects of the social composition of St Petersburg were in practice evaded or ignored. The category of 'real citizens' could in principle have meant that all property owners in the city were represented in municipal government. This could have included nobles and officials, that is people who were not normally regarded as members of the 'urban community'. If this was an attempt to make urban administration reflect the reality of the social composition of the city then it was not fully realized. Information on the men chosen as 'real citizens' in St Petersburg is not available (up to ten served on the general town *duma* in the years 1788, 1789 and 1791). But the evidence from other parts of the empire suggests that nobles did not participate willingly in urban government.

In Moscow, two men elected as real citizens declined to take up the post because they were not involved in trade (and article 172 of the Charter had specified this requirement); they were finally replaced by a merchant.[13] In other towns, it seems that minor officials and also merchant and artisans houseowners were included in this category. Furthermore, the overwhelmingly *peasant* composition of the towns – of St Petersburg as much as of other towns in the empire – was not taken into account. Peasants remained outside the urban community, and were not only able to evade urban taxes but also continued to undercut the prices of hand-made goods and, in effect, prevent the development of exclusive and specialized urban trade guilds.

There is a less obvious link between other aspects of Catherine's administrative legislation between 1775 and 1785 and the St Petersburg experience, but some of the particular issues facing St Petersburg may account for the scope of activities of the new institutions. The six-councillor *duma*, the most important executive body, was supposed to deal with all economic aspects of the life of the town and its inhabitants and to preserve peace and order (article 167). These very general, and vague, responsibilities could apply to all towns but possibly the requirement to supervise the soundness of 'public buildings' and to establish and maintain trading establishments (point 6 of article 167) reflect the particular needs of the capital and major trading centre and the requirement to encourage 'imports' to meet the needs of the population (point 5) reflects the constant need in St Petersburg to supply foodstuffs for the urban population.[14] The Police Statute of 1782, with its detailed instructions on the maintenance of buildings, river crossings, and for establishing good order in trading areas and for the maintenance of public decency and order may also have been a response to the particular conditions, or vitality, of St Petersburg as a growing city and commercial centre.[15] Law and order in St Petersburg may well have been a greater problem than in smaller towns with a less transient population. In 1785, 1,749 persons were in prison in St Petersburg awaiting trial for crimes ranging from murder to begging for alms;[16] the number of cases passing through courts analysed below is also a reflection of a high level of criminal as well as civil cases in the city.

The Statute of Provincial Administration of 1775 was concerned, of course, not only with all the country but with administration on a provincial level rather than at an urban level. Nevertheless, the detailed provisions in that act for welfare institutions – hospitals, asylums, almshouses, workhouses, houses of correction, orphanages – set up under a special board of general welfare, reflect urban and not rural concerns and could also be a product of the particular urban distress in a major city like St Petersburg.[17] Catherine's confidence in the feasibility of establishing national state schools (in 1775 and, more concretely, in 1786) possibly also stemmed from the relative success in St Petersburg of establishing schools and the availability there of potential teachers. The Statute of 1775 did at least make a concession to the different social structure of St Petersburg by establishing special courts – at the level of the first and second courts of instance – for sectors of the population which did not fit the estate categories of the new court structure (that is, for nobles, townspeople and state peasants). These so-called *nadvornye* courts were set up in St Petersburg and Moscow for an odd assortment of 'extras' – people working at court, occupied in industry, *raznochintsy* and a vague group of 'citizens' (*grazhdanskie*) who did not own immovable property but who were not subject to the urban courts. This category of court was an addendum to the main Statute and very much an afterthought; no such provision was made for population in other towns and provinces which fitted awkwardly into the new structure (although *nadvornye* courts were also established in Archangel *guberniia* in 1784).[18] Finally, it should be noted that the extent of *noble* population of the city may have encouraged Catherine to believe that noble assemblies could and would flourish in other towns in the empire and provide a focus at least at election time which could encourage the development of a cultural and social life for the provincial nobility. Noble assemblies, first established in 1767 in order to elect representatives to the Legislative Commission, became an important ingredient of the Statute of 1775. They became the forum for the conducting elections of nobles to posts in local administration, and were also of central importance in the Charter to the Nobles in 1785 for the recording and registering of the provincial nobility.

Given the size and social composition of St Petersburg, and the fact that Catherine was in residence in the city, it is clear that if Catherine's new administrative institutions were to work at all, then St Petersburg would be the city (and the province) where they could be expected to operate most fully and with the most vitality. Within a decade of the promulgation of the Statute of Provincial

Administration senators and other notable individuals were dispatched to check that all the institutions had been established and were functioning correctly. It will be of no surprise to learn that St Petersburg *city* (but not necessarily the districts in the St Petersburg *guberniia*) was one of the areas where the full range of institutions was established. In 1786, an inspection of St Petersburg reported that all the institutions had been established in the city – courts, fiscal bodies, urban *duma*s, police, welfare institutions (including national schools) and that everything was apparently in 'good order' (although urban institutions had not been set up in all district towns, this, of course being more typical of the empire as a whole).[19]

The establishment of the appropriately titled institutions did not itself, of course, ensure that the legislation was implemented in full or as desired. The failures of the composition of the town *duma*s to correspond to the legislation of 1785 has already been noted, in St Petersburg as much as anywhere else. In addition, institutions had to be staffed according to the legislative requirements, something which required appointed officials at the top, elected officials in the courts of lower instance (and urban institutions) and a new influx of clerical staff. It has been estimated by Robert Jones that the number of posts in provincial administration rose from 12,712 in 1774 to 27,000 by the end of Catherine's reign.[20] The city of St Petersburg should, of all places, have been able at least to staff these institutions adequately. By the end of the century St Petersburg was an attractive place to live in, albeit expensive, but the higher costs of living in St Petersburg had been acknowledged by higher rates of pay for posts there (along with the *gubernii* of Riga, Reval, Vyborg, Kursk and Irkutsk). The salary scale affected posts from top to bottom: the governor received 4,000 roubles, compared with 3,000 elsewhere; the presidents of the upper land court (noble court of second instance), 750 instead of 600 roubles; the judge of the district court (noble court of first instance), 600 instead of 360 roubles; the urban assessors in the *guberniia* magistracy (an urban court of second instance), 300 instead of 200 roubles; the secretary in the lower *rasprava* and district courts (first instance courts for state peasants and nobles), 250 instead of 200 roubles.[21]

On the whole, St Petersburg city was able to staff the new institutions. In this respect it was quite different from other *gubernii* and towns where for the most part the structure of the institutions of 1775 and 1785 were established but not fully staffed. Distant *gubernii* and those with a low population density were particularly vulnerable, such as Olonets, Kolyvan and Vologda (all of which, amongst other things, lacked the nobility to fill elected noble posts) where not all institutions were opened. The many small district towns which comprised mainly, or entirely, peasants could not staff the new urban institutions. Even in St Petersburg *guberniia*, the district town of Oranienburg was not able to set up its town magistracy or its orphan's court.[22] Many *gubernii* were unable to establish the full range of welfare institutions required by the Statute of 1775. In 1786, it was reported that Olonets *guberniia* the board of social welfare was not yet opened and the only welfare institution was the hospital in Petrozavodsk catering for 25 patients, although boards had been set up in all *gubernii* by the end of the century.[23] There was also a severe shortage of clerical staff in other parts of the empire (and, indeed, the *St Petersburg News* advertised clerical vacancies in other *gubernii*, quite possibly in an attempt to attract qualified candidates in the city to seek posts elsewhere).

The composition of the municipal *duma*s, and the exceptional position of St Petersburg here, has already been mentioned. Difficulties in filling elected posts in urban courts occurred in the district towns of the St Petersburg *guberniia*, as noted above, rather than in the city, for the same reasons as the difficulty in fully manning the municipal *duma*s. The city of St Petersburg at least had the noble population to support the elected and appointed posts for institutions for this estate. Indeed, it was one of the features of St Petersburg that the ranks held by noble appointed office holders was often higher than the rank attached to the post. In 1782, the seven St Petersburg elected noble assessors in the district court (a post ranked 9) all already held higher ranks, through military or civil service (four were rank 8, three were rank 7 and one was rank 5). In the same year, ten of the noble assessors in the lower land court (a rural police institution with both administrative and minor judicial functions) had ranks above the rank allocated to the post, while four were ranked below. This may well have an exclusive feature of the existence of large numbers of highly ranked nobles in St Petersburg city and *guberniia*. Comparative figures for other *gubernii* are too vague to be conclusive but some comparative figures acquired for the noble marshals of the nobility suggested that marshals in St Petersburg were consistently of higher ranks than marshals in other *gubernii*.[24]

The noble assemblies in St Petersburg also attracted relatively high attendance. In 1780, that is after the introduction of the Statute but before the functions of the assemblies were extended by the Charter to the Nobles, 108 nobles attended the assembly in St Petersburg city; the district assemblies saw attendance of between 10 and 15 nobles but here numbers of those absent were higher than those present.[25] The district experience of St Petersburg is, not for the first time, more typical of the experience of the whole country. Nobles, often resident in St Petersburg or in the army, often chose not to return at the time of elections to vote, so leaving the assemblies to the poorer and less well-educated nobles who had retired to the countryside or who lacked the skills and influence to find posts for themselves, or their sons, in the capitals. Attendance in noble assemblies outside St Petersburg declined as the initial enthusiasm waned – in Iaroslavl', for example, the level of attendance dropped from 705 in 1777 to 301 in 1783.[26]

It was also relatively easy to attract experienced and high-ranking nobles to the top posts in St Petersburg, which was not only a prestigious and attractive post but was a good career move. The distinguished governors of St Petersburg included: U.S. Potapov, who had been the vice-governor of the *guberniia* and moved on from being governor to become the president of the census college and was awarded the orders of St Vladimir fourth class, P.P. Konovitsyn, an experienced administrator who had been governor of Tambov and Novgorod *gubernii* before the post in St Petersburg and then moved on to become governor-general of Archangel and Olonets *gubernii*; N.I. Ryleev, another experienced administrator who had served in the police department in St Petersburg before taking the post and was awarded with the order of St Vladimir third and second class in 1793 and 1796.

At the other end of the scale, it also proved possible to find clerical staff in St Petersburg. Clerical staff came from different social backgrounds (including the sons of clergy, townspeople, poorer nobility and soldiers) but were often themselves the children of clerks and St Petersburg, of course, was the location of the central state institutions with the largest clerical staff. The national schools, set up technically in 1775 but more firmly after the Statute on National Schools of 1786, taught mostly the children (mostly, but not exclusively, the sons) of merchants, artisans and minor officials, at least some of whom might seek clerical posts in the new institutions. In 1789 a report was made to the Senate listing some 100 minor office holders in St Petersburg; those in the civil chamber (the highest court of instance for civil cases) were commended as 'each had the ability to undertake their tasks'. The junior office holders in St Petersburg came from a varied background – sons of clerks, officers, soldiers, merchants, court peasants, clergy – but were almost all young, and were mostly in their late teens.[27] Catherine's reforms had at least opened up opportunities for some.

Opening and fully staffing the new institutions does not, of course, ensure that they would function well. This is naturally more difficult to assess. What can be established is that the St Petersburg institutions certainly transacted vast amounts of business, which in turn, absorbed a large amount of time of the officials involved (appointed and elected). To this extent – and it is a limited extent – it can be said that Catherine's institutions worked, at least in St Petersburg and, in fact, to a greater extent in the city and *guberniia* in St Petersburg than elsewhere in the empire. It is often stated that the problem with the Russian empire was that it was 'undergoverned' rather than 'overgoverned'.[28] Over the whole imperial period, and over the whole empire, this is probably true; it is less true, however, for the city of St Petersburg in the aftermath of Catherine II's reforms of local and municipal administration.

In order to illustrate this, the performance of various institutions can be assessed. The Statute of Provincial Administration set up an elaborate structure of courts of three instances by social estate. The highest courts in the *guberniia* were the civil and criminal chambers, which heard civil and criminal cases respectively, and below them were established first and second instance courts – the district and upper land courts for nobles, town and *guberniia* magistracies for townspeople, upper and lower *rasprava* for state peasants,[29] and, in St Petersburg at least, upper and lower *nadvornye* courts for a variety of other persons. In addition, Catherine established a conscience court (*sovestnyi sud*) for cases which fell outside the normal confines of Russian law and legal practice,[30] a lower land court which dealt with minor infringements of the law in the countryside (which will be discussed further below) and oral courts for minor cases in towns. In 1782, the Police Statute also gave the police the right to investigate and adjudicate minor criminal offences (thefts under 20 roubles).

The evidence from St Petersburg demonstrates the extraordinary amount of work carried out by these courts. In 1786, for example, the courts in St Petersburg heard the following number of cases: civil chamber, 1,756 cases; criminal chamber, 400 cases; conscience court, 202 cases; upper land court, 874 cases; upper *nadvornyi* court, 946 cases; *guberniia* magistracy, 874 cases; upper *rasprava*, 276 cases; lower *nadvornyi* court, 1,961 cases; district court, 228 cases; town magistracy, 3,272 cases; lower land court, 411 cases; oral courts, 4,517 cases; police board, 15,554 cases. In addition the fiscal chamber handled almost 5,000 cases involving state interests and almost 12,000 cases reached the *guberniia* board, the highest executive office in the *guberniia*, on appeal. In the whole *guberniia* for that year over 50,000 cases reached district or *guberniia* courts and institutions of law and order.[31] The size of St Petersburg largely accounted for the extent of business; only Moscow could be expected to handle such a workload. Other *gubernii* had fewer cases, although the courts were kept busy – in 1789 some 34,000 cases were recorded in Tambov *guberniia* and some 19,000 in Kaluga *guberniia*.[32] Of course, many of these cases were on appeal, and in themselves reflect something of the inefficiency and time-consuming features of the Russian legal structure. Some cases were also outstanding at the end of the year, although these records, if fully accurate, record relatively few of these (35 from the criminal chamber, 74 from the civil chamber, 11 from the upper land court, 26 from the upper *nadvornyi* court, 124 from the *guberniia* magistracy, etc.). Cases which had been passed to a higher court on appeal, of course, would be recorded here as 'settled' rather than 'unsettled', so the figures may present a very rosy picture of the operation of the Russian legal system.

Another indication of the sheer workload generated by Catherine's institutions is the number and frequency of meetings which took place. The six-councillor *duma*s were supposed to meet at least once a week. In St Petersburg the number of meetings of the general town *duma* fluctuated sharply from month to month and year to year, but the six-councillor *duma*s, which conducted the main business of the town, regularly met several times a week, and in excess of the requirements stipulated by the Charter. The St Petersburg city six-councillor *duma* met 105 times in 1788, 100 times in 1789, 120 times in 1791 and 317 days in 1794. Absences and the reason for absences were noted in all institutions. Attendance at the six-councillor *duma* meetings was very high in St Petersburg *guberniia*, in the city as well as in the district *duma*s.[33]

Officials were supposed to attend for 225 days of the year in the chambers and the courts of second instance. A record exists of the attendance patterns of officials in all *gubernii* for the year 1789. An analysis of this record with regard to the higher institutions in St Petersburg (the *guberniia* board, the chambers, the courts of second instance) showed that these St Petersburg institutions were less well attended than the municipal organs, and also that absenteeism in St Petersburg was higher than in some other *gubernii* (I made a particular study of the *gubernii* of St Petersburg, Tver', Tambov, Kaluga, Novgorod and Iaroslavl'). The comparative figures for absenteeism in that year were: St Petersburg, 28 per cent; Tambov, 24 per cent; Kaluga, 23 per cent; Iaroslavl', 22 per cent; Novgorod, 14.5 per cent. The reason for this may be that the more prestigious higher officials in St Petersburg were also given special and additional functions to perform. St Petersburg absences were accounted for by the demands of 'other business' (2,543 days), 'illness' (1,163 days) and 'leave'. This pattern was different in the other *gubernii* studied where absences were more likely to be due to leave and illness.[34]

Finally, the number of people in welfare institutions and schools in St Petersburg indicate a high level of activity, which was not always reproduced elsewhere. Accurate figures for inmates are impossible to determine but it is clear that the St Petersburg city institutions were active. In 1785, Governor Konovitsyn stated that the number of inmates in St Petersburg institutions were as follows: hospital, 1,282; lunatic asylum, 64; workhouse, 617; house of correction, 446. The following year, A.R. Vorontsov reported the numbers rather differently: hospital, 1,654; lunatic asylum, 69; orphanage, 516; almshouse (for incurables), 1,233; other almshouses (including the sick from the workhouse), 278; workhouse, 546; smallpox hospital, 139.[35]

Catherine had personally donated two buildings in St Petersburg for national schools. By the end of her reign there was one major national school and twelve minor national schools in the city. Between 1786 and 1796 the number of pupils in schools in the St Petersburg *guberniia* rose from 3,123 to 3,902 (and reached 4,136 in 1802).[36] No other town in the empire was so well served by state education. Furthermore, the St Petersburg board of social welfare, the body which had been set up to supervise the new welfare institutions, received the highest level of charitable donations in Catherine's reign from various sectors of society – over 35,000 roubles. The boards were supposed to act as banks and to lend out money at interest from their initial capital of 10,000 roubles in order to increase their income and were also authorized to raise money from other sources. By 1802 the St Petersburg board had by far the largest income of all boards in the empire – over 130,000 roubles.[37]

The activity of the St Petersburg institutions can be established, but this does not necessarily mean that they functioned productively. The *quality* of the St Petersburg administration as opposed to the *quantity* is far more difficult to establish. The task is made more difficult by the limitations of the evidence. The nature of the records on local administration – detailed reports for each session dryly recorded – gives no indication of how business was conducted or how long it took for a case to reach a court either for the first hearing or for appeal. There is no record of the level of satisfaction, or dissatisfaction, with the work of the town *dumas*. We have some evidence of the attendance by officials at institutions, which has already been noted, but not of their level of competence. Memoirs of those who served in local government are few. Some exist for senior figures, for some noble officials and a few clerks, but I have not come across any which relate to St Petersburg. We know that the civil service was regarded by most nobles as inferior to military service and that young nobles usually only entered civil service if they lacked the physical ability or the influence to join a regiment, and that some nobles only considered posts in the civil service at the point at which they retired from the army. There is, however, no direct record of the motivation for any of the nobles in St Petersburg who took elected or appointed posts in local administration. No one who served in the St Petersburg municipal organs has left a record of his life. Nevertheless, despite these qualifications, at least some tentative conclusions can be drawn about the performance of St Petersburg local government institutions.

A fundamental problem which militated against efficient operation of local administration was the overlapping of functions between institutions. This was true of all local government but was particularly evident in the city of St Petersburg because it was here that the full array of institutions operated. These overlapping jurisdictions occurred both within institutional structures and across them. The elaborate court structure, for example, led to confusion rather than simplification. The courts of the first and second instance were divided by social estate, but this in itself led to confusion when litigants were of different social estates, which was a frequent occurrence in a city like St Petersburg. Catherine was slow to legislate for this scenario. In 1786 it was established that in such cases the case should be heard in the court of the defendant; only in 1796 was it clarified that in criminal cases the courts should sit together to hear the case.[38] In fact, the evidence from St Petersburg, and from other *gubernii*, suggest that the practice was fairly arbitrary, although it has to be said that the court records did not always clearly indicate which litigant was the defendant. St Petersburg courts rarely sat together, although cases frequently involved members of different social estates. There seemed to be no pattern in St Petersburg: nobles appeared in town courts; merchants appeared in noble courts; peasants appeared in both. The operation of the courts specifically designed to deal with the unique social composition of the city of St Petersburg – the *nadvornye* courts – is vague, but a survey of the social estate of the litigants appearing in the St Petersburg *nadvornye* courts in 1786 and 1796 suggests that they did not cater for a narrowly defined group. Nobles, officials, palace officials, foreigners, merchants, artisans and peasants (either specifically state peasants or undifferentiated 'peasants') appeared before these courts but, in fact, as cases were heard in the court of the defendant anyway and the defendant in civil cases is not always clearly specified in the records this evidence can only be used in the most tenuous way to suggest at least a degree of confusion in the implementation of legislation.[39] Appeals should have progressed from the court of first instance to the matching court of second instance but did not always follow this pattern in St Petersburg, or elsewhere.

Further legal confusion was caused by the duplication of functions between courts and other institutions. The intended and actual role of the lower land court is unclear – it was primarily a police organ responsible for law and order and it was supposed to investigate offences and pass cases onto the courts but it seemed also to have acted as a court itself for minor offences. The police after the Statute of 1782 also had powers to investigate and pass sentence on minor crimes, including thefts of under 20 roubles. The welfare institutions had both a charitable and punitive function. The house of correction was supposed to force the idle to work, while the workhouse was supposed to provide work for the deserving poor. But in St Petersburg the function of the two institutions merged and the courts and the police sent rowdy inhabitants to workhouses and houses of correction seemingly indiscriminately.[40] The St Petersburg fiscal chamber, the highest body in the *guberniia* for financial matters, heard a very large number of cases involving financial transactions which could have been the province of the civil chamber; in 1786 it heard 4,618 cases involving a 'state' interest (almost certainly contracts) and 356 civil cases.[41] Disputes between townspeople over contracts and bills of exchanges also came to the municipal administrative organ, the six-councillor *duma*. Civil cases concerning the property of orphans were heard in a special orphans court. Finally, the conscience court was an extraordinary institution. Set up outside the normal legal structure it was supposed to deal with crimes which fell outside the normal jurisdiction of the courts but also introduced for good measure an element of *habeas corpus* in that all cases involving those who had been held without being charged for more than three days. The operation of this court has been analysed;[42] suffice to say that this institution did nothing to simplify the legal system.

Conflict of interest also arose over administrative functions. The functions of the general town *duma*s were poorly defined in 1785 but in practice in St Petersburg they discussed many of the same economic concerns as the six-councillor *duma*s. In the district town of Novoladoga in the St Petersburg *guberniia* there is no evidence that a six-councillor *duma* was set up at all and the general town *duma* handled all aspects of urban administration. The issue of passports to trading peasants – a frequent and onerous task particularly in a *guberniia* like St Petersburg with a large transient, trading population – was undertaken by the *duma*s and by the police. Indeed, the police (particularly after the Statute of 1782) and *duma*s shared responsibilities for the economic and social order of the city which inevitably meant an overlapping of duties. Finally, the magistracies, supposedly purely courts of first and second instance, in practice in St Petersburg became involved in administrative matters which should have been solely the preserve of the *duma*s. The reason for this was that magistracies, as established by Peter I, had originally been administrative and not judicial bodies. The change in their function in 1775 and then the ten-year delay before the introduction of *duma*s in 1785 led to an inevitable overlap between the two sets of institutions.

The magistracies in St Petersburg dealt with '*duma*' matters such as the issue of passports, fairs, trade, grain supply, the fishing industry, town meadow land, the salt monopoly and the condition of buildings.[43]

The overlapping of functions in part contributed to the workload of the local government institutions in an entirely negative manner. Cases were passed from court to court; administrative matters were passed from institution to institution or from institution to a court. This does not mean that, of course, all business was constantly recycled to little purpose. The *duma*s, particularly the six-councillor *duma*s, do seem to have performed a useful function to the extent that they were involved in many aspects of the urban economy and life of the city, including the level and price of supplies, condition of taverns, bridges and ferries, and provision of welfare institutions. To an extent the very vagueness of Catherine's legislation enabled the *duma*s to deal with matters which were of importance to the town.[44] The impact of Catherine's reforms on the quality of urban life are hard to judge, but the new urban institutions played some role, in combination with building projects, better fire prevention, the construction of street lighting and increased policing, in at least making some improvement to the infrastructure. The quality of care in the St Petersburg welfare institutions, and the quality of teaching in national schools, is a different matter but there is no doubt that the provision increased significantly.

The evidence above shows that the courts were efficient in terms of the number of cases they handled, even if many of these were simply passed upwards on appeal. A report of 1785 noted that there were 300 cases outstanding in the St Petersburg lower *nadvornyi* court,[45] but such delays were the exception. Whether justice was applied in the process is harder to judge. The Russian judicial system suffered from a number of well-known major weaknesses – the slow development of a legal profession in Russia, the lack of higher education facilities, the failure to codify the laws until the mid-nineteenth century, the nature of legal proceedings which left the initiative with the clerks and secretaries, the use of nobles as judges and assessors whose training had been entirely military, the prevalence of bribery at all levels – all led to the assumptions that, in the words of Martha Wilmot in the early nineteenth century: 'As for justice, 'tis a joke. No such thing exists and its *shadow* covers vice enough to make me shudder.'[46] St Petersburg had its own particular scandal in this period. A.V. Markov, the Secretary of I.I. Chicherin, the Chief of Police in St Petersburg, recalled that a friend of an accused man fell at his feet with the words: 'I know everything depends on you: save us father! And here to show my gratitude in advance, 50,000 roubles in gold!' Markov was, in his words, 'perplexed' but accepted the bribe. The accused was freed and his accusers in turn found guilty of slander, whipped, had their nostrils split and were sent to Siberia.[47] There were, of course, some dedicated and conscientious officials in the courts in Catherine's reign and the slow development of what can be termed a 'legal consciousness' was taking place but it is hard to demonstrate that the structures created in 1775 – and this was essentially an *institutional* rather than a *judicial* reform – greatly aided this process.

The city of St Petersburg provides an example of both the best and the worst aspects of Catherine II's legislation on local administration. On the one hand, this was the place where the legislation was implemented most fully and where all institutions were set up and were fully, or almost fully staffed. The business transacted by these institutions and the level of activity was impressive and demonstrated the vitality of local administration. The city of St Petersburg was certainly 'governed' in this period. On the other hand, the very diversity and complexity of the St Petersburg situation exposed the weaknesses in Catherine's reforms. The overlapping of functions was even more acute in St Petersburg than anywhere else in the empire (with the probable exception of Moscow) as all institutions were active and the additional courts, the *nadvornye* courts, only served to make matters more complex. The judicial structure remained essentially the same in Russia until the reforms of 1864. But it is no surprise that when attempts were made to reform municipal government in the reign of Nicholas I that they should start with an investigation and then the restructuring of the municipal organs of the city of St Petersburg, where administration and urban finances by this stage seem to have been in disarray.[48] The structure of municipal government put in place by Catherine may have allowed the city to function adequately in the early years after its introduction but did not provide the basis for efficient and effective 'government' in the long term.

Notes

 1. G.E. Munro, 'The Development of St Petersburg as an Urban Center during the Reign of Catherine II (1762–1796)' (PhD thesis, North Carolina, 1973), p. 280.
 2. George Munro, 'The Charter to the Towns Reconsidered: the St Petersburg Connection', *Canadian-American Slavic Studies*, XXIII, 1 (1989) 17–35.
 3. *Polnoe sobranie zakonov Rossiiskoi imperii* (hereafter *PSZ*), XX, 229–304, no. 14,392; *PSZ*, XXI, 461–88, no. 15,379; *PSZ*, XXII, 646–68, no. 16,421.
 4. *PSZ*, XXII, no. 16188, 21 April 1785.
 5. Rossiiskii gosudarstvennyi arkhiv drevnikh aktov (hereafter RGADA), Moscow, fond 16, delo 530, f. 16, report by N. Saltykov from St Petersburg *guberniia*, 1786.
 6. H.F. von Storch, *The Picture of Petersburg* (London, 1801), p. 88.
 7. D.I. Bagalei and D.P. Miller, *Istoriia goroda Khar'kova za 250 let ego sushchestveniia (s 1655 po 1905-y god)*, I (Khar'kov, 1905), 110.
 8. F. Ia. Polanskii, *Gorodskoe remeslo i manufaktura v Rossii XVIIIv* (Moscow, 1960), p. 34.
 9. RGADA, fond 16, delo 508, f. 86v, information collected on St Petersburg *guberniia*, 1780.
10. RGADA, fond 16, delo 530, ff. 266–66v, report by N. Saltykov to the Senate, 1786.
11. St Petersburg, Sankt-Peterburg Filial Instituta russkoi istorii (hereafter SPgFIRI), fond 36, delo 477, f. 644, report by A.R. Vorontsov from St Petersburg *guberniia*, 1786.
12. The composition of the St Petersburg general town *duma* is discussed in more detail in my 'Town Government in Saint Petersburg Guberniya after the Charter to the Towns of 1785', *Slavonic and East European Review*, LXII (1984) 71–4.
13. A.A. Kizevetter, *Gorodskoe polozhenie Ekateriny II 1785 g.* (Moscow, 1909), pp. 358–62.
14. A point well developed in Robert E. Jones, 'Getting the Goods to St Petersburg: Water Transport from the Interior 1703–1811', *Slavic Review*, XLIII (1984) 413–33.
15. On the police see, in particular, John P. LeDonne, *Ruling Russia. Politics and Administration in the Age of Absolutism 1762–1796* (Princeton, 1984), pp. 91–101 and by the same, 'The Provincial and Local Police under Catherine the Great, 1775–1796', *Canadian-Slavic Studies*, IV (1970) 513–28.
16. RGADA, fond 16, delo 523, f. 13v, report by M. Dolgorukii and A. Naryshkin on institutions in St Petersburg, 1785.
17. For the operation of welfare institutions see my 'Philanthropy in the Reign of Catherine the Great: Aims and Realities', in R. Bartlett and J.M. Hartley (eds), *Russia in the Age of the Enlightenment. Essays for Isabel de Madariaga* (London, 1990), pp. 167–202.
18. *PSZ*, XXII, 208, no. 16059, 5 September 1784.

19. SPgFIRI, fond 36, delo 478, ff. 3–8, report by P. Zavadovskii and M. Dolgorukii on St Petersburg, 1786.
20. R.E. Jones, 'Catherine II and the Provincial Reform of 1775 – a Question of Motivation', *Canadian Slavic Studies*, IV (1970) 511.
21. Material drawn from *PSZ* XLIV, pt 2, 254–7, Knigi shtatov.
22. RGADA, fond 16, delo 508, f. 29v, report on institutions in St Petersburg *guberniia*, 1780.
23. SPgFIRI, fond 36, delo 478, f. 126, report from A. Vorontsov from Olonets *guberniia*, 1786. See also Janet Hartley, 'The Boards of Social Welfare and the Financing of Catherine II's State Schools', *Slavonic and East European Review*, LXVII (1989) 211–13.
24. The material here is drawn from lists of noble office holders by M.M. Turkestanov, *Gubernskii sluzhebnik ili spisok general-gubernatoram, praviteliam, poruchikam pravitelia, dvorianskim predvodateliam v 47 namestnichestvakh (1777–1796)* (St Petersburg, 1869). The material has, however, to be treated with caution as there could be many unpredictable reasons (such as age, family, health) which led to nobles taking posts beneath the rank they currently held.
25. RGADA, fond 16, delo 508, ff. 55v–64v, material on institutions in St Petersburg *guberniia*, 1780.
26. See J.M. Hartley, *A Social History of the Russian Empire 1650–1825* (London and New York, 1999), pp. 94–6.
27. RGADA, fond 16, delo 533, chast 2, ff. 139–49, report by A. Brius from St Petersburg.
28. This is a point made by several authors on local administration in imperial Russia. A general survey of local administration and of, *inter alia*, the question of over- or under-governing of the country is given in my chapter on 'Provincial and Local Government, 1682–1917', in D. Lieven (ed.), *Cambridge History of Russia*, vol. 2, forthcoming.
29. For information on the operation of these courts see my 'Land, Law and the Peasant in Pre-Emancipation Russia' in *Sudebnik*, V (2000) 99–118.
30. For information on the operation of this court see my 'Catherine's Conscience Court: An English Equity Court?', in A.G. Cross (ed.), *Russia and the West in the Eighteenth Century* (Newtonville, Mass., 1983), pp. 306–18.
31. SPgFIRI, fond 36, delo 478, ff. 10–12, report by A.R. Vorontsov from St Petersburg *guberniia*, 1786.
32. RGADA, fond 16, delo 386, ff. 130–130v, 56–56v, report on settled and outstanding cases in various *gubernii*, 1789.
33. Hartley, 'Town Government', pp. 80, 75.
34. This statistical information is taken from my thesis, 'The Implementation of the Laws relating to Local Administration, 1775–1796, with Special Reference to the Guberniya of Saint Petersburg' (PhD thesis, London, 1980), pp. 97–9, and is drawn from RGADA, fond 16, delo 386, a list of attendance figures for 1789, with the folios 145v–48 relating to St Petersburg. The statistics are reproduced in an appendix to my thesis, pp. 341–4.

35. Hartley, 'Philanthropy', pp. 181–2 from the following archival sources: RGADA, fond 16, delo 526, ff. 319v–20, report by P. Konovitsyn on St Petersburg, 1785–86 and SPgFIRI, fond 36, delo 478, f. 23, report by A. Vorontsov from St Petersburg *guberniia*, 1786.
36. A. Voronov, *Istoriko-statisticheskoe obozrenie uchebnykh zavadenii S. Peterburgskago uchebnago okruga s 1715 po 1828 god vkliuchitel'no* (St Petersburg, 1849), p. 69.
37. Hartley, 'The Boards of Social Welfare', pp. 225, 216–17, 220.
38. *PSZ*, XXII, 558, no. 16357, 19 March 1786; *PSZ*, XXIII, 920–2, no. 17493, 7 August 1796.
39. Material, which is rather sketchy, on the *nadvornye* courts was taken from the records of the St Petersburg upper and lower *nadvornye* courts held in St Petersburg, Tsentral'nyi gosudarstvennyi istoricheskii arkhiv – Sankt Peterburg, fond 1715, opis' 1, delo 4, fond 1716, opis' 4, delo 3.
40. Hartley, 'Philanthropy', p. 185.
41. SPgFIRI, fond 36, delo 478, f. 10, report by A. Vorontsov from St Petersburg *guberniia*, 1786.
42. See Hartley, 'The Conscience Court'.
43. These problems are discussed in more detail in Hartley, 'Town Government', pp. 67–84.
44. I make this point in Hartley, 'Town Government'. It is also made for early nineteenth-century municipal government by Boris Mironov, 'Bureaucratic or Self-Government: the Early Nineteenth-Century Russian City', *Slavic Review*, LII (1993) 232–55.
45. RGADA, fond 16, delo 523, f. 5, report by M. Dolgorukii and A. Naryshkin from St Petersburg, 1785.
46. Marchioness of Londonderry and H.M. Hyde (eds), *The Russian Journals of Martha and Catherine Wilmot 1803–1808* (London, 1934) pp. 308–9. I discuss Russian justice in the context of bribery in Russia in more detail in my 'Bribery and Justice in the Provinces in the Reign of Catherine II' in S. Lovell, A.V. Ledeneva and A. Rogachevskii (eds), *Bribery and* Blat *in Russia. Negotiating Reciprocity from the Middle Ages to the 1990s* (London, 2000), pp. 48–64.
47. P.G. Kicheev, *Iz nedavnei stariny – razskazy i vospominaniia* (Moscow, 1870), pp. 99–103.
48. W. Bruce Lincoln, 'N.A. Miliutin and the St Petersburg Municipal Act of 1846: A Study in Reform under Nicholas I', *Slavic Review*, XXXIII (1974) 49–68.

7
Petersburg Actresses On and Off Stage (1775–1825)

Wendy Rosslyn

In the half-century ending in 1825, theatre was one of the chief forms of public entertainment in Russia, particularly in St Petersburg, and actresses therefore played a prominent part in the social life of the upper classes, in both its 'respectable' and its covert manifestations.

Theatre audiences were socially diverse, spectators ranging from peasants to grandees, but the largest and best documented was the upper-class segment, particularly male spectators, whose memoirs, letters and poems give frank insights into their relations with actresses. Audiences, of course, included women; indeed, special areas of the theatre were identified as suitable seating for them. But women's responses to theatrical performances – what they enjoyed or were shocked by, how they perceived actors and actresses – are undocumented. The focus here will therefore be male–female audience–actress relations.

Actresses (meaning in the present context all female theatre performers, including dancers and singers) worked in public theatres, notably the Imperial Theatres, in private theatres and in serf theatres, where, although they lived enclosed on the estates of their owners, they often performed not only for them and their guests, but also for the public. A large number of foreign actresses worked in Russia, but this discussion of actress–audience interactions will centre on Russian actresses, not least because a few of them left autobiographies, rarities in Russian women's writing of this period, which furnish a subjective addition to the records of their careers kept by the Imperial Theatre Administration, the chief source of information.

These interactions have close parallels with those in Western European societies, both then and now. Research on British actresses of the Restoration period shows that their success on stage was partly the result of the titillating scenes which they were required to play, and that off-stage they were subject to sexual exploitation.[1] But whereas theatre life in western countries has been well explored, and is even taken for granted, this is not the case for Russia, and I shall devote much of the essay to an exposition of the evidence about it.

In Russia at this time, as in western Europe, professional actors were viewed ambivalently. They were condemned for their dissolute private lives, extravagance, and avarice. Their chief skill, the ability to dissemble, was seen as deception. And the disdain in which they were held was related to the fact that the actor engaged, to quote Rousseau, in 'a trade by which he gives himself in representation for money, submits to the ignominy and affronts which one buys the right to subject him to, and puts his person on public sale'.[2] However, others were prepared to respect male actors as purveyors of enlightenment and facilitators of public morality, and D'Alembert refers to them as 'men who are so necessary to progress'.[3] In Russia, whilst nobles engaged enthusiastically in amateur performances, professional actors were viewed by upper-class members of their audiences with disdain on account of their inferior social class. When the Director of the Imperial Theatres A.L. Naryshkin took Ekaterina Isakova as his mistress, he arranged to have her excluded from the special theatrical estate (*soslovie*) to which actors were assigned, in order to mitigate the difference in status. And the memoirist F.F. Vigel' commented on the disastrous influence of actors with regard to the nobleman, playwright and Administration official A.A. Shakhovskoi: 'his passion for the theatre threw him completely into the riff-raff from behind the scenes', who marked his actions and thinking with their 'lack of self-restraint, recklessness, and envy'.[4] On the other hand, the playwright P.A. Plavil'shchikov asserted in 1792 that 'a spectacle is a public entertainment which improves human morals',[5] and F.F. Ivanov argued in 1804 that the sale of talent in public was not in itself depraved: 'an actor does not entertain but teaches, in exchange for money but not for the sake of money, just as a professor gives classes for money and an author publishes his works'.[6]

Whereas theatre performers of both sexes mostly attracted the disdain of the upper classes, actresses were also, as in western Europe, denied respect because they were public women. Respectable women were defined by their modesty, were permitted only minimal social contact with men before marriage in order to protect their chastity, and lived their married lives in the domestic sphere; actresses, by contrast, put themselves on public view, and their perceived lack of modesty was interpreted as a lack of propriety. Rousseau argued that the profession was by nature prejudicial to female morals. A woman had immodestly to seek the gaze of the male spectator, and it was difficult for her to sell her talent on stage but to refrain from satisfying off-stage the desires which she tried to excite in her audience. When subjected to seduction, she had little chance of resisting, deprived as she was of moral values by an education focussed on coquetry and her performance of amorous roles, clothed in revealing attire, and constantly surrounded by infatuated and audacious young men.[7] This view was largely shared in Russia. Some actresses were literally public women, in that they were sexually available to members of the audience, and actresses were thought inadmissible into respectable society on account of their inferior morals, as well as on class grounds. One of the few to defend their morals was R.M. Zotov, an Administration official, who reasoned that ostracism of actors from 'decent society' was irrational, since most were educated people. He listed virtuous actresses who were both fine wives and good actresses, and pointed out that 'frivolous' wives were to be found in all sections of society.[8] But Zotov, child of an unequal marriage, had an uncommonly liberal approach to social prejudice.

Interactions between actresses and the audience in the theatre and off stage therefore brought together the inhabitants of different worlds. On stage, actresses performed in the plays, ballets and operas which were part of the social round. Off stage, they were admitted to upper-class homes to teach accomplishments such as dancing, and to provide entertainment, by giving recitations. Actresses also provided the male members of their audience with an unofficial social sphere. They were prominent figures in the underworld of high society to which upper-class males retreated in order to indulge themselves, freed from the shackles of conventional propriety.

The on-stage relationship between actress and audience was highly ambivalent. Rousseau describes the spectator as both repelled by the actress's immodesty and infatuated with her, and ambivalence pervaded the Russian theatre likewise. Actresses often played virtuous characters: right-thinking comic heroines, tragic heroines visited with undeserved suffering, or sentimental heroines possessed of fundamental innocence. Ostensibly audiences came to the theatre to admire virtue and to have their sentiments elevated. But at the same time they took pleasure in viewing the female body. The ambiguity can be seen in P.I. Shalikov's account of a ballet danced by serf women on a country estate. His eye dwells lovingly and constantly on the female body, seen at close quarters in good lighting: 'Their art, lightness, pliancy, and the pleasantness of the movements of their bodies were even more captivating, *more interesting* to the eye close up than in the theatre, in a large gallery lit by many candelabra.' In the next breath Shalikov exalts his pleasures in the chief dancer's soul:

> Now, my friends, let me tell you what was most precious and dear to my sensitive heart: Virtue, sacred virtue!...she descends from her shining throne to the last of the applause – to comfort the sorrowing and help the poor and she gives them all she has...I can say no more...tears burned in my breast...[9]

Since the display of female sexuality was not publicly approved, it was presented on stage for covert enjoyment. Female performers were required to participate in titillating scenes – one of the staple opera scenarios in the 1810s and 1820s involved a tyrant imprisoning his female victim who was obliged to defend her honour.[10] Audiences were also titillated by the actress's bold return of the male gaze. Instead of decorously casting her eyes down, she looked back, suggesting her willingness to engage with the spectator in reality. Elizaveta Sandunova, we are told, 'turned the heads of the young men from the court and the guards with the charm of her acting and singing, but still more by sweeping her flashing glance over all their sharp-sighted eyes and arrogant hearts'.[11] In his poem 'To a Young Actress' ('K molodoi aktrise', 1815) Pushkin unmasks the dynamics of the interaction between spectator and actress, in this case a serf: the actress may lack professional skill, but her success with the public is determined by her beauty, and the promise of its availability to the audience, seen in the public display of passion.

Women were often required to expose their bodies on stage in ways unacceptable in polite society, not infrequently by playing cross-dressed roles, which allowed the contours of their buttocks and legs to be seen. Costumes for female roles could also be made to reveal the body, notably in ballet. Dancers, who until about 1795 wore long heavy costumes with farthingales,[12] not unlike respectable women, were dressed thereafter in the gauzy skirts imitated from the French ballet, and choreographed into sensual movements:

> The costumes of the nymphs, naiads, and the other divinities of Olympus were extremely picturesque and pleasing to audiences, since they delineated the bodies of the [female] dancers. Dresses became still shorter and pink tights completed the illusion. This was the beginning of pirouettes, entrechats *en quatre*, and even *en huit*; of raising the foot above the head, and all the refinements of the newly created art, for which... the... destroyed all sense of modesty and bashfulness with poses and groupings...[13]

Another sign of the covert attractiveness of the female body to audiences was the popularity of the youth theatre formed by Shakhovskoi in about 1813, the draw being the chance to look at pretty girls.[14]

Not surprisingly, less insightful spectators assumed that the allure of the artist on stage signalled a looseness of morals off-stage. Captivated by the actress, they wanted to enjoy her exciting stage qualities in an intimate relationship, or at least in infatuation at a distance. Adulation took literary forms. In 1805 the theatre enthusiast S.P. Zhikharev noted: 'our comrade Morozov is hopelessly in love with Sandunova and goes secretly to the theatre every time she performs. Today we found a whole pile of epistles, madrigals and sonnets to the famous actress...'[15] The premature death in 1810 of the dancer Mar'ia Danilova resulted in a flood of sorrowful verse.[16]

In the early years of the nineteenth century theatre audiences were highly partisan, and groups of young male devotees formed round their favourite actresses to savour their performances, support and applaud them. Zotov recalls: 'all theatre-goers divided into parties and stood up for the actresses boldly. I remember in 1810 there were Semenova and Val'berkhova parties. They would run after their carriages, stop them, express their praises, and quarrel in the street about their respective superiority'.[17] These groups of admirers could be manipulated by actresses, who could hire a prime mover and provide his associates with free tickets, so that they would applaud, shout and stamp their feet, regardless of the merits of the performance, and even trade blows with opposing supporters; popularity with the audience could then be traded for favourable treatment from the theatre management.[18]

The behaviour of young men with actresses of course differed radically from their behaviour in polite society, as can be seen from the fact that their rowdy behaviour extended to violence – admirers of the actress Aleksandra Kolosova, antagonized by Shakhovskoi's ill-treatment of her, stopped him in the street and gave him a whipping.[19] The prime characteristic of this alternative mode of behaviour was the hedonistic pursuit of pleasure in wine, women and indecent writing.

Young men presented themselves as virile connoisseurs of female beauty. Pushkin recalls:

> Before the beginning of an opera, tragedy, or ballet young men walk along all ten lines of armchairs, tread on everyone's feet, and talk to all their acquaintances, and also to those who are not acquaintances.
> 'Where have you come from?'
> 'Semenova's, Sosnitskaia's, Kolosova's, Istomina's.'
> 'How lucky you are!'
> 'She's singing today – acting – dancing – let's applaud – let's give her a curtain call! She's so lovely. She has such eyes! such lovely little feet! such talent!'[20]

More aggressively, they presented themselves as rakish libertines, asserting their sexual prowess. Pushkin summed up the culture in a letter to Nikita Vsevolozhskii, a friend of his youth and host to the Green Lamp circle, reminding him of himself, and what they had shared:

> you remember Pushkin ... whom you saw both drunk and in love, who ... was your constant companion at the theatre, the confidant of your pranks [draft: passions in the wings], Pushkin, who sobered you up on Good Friday and took you by the hand to the church of the Theatre Administration, so you could pray to the Lord God and have your fill of looking at Miss Ovoshnikova ...[21]

Of course, pleasure required sexual behaviour unacceptable in polite society. The young men preyed on the trainee actresses at the theatre schools, who were deemed to be sexually available and even legitimate objects of sexual experiment and self-indulgence. Their treatment of the girls shows not only ingenuity in circumventing the schools' arrangements for preserving the pupils' chastity, but also the deliberate flouting of limitations on public behaviour, extending to blasphemy. Praskov'ia Orlova-Savina (*née* Kulikova), a pupil at the Moscow theatre school from 1824, recalls:

> they looked at us from a distance (those who had no chance of approaching closer), sighed, walked up and down past the windows, or met [us] in church on festival days. And here on Palm Sunday or Easter Sunday, sinners!, they used to light candles in the choir, where I always stood, and say 'We are lighting up our tsaritsa'...[22]

Similar things took place in St Petersburg. According to the daughter of the actor Ia. Brianskii, who was a pupil at the theatre school:

> Those who were infatuated (*vliublennye*) with the pupils walked up and down past the windows of the school along the canal embankment innumerable times... The pupils kept watch at the windows and counted how many times their admirers went by, and the degree of infatuation was measured by the number of times they passed.[23]

The young men also ogled the girls from hidden vantage points. Pushkin's scabrous letter of 1819 to his absent friend Mansurov, telling him about the dancer Mariia Krylova, then aged fifteen, reveals them sharing sexually arousing observation of her (the Petersburg theatre school was sited near Vsevolozhskii's home):

> what is he doing now in great Novgorod? envying us and weeping because of Kr. (of course with his lower duct). Every morning the winged maid flies to rehearsal past our Nikita's windows and as before telescopes and *** rise to her but, alas, you cannot see her and she cannot see you.[24]

Bawdy texts of this kind paraded rebellious masculinity.[25] Voyeuristic indulgence was augmented by insubordinate self-assertion against senior males through stealing the pleasure in their bodies reserved for themselves:

> I well remember the trips to Ekateringof and to Gutuev Island made by sworn theatre-lovers with the sole aim of looking, albeit from a distance, down a telescope at the adored one. I say Gutuev Island because Ral''s dacha, where Shakhovskoi spent the summer, always surrounded by his thespian flowers, was on the shore of Gutuev Island, and there, in the tall grass, armed with telescopes, sat the admirers, waiting, sometimes for hours on end, for some nymph to come out into the garden on the opposite side, and this just to have our fill of looking at her...[26]

Naturally, imagination played its part in the relationship with the girls, and a sample of the sexual fantasies they engendered is provided by Pushkin's poem 'To Mansurov' ('K Mansurovu', 1819), in which he envisages Krylova throwing off her uniform and lying down naked on velvet before her admirer. Dishonourable behaviour did not, of course, stop short of seduction and pregnancy. Avdot'ia Ovoshnikova, for example, gave birth to the first of her illegitimate children by Vsevolozhskii soon after leaving the theatre school, aged eighteen.[27]

Theatre, Iu. M. Lotman suggests, provided models on which people of the late eighteenth and early nineteenth centuries could construct their speech and behaviour,[28] and actresses became involved in dramatic 'plots', which even contained abductions, deceptions and duels.[29] One such 'performance' involved the suspected infidelity of the dancer Avdot'ia Istomina which led her jealous lover, the guards officer Vasilii Sheremetev, to challenge an innocent man to a duel, in which Sheremetev was killed.[30]

Of course, some actresses led impeccable private lives. But the fact that they were admired for their virtue shows how common it was for actresses to be sexually available. Pushkin provided the paradigms of promiscuous and virtuous actresses in his sketch 'Les deux danseuses' in which he contrasts two sisters. One is in fashion with the audience, has a lover in the gallery (not a man of substance), but becomes the kept mistress of another, marries, and is able to live well, though she is ostracized by society; the other marries the prompter, and finds herself in straitened circumstances.

Whilst men were assumed to have sexual needs, 'respectable' women were not, and upper-class married men often sought sexual pleasure elsewhere, particularly with lower-class women, sex with whom was acceptable behaviour. Actresses were alluring, especially when compared to house serfs and prostitutes; indeed, actress-mistresses conferred prestige.[31] Actresses had special training in accomplishments valued by society, such as singing and dance. They were not only more accessible than young women of high standing,[32] but their stage roles provided tantalizing glimpses of their assumed off-stage sexuality. They offered the prospect of an exciting, reputation-enhancing relationship which facilitated the display of affluence and carried no obligation to marry or maintain children. In effect many relationships involving actresses amounted to prostitution, since they involved payment. Whilst overt prostitution usually entailed working in a brothel, control by its proprietor, numerous clients and a way of life determined by the sex trade, this was covert prostitution, which involved women working alone, and combining trade in sex with other employment.

Sexual relationships between actresses and spectators for gain, whether in the form of payment, favour or maintenance, were apparently routine. Relationships were struck up when upper-class male spectators were allowed backstage to inspect actresses at close quarters and proposition them. F.F. Kokoshkin, Director of the Moscow Imperial Theatre, used to take men backstage himself.[33] Clients included spectators from the highest levels of society. The letters of the ballet-master Ivan Val'berkh and his dancer wife Sof'ia, parents of the actress Mariia Val'berkhova, show one such event in 1808. Sof'ia wrote that after a performance at the Hermitage Theatre A.L. Naryshkin had taken Grand Duke Konstantin Pavlovich into the dressing room, where he talked to Mariia in French and was impressed with her. Sof'ia found this unpleasant and would have preferred, she said, to stay in the auditorium, had she known they were coming.[34] To this her husband replied: 'I myself find it unpleasant that Konstantin Pavlovich spoke with Masha, and if when I come back I hear anything else, I swear to you she will be in the theatre no longer.'[35]

Such relationships did not have to be concealed, but for official purposes were referred to as patronage, which was consistent with the fact that the women often received maintenance or preferential treatment rather than monetary payments. Inasmuch as they were a form of patronage, the relationships were not just private liaisons but part of the man's network of influence, which could be exerted on the Administration to privilege the mistress and disadvantage her rivals. An actor of the period commented:

> The Theatre Administration pandered to keepers of mistresses by letting their favourites have preference and pushing their rivals on stage to the back... The least disrespect to the odalisks in the ballet from their peers called down cruel persecution from the Administration.[36]

When relationships ended, the woman could be handed down the ladder of patronage. The ballet-master Glushkovskii tells the story of Agrippina Bel'o, who was performing a gypsy dance on stage when she caught the attention of Konstantin Pavlovich, who made an excuse to visit the theatre school where she was a pupil. Soon after she was allowed to graduate early and move to Strel'na, where she led such a life of luxury that her patron reproached her with running up 'more debts than a guards' general's salary for ten years'. However, the relationship ended, and then 'General Opochinin, the above-mentioned person's favourite, began to show her special favour'.[37]

The exchange of sex with officials in the Administration for favour was also routine, and in this respect practice in Russia was identical to that elsewhere. Glushkovskii reported:

> One foreign dancer who had travelled round nearly all the theatres in Europe told me how most young women in the ballet companies make their way. At first the young woman does everything to get into the favour of the ballet-master, so that he will make up good steps for her and give her good parts. If she has sufficient talent and the public likes her, patrons of her talents appear immediately. If old men offer their services, she tries to choose the richest. If aristocrats who have squandered their wealth offer, she chooses the one who has most weight in public so that he can shout about her talent. If a gambler turns up, she makes use of the fact that punters gather at her house for breakfast and arranges lotteries, and sells tickets at high prices. If someone wins, she cunningly arranges for the things to remain in her possession. If fortune smiles on her and purses full of guineas appear, she immediately

gives gifts to the ballet-master and journalists: to the former to pull strings for her at the theatre and to the latter to extol her talent to the skies, and she hires an applauder in chief...[38]

It was common practice for officials of the Administration to establish liaisons with actresses in the course of their work. Zotov recalls that the rare persons of integrity showed up the general state of corruption:

> All the Directors of the Theatres were distinguished by their philandering, and if they did not live with actresses and dancers openly, they did not make much attempt to conceal their liaisons. Even second-rank officials of the Administration liked to boast of their liaisons. [S.S.] Gagarin was the first who did not wish to submit to this dirty habit, out of pride and sincere love for his wife (*née* Valevskaia). During his three-year incumbency he was invariably fully clothed and standing when he received actresses and dancers. He did not invite them to sit down, and only listened to their petitions.[39]

The dancer Anna Osipova, for example, received a dress embroidered with silver from the Director P.I. Tiufiakin in recognition of her zeal and a particularly successful performance.[40] Doubts about the innocence of the gift are confirmed by the fact that when she graduated from the theatre school she was given a higher salary than usual, a payment of 200 roubles was made to her mother, and Osipova was required to take an extra year's training.[41] The payment was probably a bribe to buy her mother's consent to the affair, and the further year in the school ensured that she was at the Director's disposal. One of the favourites of M.A. Miloradovich, the dancer Ekaterina Telesheva, was appointed to the ballet company in 1825 on advantageous terms with a high initial salary of 1,500 roubles, a 350-rouble accommodation allowance, and firewood. She was also credited with two additional years of service. When she moved into an official flat she was given four rooms, a kitchen and a laundry because she was a soloist, instead of the usual two rooms and kitchen she paid 200 roubles' annual rent for the extra accommodation. Six months later she petitioned not to pay, as she could not afford the extra rooms, and this was agreed.[42] She was also given roles belonging to her rival Anastasia Novitskaia.[43]

Another venue for introducing clients to young women from the theatre was the social gatherings hosted by Shakhovskoi and the actress Ekaterina Ezhova, of which Iu. Oksman rightly observes that 'at times it was difficult to draw a demarcation line between an influential literary and theatrical salon and a house of assignations for high society'.[44] The young women, most of whom graduated from the theatre school in 1823, were the actress Liubov' Diurova, the dancer Mariia Azarevicheva and her actress sister Nadezhda (illegitimate daughters of the Director A.A. Maikov and the serf dancer Ekaterina Azarevicheva), Monrua, and the dancers Vera Zubova and Ekaterina Telesheva,[45] the latter a relative of Ezhova.[46] The men they met there are listed by Zotov as Miloradovich and the writers Khmel'nitskii, Griboedov and Zhandr,[47] whilst Aleksandra Asenkova, one of Shakhovskoi's pupils, who says that she also attended, mentions Pushkin, Zhukovskii, Batiushkov, Griboedov and Krylov. Griboedov, she says, lived on the same staircase and came most often.[48]

Vigel' saw nothing unusual in these gatherings, though a question arose over their economics:

> His [Shakhovskoi's] partner Ezhova received actresses, dancers, and girls from the theatre school at her home every evening; principally the last, so as to improve their social graces. A few of the elderly and a large number of the young people of Petersburg claimed the honour of being received in her salon. Lighting and hospitality, at least a cup of tea, entailed expense. By what means she recompensed herself for this I do not know.[49]

Asenkova also construed them innocently. She interpreted Shakhovskoi's demands that she attend as his wish to develop her talent, and she obeyed willingly, because the gatherings were 'extremely pleasant and entertaining'.[50] The playwright P.N. Arapov ascribed the favour shown to the young women to their special artistry,[51] but felt it necessary to add that no liberties were taken with them.[52] But P.A. Viazemskii observed that Pushkin had to join the circle of Shakhovskoi, the 'Cerberus of the wings', in order to meet actresses and dancers,[53] and Pushkin refers to Shakhovskoi as 'a good fellow, a fine writer, and an excellent pimp'.[54] In fact, Arapov's account seems to suggest that symbolic payments for the girls' services were made at the salon. While some guests were engaged in conversation,

Ezhova 'poured tea and invited the remaining guests to play billiards; this game usually came out luckily for Katin'ka, or Nadin'ka, or Liubushka, or Mashin'ka, the most interesting of the theatre-school girls, from ten to twenty roubles a game; the loser settled up on the spot and Kat. Ivan. put the money into a box for those she was patronising...'[55] In effect, Ezhova functioned as the procuress, and Shakhovskoi was bound to her, it was said, by 'cohabitation, habit, and shared advantage'.[56] Griboedov revealed the sexual encounters stemming from these gatherings:

> For a long time I have lived in isolation from everyone, and suddenly longing got the better of me, where to, if not to Shakhovskoi's? There at least you can run a bold hand over the swansdown of sweet breasts etc. In three or four evenings T[elesheva] drove me mad, the more easily because she herself had just become accustomed for the first time to that feeling which had burned me blacker than coal in my sinful life. And the alluring thing for me was that my rival was Miloradovich, stupid, boastful Miloradovich, the idol of Shakhovskoi, who behaves like a scoundrel. Both are swine! I maddened this *chevalier bavard* every day, aroused the indignation of the whole house against me, then fired some rag of a gift at Ezhova and then made peace, and then quarrelled again. Meanwhile T. had made such progress in the three weeks of our affections in... dance, that no-one here could express enough surprise – everyone asked her what had caused such a charming change, such perfection?[57]

The gatherings at Shakhovskoi's dacha were the summer season of the same enterprise. Zotov recalls that 'the most talented girls from the theatre school stayed there ... with their overseers, both to enjoy the summer air at the dacha and for daily lessons and rehearsals. ... Prince Shakhovskoi worked with them every day, and Count Miloradovich was often at the lessons, encouraging their great successes with words and rewards.[58] A.I. Vol'f, author of a chronicle of the Petersburg theatres, saw that Shakhovskoi's pimping was an element in securing patronage from Miloradovich; and in return for their services he patronized the girls:

> Count Miloradovich and Prince Shakhovskoi made themselves the complete masters of the theatrical world. All matters, whether

of administration or repertoire, were decided in the Prince's study, where the Governor-General [Miloradovich] came every evening. So that the Count would not be too bored with these matters Shakhovskoi's housekeeper and favourite the actress Ezhova, who played comic old women, invited pretty young actresses, and especially dancers, to her home in the evenings. Entertained by the beauties who were in his power, Miloradovich of course confirmed all Shakhovskoi's proposals, and, under the influence of beautiful eyes, found that everything was capital in his new kingdom.

However, this was not quite the case. Money was spent in the most thoughtless manner on the production of ballets, which the Count loved passionately, and on the empty dramas rehashed by Shakhovskoi from Pushkin's poems and Walter Scott. Miloradovich's favourites and the other dignitaries who visited Ezhova's salon received significant rises in salary, benefits, and single payments, and other, less fortunate, artists received salaries which, as the saying goes, would not keep a cat in milk.[59]

The philandering of Miloradovich, who was Governor-General of St Petersburg, was also exploited by political opponents. Kolosova, who had earned the displeasure of Shakhovskoi and Miloradovich, noted that the latter allowed breaches of security. He would take papers of the State Council to Shakhovskoi's home and while he was calmly paying court to Telesheva, they were left unattended, to be leafed through by the girls from the theatre school, Bestuzhev-Marlinskii, and Iakubovich.[60]

Actresses had much to gain from being kept mistresses. Nimfidora Semenova, for example, mistress of V.V. Musin-Pushkin, lived in grand style with liveried servants.[61] Of course, the relationships rarely led to marriage. The men often had multiple favourites – Naryshkin, for example, invited comparison with a sultan surrounded by 'the brilliant galaxy of his wives and odalisks',[62] and unequal marriages were frowned upon. But there were exceptions. The great tragic actress Ekaterina Semenova, by birth either the daughter of serfs or the illegitimate daughter of landowner and serf,[63] became the mistress of I.A. Gagarin, member of the repertoire committee, aristocrat, courtier and squanderer of inherited wealth;[64] he encouraged the playwrights and translators of plays she acted in, and those who helped her learn her roles, protected her against arbitrary treatment by the Administration, and gave her a luxurious lifestyle.[65] Semenova had four children by him and eventually married him, at which point she left the theatre. The relationship between Shakhovskoi and Ezhova was a common-law marriage. She was his housekeeper from 1817, and bore his children. Vigel' considered that she 'ruled him, as they say, with a rod of iron: she wound herself round his huge torso like a snake',[66] and the relationship brought her a great deal: she enjoyed a more luxurious lifestyle than she could otherwise have expected, Shakhovskoi created roles for her,[67] and she had the advantage of his connections in the theatre world as head of the repertoire section of the Administration almost continuously from 1802 to 1825. She also came in for patronage from Miloradovich, who, for example, ordered a foreigner who booed her to be deported.[68]

One aspect of Russian theatre life, not paralleled in Western Europe, was recruitment into prostitution at the theatre schools. Bel'o was not unique in being introduced to trading in sex at an early age. The pupils were under the protection of the schools whilst living apart from their parents, and the Administration, which was responsible for keeping order, appointed boarding staff to supervise them, since most of them were minors.[69] For the 80 or so girls, the staff employed in 1820 included five female overseers[70] and other workers, who were to supervise the girls day and night.[71] The girls were to be locked into their rooms at night and the keys kept on the person of the chief overseer, and they were to be excused work and study only on certification by the chief doctor.[72] Even so, female pupils were subjected to the harassment described earlier, and some were initiated into trading in sex by those who had care of them. The girls had little defence because contact with families was minimal. Parents were allowed to visit on Sundays,[73] but many were too poor, too far away, or, as serfs, had no freedom of movement. Asenkova, who was at the Petersburg theatre school until 1814, remembered that she saw her father only about four times a year.[74]

Staff of the Administration used their authority to extort sexual services for themselves. When Miloradovich became Director in 1824, Vigel' considered that he treated the theatre school as his harem:

> Miloradovich ... wanted to have his Parc aux cerfs (the deer park at Versailles where the French kings kept their harems) and the

long-deserted wood at Ekateringof was chosen as the place for his entertainments. He demanded more than a million roubles from the city to decorate it, and had little dachas nearby rented for the young actresses and the theatre-school girls, and in the completed hall, called a pleasure garden, he began giving balls, not of course at his own expense, at which odalisks, bayadères and almées danced before him, and he threw them his handkerchief [to indicate his choice for the night] at whim.[75]

Staff at the school also profited from the bodies of their charges. The Director of the Moscow school hired out female pupils for private performances, at one of which a girl was required to play Venus in a scene called Venus Bathing, in which she had to wear a gauze tunic directly over her tights, without underskirts,[76] revealing her body. In Petersburg the girls were obliged to attend masquerades at the Bol'shoi Theatre. According to Asenkova they were put into the boxes of the fourth circle, and dozed there until three in the morning; some guests took pity on them and sent them fruit and sweets.[77] It seems unlikely that so much insistence was placed on having the girls there to doze and eat sweetmeats and the boxes were probably used for assignations.

The pastoral staff, who must have taken their cue, if not their instructions, from above, were also implicated. The memoirs of Praskov'ia Kulikova, who recalls becoming involved in assignations between pupils and clients when she was aged twelve or thirteen,[78] show that overseers at the school, bribed by the men, acted as go-betweens or passed gifts or notes to the girls. Kulikova remembers being summoned in the evening to take tea with an overseer and two men; they ate delicious buns, listened to sweet talk and the overseer 'compelled her to be affectionate' against her will.[79] There were also night-time assignations. One girl was seen to dress up and leave the dormitory to visit her admirer, who lived in the house opposite.[80] Another girl was abducted from the Petersburg theatre school, which caused particular consternation since she had attracted the attention of Grand Duke Nikolai Pavlovich.[81]

Some of the staff were corrupt and exerted pressure on the girls. Kulikova records that when an 'old man' was making advances to a girl and sent 'very many presents' which she did not want to accept, the overseer, whom he had probably bribed, took the presents regardless.[82]

Others were opposed to what went on, but unable to stop it. When told by Kulikova of the tea-drinking sessions, the senior overseer caught the bribe-taker in the act, and dismissed her.[83] However, dismissals of overseers, who would be replaced by others subject to the same temptations, were unlikely to resolve the problem.

The theatre schools were also hunting grounds for pimps recruiting minors for prostitution. This required parents to co-operate and hand over control of their daughters. One girl records an attempt by Prince Lobanov-Rostovskii to recruit her, when she was twelve:

> I saw him about twice, and only afterwards discovered that... he had thought of trading in me!... For this he had sent to my father with a proposal: a wooden house, 15 thousand, and all maintenance for them [sic], and he promised me mountains of gold!... But the emissary, even though my father knew him, was almost thrown down the stairs...[84]

An attempt by the writer and theatre-enthusiast S.P. Potemkin, who had squandered a large inheritance, to recruit another pupil by bribing her mother, a hospital nurse, with money, gifts and sweetmeats was frustrated by the girl's own refusal.[85] She was fortunate to escape, unlike another girl, whose parents connived: the dancer and actress Litavkina was sold to Potemkin, in return for a house, by her father; the latter was influenced by his second wife, who wanted to secure her own children's future. Litavkina was subjected to pressure, 'the tricks of the devil', by A.N. Verstovskii of the Moscow theatre administration.[86]

Pimping and procuring of theatre-school girls was also done outside the schools. An early case was in the private theatre company managed by Karl Knipper, proprietor of the German theatre in St Petersburg. In 1779 Knipper took on 50 young actors and musicians who had been training at the Moscow Foundling Home, with the aim of forming a new Russian company. It was alleged that Knipper had depraved the girls himself and sold their bodies to others for money. An investigation by the Foundling Home concluded: 'it is known in what depraved behaviour and debauchery, to the dishonour of [good] upbringing, in which the proprietor himself participated, the foundlings of both sexes were allowed to indulge; in view of their inexperience they should have had skilled guidance, without which their ruin was inevitable...' The young people were returned to Moscow in disorder, debt and poverty, with three of the thirteen girls pregnant.[87]

The girls, controlled by the staff of the schools and the Administration, or their employer, were in no position to assent freely, or to dissent, to the advances made to them, and they were poorly served by the law. The law of 1716 prescribed severe penalties for rape, but females were deemed to have consented to intercourse unless it was established that they had tried loudly and forcibly to resist. It was not until 1845 that females thought to be sexually immature could fail to resist, but not be thought to have consented.[88] Moreover, the girls were probably undermined by the perception that they were sexually mature: in 1774 the Orthodox Church set the marriageable age for women at thirteen.[89]

Where parents were concerned, relatively substantial payments were made, but the theatre-school girls themselves were poorly recompensed for their sexual services. Kulikova mentions buns, sweets, books, a small barrel of grapes, a belt decorated with silver and embroidered slippers.[90] These were no doubt intended as appealing luxuries. Actresses, and the trainees at the theatre schools, did not live in dire poverty. Indeed, actresses in the higher echelons were relatively well paid.[91] When Istomina, aged seventeen, cohabited with Sheremetev, he lived with her, since she had a good salary and his means were modest.[92] But the trainees lived in harsh and spartan conditions. The girls had only stockings, handkerchiefs, drawers, kerchiefs, aprons and three dresses.[93] One girl was boxed round the ears so hard by an overseer that she had to go to the infirmary.[94] On occasion they themselves were able to exercise patronage: when in 1822 the actor V.A. Karatygin was arrested for alleged disrespect to the Director (Maikov), he was freed after their pleas to Miloradovich.[95] But they were inadequately recompensed for the services they were required to supply.

The main incentive to covert prostitution must have been the prospect of a more luxurious lifestyle as a mistress of an upper-class man. A contemporary recalls that in the reign of Nicholas I the trainees, imbued with the traditions of their predecessors, thought constantly of finding rich admirers so that on the day they left the school they could step into their own carriage and proceed to a flat ready prepared with a dowry of linen and a rich toilette.[96] In effect they were launched and socialised into covert prostitution by the pressures and temptations of the theatre schools. The fact that the girls were the objects of sexual harassment may well have served to plant the idea of seduction in their minds at an early age and to define them to themselves as prostitutes in the making. Having seen other pupils engage in covert prostitution, they were sufficiently worldly-wise not to be deceived into it, but they were certainly subject to pressure. As well as motivation, actresses had ample opportunity to enter into liaisons, as nearly all the young unmarried ones lived in official accommodation and were free of parental control.

How are the interactions between actresses and members of their audiences to be contextualized? First, what I have described illuminates Lotman's division of the everyday lives of nobles in the late eighteenth and early nineteenth centuries into two categories: normal and transgressive behaviour. Lotman sees their lifestyle as a collection of different types of behaviour, such as those appropriate to the estate, the ball, female company, and so on; these were regulated by norms of honour, tradition, state discipline and class custom. But regulated behaviour generated the desire for liberty and rejection of conventions. These deviations from normal behaviour included drunkenness, erotic adventures, vice, perversion and 'escape into the world of gypsies, and attraction to artists'.[97] The behaviour of the young nobles described above is a manifestation of this deviant culture.

Prescriptions for virtuous behaviour at this time focused on self-restraint. Catherine II's *Nakaz* of 1767 called for fathers to teach their children, amongst other things, fear of God, obedience to the ten commandments, respect for law, love of labour, decorum, civility, sympathy for the unfortunate, and economy, and to deter them from injustice, violence and lies.[98] With differing ideology, the mason N.I. Novikov taught that virtue was the art of restraining passion and controlling desire.[99] Conduct books of the early nineteenth century prescribed similar behaviour.[100] Whilst submitting to these moral imperatives in some areas of their lives, in others young men asserted their freedom from them.

One of these alternative spheres was youth culture in rebellion against elders, obedience, restraint and chastity. Whilst observing propriety in the classroom, young men ignored it in their private time. The process began in educational institutions. In the 1820s A.N. Vul'f writes of the Cadet Corps as 'a world apart: half a barracks, half a monastery, where the vices of both are combined':

> All vices find entry here, whilst not a single measure is taken to eradicate them. The pupils, who are accepted without any selection, very

often bring with them all the vices which we encounter in young men who have been nurtured in idleness amongst their house serfs, from whom they have already picked up everything, and they pass it on to their comrades. Thus, every day, over several decades, vices are collected together until they merge into a single whole and constitute a type of custom and law, hallowed by time (always a powerful factor) and by general example.[101]

Released from educational institutions and parental oversight, young men entered homosocial networks, which provided a means for them to react against constraints, and declare their masculinity through sexual prowess, acquiring peer approval, rejecting dignified self-control and displaying bravado. Pushkin's biography, which can be taken as representative of young men of his class, reveals him, before he came of age, betting on his prowess in excessive drinking, quarrelling over women, running after actresses, visiting prostitutes, duelling, gambling, issuing challenges to duels and enjoying the society of like-minded young men.[102]

Another of the social spheres which accommodated deviance was the backstage world of the theatre. Here upper-class men, young and old, met with a caste of people they defined as inferior in social class and moral sense, who could be treated with impunity, much as they could treat their serfs. The resulting opportunity for libertine conduct was evidently fully exploited.

'Bad' society bordered closely on 'polite society' inasmuch as it happened in contiguous spaces – on and behind the stage. Patronage brought covert prostitution in its wake: pimping allowed men to obtain patronage, just as offering sex was a means for women to obtain it. The sexual element in patronage was not thought undesirable, and was not restricted to the theatre world. Zotov, springing to the defence of actresses' morality, pointed out that young ladies of quality who were concerned about decorations for their spouses did just as actresses did, 'only in their case everything is done behind a screen and not publicly'.[103]

This account of covert prostitution amongst actresses must be put into the context of prostitution in general in the eighteenth and early nineteenth centuries. Information about prostitution in Russia at this time is scattered and sparse,[104] and it is therefore worth outlining what is known. Prostitution began in the city almost from its foundation, and flourished thanks to the inflow of foreigners, particularly women whose manners were unlike those of Russian women. Initially prostitution centred on taverns and bathhouses,[105] but brothels soon appeared, one of the first fruits of westernization.[106] Secret brothels were in existence by 1718, and Peter I directed 'obscene establishments' to be eradicated.[107] Measures were taken in 1728, but the question was reconsidered in 1730, when brothels were thought necessary for the large population of military men living apart from their families, but to limit disease a senate decree of 1736 ordered prostitutes to be flogged.[108]

In 1750 Elizabeth ordered the deportation of women who ran secret brothels. Her commission of investigation discovered men of distinction amongst the clients, and police estimated the number of prostitutes working in St Petersburg, most of them foreigners, at about 500. Most of the foreigners were deported, and the Russian women were exiled to Orenburg and other towns.[109] The Russians were mainly abandoned spouses, such as soldiers' wives, and widows and daughters of lower ranks. Wives of army recruits were often driven out of their villages by other women, who saw them as a threat, and the soldiers' wives then went to the cities, where, finding little chance of other employment, they took to prostitution.[110] A case study of a procuress shows the foreign dimension. Anna-Kunigunda Felker, known as Dresdensha, had come to Russia to work for a military officer, who forced her to live with him. She married another man, but her husband went into the army and she was left without subsistence, and took up procuring, bringing in girls from abroad, whom she placed in distinguished homes in the guise of servants. She also ran a brothel and organized balls, which were a common site of covert prostitution: payment was made through expensive entrance tickets, which entitled the clients (seamen, ship-owners, merchants and officers) to take the young female 'guests', often foreigners, home.[111]

In Catherine II's reign graver measures were taken against prositition and venereal disease, the seriousness of which was recognized. Of the patients in the Petersburg General Infantry Hospital in 1763, 20 per cent had venereal diseases,[112] and that year women named by soldiers as the source of their disease were ordered to be confined in hospital.[113] From 1765 to 1774 treatment for them was provided in a special hospital on the Vyborg side, which opened with two patients and a year later had forty. The patients were held under arrest, and if they were discharged, were sent to the mines at Nerchinsk.[114] In 1780 a decree prescribed that debauched women in both capitals should be sent to Irkutsk,[115] and the laws of 1775 and 1782 which established the houses of correction provided for dissolute women to be sent to them[116] – although there seems to be no record that this was done.[117] The law of 1782 was one of the few attempts in history to control prostitution by punishing clients as well as prostitutes: it became an offence not only to engage in prostitution or run a brothel, but also 'to open one's own home or to use a rented home day or night for indecency; to enter a home day or night for indecency'.[118] The threat to both prostitutes and clients was now markedly greater than before. However, at the same time, certain areas of St Petersburg were designated as suitable for 'free houses',[119] and clients were evidently not deterred from using prostitutes. Catherine II's secretary A.A. Bezborodko, for example, went to 'the most indecent houses' every Saturday, taking with him a hundred roubles, and in winter spent his Sunday nights at the masquerades at Lion's, amongst the 'beauties'.[120]

Repression of overt prostitution continued in Paul I's reign, when prostitutes were obliged to wear distinguishing yellow dresses,[121] and a decree of 1800 repeated the requirement for dissolute women in the capitals to be sent to the Irkutsk factories.[122] Many of them were soldiers' wives,[123] as before, but foreign women still played a large role in prostitution. John Carr, who visited Russia in the early years of the nineteenth century, observed the prostitutes:

> they live in a quarter by themselves, and I believe are not very numerous ... some of them are Polish, of course handsome; some Germans, of course fascinating; and some, the most of them, fair and frail wanderers from the upper parts of Finland, which ... is said to possess many pretty faces and good persons amongst the females ...[124]

This brief account makes it possible to speculate that the measures taken in Catherine's reign led to an increase in covert prostitution, and that the prevalence of venereal disease amongst prostitutes both covert and overt resulted in the pursuit of very young girls, who were assumed to be free of infection. Second, it makes it possible to refine the generalization made by N.B. Lebina and M.V. Shkarovskii, historians of prostitution in St Petersburg from the nineteenth century, that Russian prostitutes had more lowly clients than foreign prostitutes.[125] Indubitably there were famous cases of glamorous foreign actress-mistresses, notably the French singer Mme Chevalier, who was tempted to St Petersburg in 1798 with an exceptionally high salary and generous benefits, and immediately became the mistress of I.P. Kutaisov, favourite of Paul I, and also enjoyed Paul's personal patronage, and indeed was rumoured to be his mistress too; she used her considerable influence to advance her husband's career and for her own financial advantage, lived in great luxury and eventually came to be considered a member of the Russian aristocracy – at least until Paul's death.[126] But Russian women – actresses – also played a part in high-class prostitution, working covertly. Moreover, this picture of covert, casual and episodic prostitution coincides with the emerging picture of eighteenth-century English prostitutes. Recent research challenges the idea that the latter were typically professionals working in brothels, controlled by a pimp or procuress, and shows instead that they were young women who worked for themselves, interspersed spells of prostitution with employment, and probably went on to marry and leave the trade.[127]

Finally, this description of the interactions between actresses and male spectators should be put into the context of male attitudes to prostitution at this time. In religious terms, the view of women, long propagated by the Church, as the sinful daughters of the temptress Eve, still held. In secular terms, the legislation which aimed to punish both prostitute and client failed to persuade the latter of his guilt, but made the former seem deserving of ill-treatment. If any party was deemed guilty it was the young woman. Griboedov identified Telesheva, whom he seduced, as the cause of his desire and was persuaded that he had done her good. Similarly, after an episode in which a girl at the Moscow theatre school had been importuned, the girls were told by their carers 'how shameful and improper it is for girls to listen to overtures from rich men and men of quality, knowing that such a man cannot marry [them] and may ruin honest girls'.[128] It is difficult to tell from the few pieces of writing by the young women who engaged in covert prostitution how they perceived themselves and their clients. Kulikova records that the girls did not like those who went straight from the theatre school to a flat. She remembers that they 'could hear them devouring the sweets given them by the nursemaids who had taken the bribes';[129] perhaps they were envious, but they certainly expressed no indignation at their treatment. Neither did Asenkova or Kulikova. In fact when she wrote her memoirs in 1885, Kulikova, now married to a nobleman, denied that she had been seduced, defending her reputation:

> how stupid little minds can be. I was eleven or twelve, many people loved me as a talented little girl, but I thought that they were real admirers, who were seeking my downfall... Later I found it amusing that I had been afraid of all those [men] who caressed me like a child, imagining that they were all running after me![130]

She cited the fact that she had been in love with one of the boys at the school, and had the support of her brother, who was also there. In her autobiography, where her declared aim is to call souls to faith, she presents herself as a sentimental heroine who is exposed to sin but survives unscathed thanks to her innocence and virtue. But it is perhaps unlikely that when others fell victim to coercion, she did not.

In the early nineteenth century the time when prostitutes came to be considered victims of sexual violence and capable of living moral lives was still some way off, as were campaigns for their rehabilitation and for abolition of the trade. At the end of the eighteenth century and the beginning of the nineteenth actresses played a large part in Petersburg social life as providers of artistry and entertainment. Some rose to be stars. But as the theatre generated a space in which the usual conventions of behaviour for nobles and aristocrats were suspended, actresses also populated an underworld in which young bachelors indulged in libertine behaviour and married men in infidelity. Actresses were in effect covert prostitutes. The history of prostitution at this time is not well established, but it has been suggested that upper-class men turned to foreign prostitutes whilst Russian women attracted lower-class clients. However, in the elaborate mechanism of prostitution within the theatre, Russian women also participated in the high-class sector of the trade.

Acknowledgements

The author wishes to acknowledge funding from the Arts and Humanities Research Board, the British Academy, and the University of Nottingham, and the various kindnesses of M. Sh. Fainshtein, Rebecca Friedman, Janet Hartley and Mary Zirin.

Notes

1. Elizabeth Howe, *The First English Actresses: Women and Drama 1660–1700* (Cambridge, 1992); Sandra Richards, *The Rise of the English Actress* (Basingstoke and London, 1993), p. 4.
2. J.-J. Rousseau, *Lettre à D'Alembert sur les spectacles* [1758] (Lille and Geneva, 1948), pp. 101, 106.
3. *Ibid.*, p. 5.
4. F.F. Vigel', *Zapiski*, I (Moscow, 1928), p. 330.
5. Quoted in Victor Borovsky, 'The Emergence of the Russian Theatre, 1763–1800', in Robert Leach and Victor Borovsky (eds), *A History of Russian Theatre* (Cambridge, 1999), p. 58.
6. *Severnyi vestnik*, part 4 (1804), 291, quoted in A. Ia. Al'tshuller (ed.), *Ocherki istorii russkoi teatral'noi kritiki: konets XVIII–pervaia polovina XIX veka* (Leningrad, 1975), p. 57.
7. Rousseau, *Lettre*, pp. 110, 117–18, 120–1.
8. 'Zapiski Rafaila Mikhailovicha Zotova', *Istoricheskii vestnik*, LXV (1896) 306.
9. P. Shalikov, *Puteshestvie v Malorossiiu* (Moscow, 1803), pp. 80–4.
10. A.A. Gozenpud, *Muzykal'nyi teatr v Rossii: ot istokov do Glinki. Ocherk* (Leningrad, 1959), p. 420.
11. Shakhovskoi, quoted in *ibid.*, p. 407.
12. N.M., 'Biografiia Evgenii Ivanovny Kolosovoi', *Repertuar russkogo i Panteon vsekh evropeiskikh teatrov*, no. 4 (1842) 12.
13. 'Zapiski Zotova', LXVI (1897) 773–4.
14. R. Zotov, 'Materialy dlia istorii russkogo teatra. Kniaz' A.A. Shakhovskoi', *Repertuar i panteon*, 1846, XIV, 13–14; Iu. A. Dmitriev et al. (eds), *Istoriia russkogo dramaticheskogo teatra*, II (Moscow, 1977), 381.
15. S.P. Zhikharev, *Zapiski sovremennika* (Leningrad, 1989), p. 169.
16. Poems are quoted in M.V. Borisoglebskii, *Proshloe baletnogo otdeleniia Peterburgskogo teatral'nogo uchilishcha*, I (Leningrad, 1938), 66.
17. 'Zapiski Zotova', LXVI, 766.
18. A.P. Glushkovskii, *Vospominaniia baletmeistera* (Leningrad and Moscow, 1940), pp. 160, 85.
19. 'Zapiski Zotova', quoted in P.A. Karatygin, *Zapiski* (Moscow and Leningrad, 1930), p. 309.
20. 'Moi zamechaniia o teatre', A.S. Pushkin, *Polnoe sobranie sochinenii v desiati tomakh*, VII, 3rd edn (Moscow, 1964), 7–8.
21. Letter of late October 1824, *ibid.*, X (1966), 103–4.
22. P.I. Orlova-Savina, *Avtobiografiia* (Moscow, 1994), p. 79. The autobiography is discussed in Mary F. Zirin, 'Two Autobiographies by Russian Actresses as Cultural History' (unpublished).
23. 'Vospominaniia A. Ia. Golovachevoi-Panaevoi' in her *Russkie pisateli i artisty 1824–1870* (St Petersburg, 1890), p. 22.

24. Letter of 27 October 1819, Pushkin, X, 14.
25. Cf. V.D. Krenke: 'cadets in the 1820s and the first half of the 1830s produced manuscripts which they circulated containing antisocial (*tsinicheskie*) compositions ... and the more severely the institution's authorities persecuted these manuscripts, the more the cadets managed to keep them and acquire new ones. In my time as an ensign, every officer brought with him entire exercise books of these compositions from the Corps ...' ('Byt saperov 50 let nazad', *Istoricheskii vestnik*, no. 8 (1885) 290, quoted in A.I. Reitblat, *Kak Pushkin vyshel v genii. Istoriko-sotsiologicheskie ocherki o knizhnoi kul'ture Pushkinskoi epokhi* (Moscow, 2001), p. 25).
26. P. Arapov, *Letopis' russkogo teatra* (St Petersburg, 1861), p. 351.
27. Nikolai El'iash, *Avdot'ia Istomina* (Leningrad, 1971), pp. 69–70; Iu. Slonimskii, *Baletnye stroki Pushkina* (Leningrad, 1974), p. 28. Her son Iraklii Nikitin, who became a dancer, was not recognized by Vsevolozhskii as his son.
28. Iu. M. Lotman, 'Iskusstvo zhizni', in his *Besedy o russkoi kul'ture. Byt i traditsii russkogo dvorianstva (XVIII – nachalo XIX veka)* (St Petersburg, 1997), p. 183.
29. Leonid Grossman, *Pushkin v teatral'nykh kreslakh* (Leningrad, 1926), p. 10.
30. *Ibid.*, pp. 59–60.
31. Quoted in Slonimskii, *Baletnye stroki Pushkina*, p. 139.
32. An observer commented on the absence of interaction in Petersburg salons in the mid-1820s: 'At *soirées* the *ladies* group themselves around one table, presided over by the mistress of the house, the *young ladies* go and establish themselves in some corner of the room; the *men* address a few words to the ladies of the table as they enter and soon gather together; the *young men* use the liberty accorded them to converse with the *young ladies* only with extreme scruple, one might say with a certain repugnance' (M. Ancelot, *Six mois en Russie* (Paris, 1827), pp. 62, 64).
33. Orlova-Savina, *Avtobiografiia*, p. 64.
34. Ivan Val'berkh, *Iz arkhiva baletmeistera (Dnevniki, perepiska, stsenarii)* (Moscow and Leningrad, 1948), p. 123.
35. *Ibid.*, p. 123.
36. Quoted in Slonimskii, *Baletnye stroki Pushkina*, p. 139.
37. Glushkovskii, *Vaspominaniia baletmeistera*, p. 144.
38. *Ibid.*, p. 160.
39. 'Zapiski Zotova', LXV, 313.
40. Rossiiskii gosudarstvennyi istoricheskii arkhiv, hereafter RGIA, f. 498, op. 1, ed. khr. 19.
41. Borisoglebskii, *Proshloe baletnego...*, I, 106.
42. RGIA f. 497, op. 1, d. 2786.
43. Borisoglebskii, *Proshloe baletnego...*, I, 68.
44. Iu. Oksman, 'Vospominaniia P.A. Katenina o Pushkine', in *Literaturnoe nasledstvo*, XVI–XVIII (Moscow, 1934), p. 646; A.M. Karatygina, 'Vospominaniia', in Karatygin, *Zapiski*, pp. 160–1, 311–12.
45. 'Zapiski Zotova', LXV, 37. The notes to Karatygin, *Zapiski*, p. 160 assert that the girls lived at Shakhovskoi's flat.
46. A. Pleshcheev, *Nash balet 1673–1896* (St Petersburg, 1896), p. 78.

47. 'Zapiski Zotova', LXV, 37.
48. A.E. Asenkova, 'Kartiny proshedshego. Zapiski russkoi artistki', *Teatral'nyi i muzykal'nyi vestnik* (1857), No. 36, 492–4, No. 37, 492–5, No. 39, 529–32, No. 42, 578–80, No. 44, 606–7, No. 46, 642–4, No. 49, 699–700, No. 50, 709–13, No. 51, 720–5, No. 50, 723.
49. Vigel', *Zapiski*, II, 94.
50. Asenkova, No. 50, 723.
51. Arapov, *Letopis' russkogo teatra*, p. 351.
52. Quoted in Borisoglebskii, *Proshloe baletnego*, p. 96.
53. Quoted in Oksman, 'Vospominaniia P.A. Katenina o Pushkine', p. 646.
54. Letter to Viazemskii of 14 October 1823, quoted in *ibid*., p. 646.
55. Arapov, *Letopis' russkogo teatra*, pp. 349–51.
56. Vigel', *Zapiski*, II, 91.
57. Letter of 4 January 1825 to S.N. Begichev in M.P. Eremin (ed.), *A.S. Griboedov. Sochineniia v dvukh tomakh*, II (Moscow, 1971), 237.
58. R. Zotov, 'Materialy dlia istorii russkogo teatra. Kniaz' A.A. Shakhovskoi', pp. 31–2.
59. *Khronika peterburgskikh teatrov*, quoted in Borisoglebskii, p. 101. Karatygina adds: '... all the dramas and melodramas which he wrote every year for the benefit performances of his favourites flopped; but the Administration did not stint on the décor: only these had new scenery and expensive new costumes, and all other authors were refused ...' (Karatygina, *Zapiski*, p. 139).
60. *Ibid*., p. 160.
61. I. Medvedeva, *Ekaterina Semenova: zhizn' i tvorchestvo tragicheskoi aktrisy* (Moscow, 1964), p. 161; 'Vospominaniia A. Ia. Golovachevoi-Panaevoi', p. 8.
62. Glushkovskii, *Vospominaniia baletmeistera*, p. 143.
63. Medvedeva, *Ekaterina Semenova*, p. 18.
64. *Ibid*., p. 76.
65. *Ibid*., pp. 76–8.
66. Vigel', *Zapiski*, II, 91.
67. *Istoriia russkogo dramaticheskogo teatra*, II, 389.
68. 'Zapiski Zotova', LXVI, 412.
69. In 1765 the age of criminal responsibility was set at seventeen; those under ten were not deemed responsible, and those aged ten to sixteen were deemed to have partial responsibility: B.N. Mironov, *Sotsial'naia istoriia Rossii perioda Imperii (XVIII – nachalo XX v.)*, II (St Petersburg, 1999), 21.
70. RGIA, f. 497, op. 1, d. 2078.
71. RGIA, f. 497, op. 14, ed. khr. 444, 1.13 and ob.
72. RGIA, f. 498, op. 1, ed. khr. 33.
73. RGIA, f. 497, op. 14, ed. khr. 444, l. 6. The regulations date to 1809.
74. Asenkova, 'Kartiny proshedshego. Zapiski russkoi artistki', No. 46, 644.
75. Vigel', *Zapiski*, II, 178.
76. Orlova-Savina *Avtobiografiia*, p. 84.
77. Quoted in Borisoglebskii, *Proshloe baletnogo* ..., p. 98.
78. Orlova-Savina, *Avtobiografiia*, p. 64. She also suggests that assignations were made by men with boys (p. 48).

79. *Ibid.*, p. 67.
80. *Ibid.*, p. 80.
81. 'Vospominaniia A. Ia. Golovachevoi-Panaevoi', p. 21.
82. Orlova-Savina, *Avtobiografiia*, p. 44.
83. *Ibid.*, pp. 68–9.
84. *Ibid.*, p. 83.
85. *Ibid.*, p. 83.
86. *Ibid.*, pp. 87–8.
87. V. Vsevolodskii (Gerngross), *Istoriia teatral'nogo obrazovaniia v Rossii*, I (St Petersburg, 1913), 295.
88. Laura Engelstein, 'Gender and the Juridical Subject: Prostitution and Rape in Nineteenth-Century Russian Criminal Codes', *Journal of Modern History*, LX (1988) 472–3.
89. Mironov, *Sotsial'naia istoriia Rossii*, I, 167–8. The average age on marriage for women in 1780 was fifteen or sixteen.
90. Orlova-Savina, *Avtobiografiia*, pp. 80, 44, 69.
91. I.F. Petrovskaia, 'K istorii opernogo teatra v Peterburge v 1801–1840gg', *Pamiatniki kul'tury. Novye otkrytiia za 1997 god* (Moscow, 1998), pp. 193–4.
92. Slonimskii, *Baletnye stroki Pushkina*, p. 129.
93. RGIA, f. 497, op. 1, ed. khr. 1325, l. 56 (1814).
94. Borisoglebskii, *Proshloe baletnogo...*, I, 92 (1818).
95. S.S. Danilov, *Ocherki po istorii russkogo dramaticheskogo teatra* (Moscow and Leningrad, 1948), p. 198.
96. 'Vospominaniia A. Ia. Golovachevoi-Panaevoi', p. 27.
97. Lotman, 'Iskusstvo zhizni', 189–90.
98. *Nakaz*, Chapter XIV. (See Paul Dukes (ed. and trans.), *Catherine the Great's Instruction (NAKAZ) to the Legislative Commission, 1767*, II (Newtonville, Mass., 1977), 89–90.)
99. 'O dobrodeteli', in N.I. Novikov, *Izbrannye sochineniia* (Moscow and Leningrad, 1954), p. 396.
100. Catriona Kelly, *Refining Russia: Advice Literature, Polite Culture, and Gender from Catherine to Yeltsin* (Oxford, 2001), pp. 37–42.
101. P.K. Guber, M.I. Semevskii and A.N. Vul'f, *Liubovnyi byt Pushkinskoi epokhi*, I (Moscow, 1994), 266–7.
102. M.A. Tsiavlovskii (comp.), *Letopis' zhizni i tvorchestva Aleksandra Pushkina*, I (Moscow, 1999) *passim*.
103. 'Zapiski Zotova', LXV, 307.
104. Prostitution is not mentioned, for example, by Mironov, but is mentioned briefly in Janet M. Hartley's *A Social History of the Russian Empire 1650–1825* (London and New York, 1999), pp. 38, 118, 166.
105. N.B. Lebina and M.V. Shkarovskii, *Prostitutsiia v Peterburge (40-e gg. XIX v.–40-e gg. XX v.)* (Moscow, 1994), p. 19.
106. Julie A. Cassiday and Leyla Rouhi, 'From Nevskii Prospekt to Zoia's Apartment: Trials of the Russian Procuress', *Russian Review*, LVIII (1999) 418.
107. Quoted from Veniamin M. Tarnovskii, *Prostitutsiia i abolitsionizm* (St Petersburg, 1888), pp. 98–9, by Laurie Bernstein, 'Yellow Tickets and State-Licensed Brothels: The Tsarist Government and the Regulation of

Urban Prostitution', in Susan Gross Solomon and John F. Hutchinson (eds), *Health and Society in Revolutionary Russia* (Bloomington and Indianapolis, 1990), p. 46.
108. G.M. Gertsenshtein, 'Prostitutsiia', in I.E. Andreevskii (ed.), *Entsiklopedicheskii slovar'*, XXVI (St Petersburg, 1898), 479–86.
109. L.N. Semenova, *Byt i naselenie Sankt-Peterburga (XVIII vek)* (St Petersburg, 1998), pp. 125–8.
110. David L. Ransel, *Mothers of Misery: Child Abandonment in Russia* (Princeton, N.J., 1988), p. 22.
111. Semenova, *Byt i naselenie Sankt-Peterburga*, pp. 125–9.
112. John T. Alexander, 'Catherine the Great and Public Health', *Journal of the History of Medicine and Allied Sciences*, XXXVI (1981) 198.
113. Laurie Bernstein, *Sonia's Daughters: Prostitutes and Their Regulation in Imperial Russia* (Berkeley and London, 1995), p. 14.
114. A.M. Kopylov, 'Iz istorii pervykh bol'nits Peterburga', *Sovetskoe zdravookhranenie*, No. 2 (1962) 58–9.
115. S.S. Shashkov, *Sobranie sochinenii* (St Petersburg, 1898), p. 872.
116. Hartley, *Social History*, p. 118.
117. I am indebted to Janet Hartley for this information.
118. Engelstein mentions: 'Eighteenth-century laws...allowed the police to punish both parties in the commercial exchange of sex by imposing fines or brief terms of detention' (Engelstein, 'Gender', p. 485).
119. Gertsenshtein, 'Prostitutsiia', p. 482.
120. N.I. Grech, *Zapiski o moei zhizni* (Moscow, 1990), p. 76.
121. Lebina and Shkarovskii, *Prostitutsiia v Peterburge*, p. 20.
122. N.I. Solov'ev, 'Presledovanie prostitutok v tsarstvovanie imp. Pavla I-ogo', *Russkaia starina* (1916), pp. 363–4.
123. *Ibid.*, p. 364.
124. John Carr, *A Northern Summer, or Travels round the Baltic, through Denmark, Sweden, Russia, Prussia, and Part of Germany, in the Year 1804* (London, 1805), quoted in Hartley, *Social History*, p. 166.
125. '[In the reign of Catherine II] most prostitutes were foreigners, as before, whose main occupation was keeping fashion shops and millinery workshops, or working as actresses. Their services were used by people of the upper and middle classes. The "tavern girls" who satisfied the needs of the lower class, were Russian': Lebina and Shkarovskii, *Prostitutsiia v Peterburge*, p. 20.
126. Her career is described in R.-Aloys Mooser, *L'Opéra-comique français en Russie au XVIIIe siècle* (Geneva-Monaco, 1954), pp. 187–99.
127. Tim Hitchcock, *English Sexualities, 1700–1800* (Basingstoke and London, 1997), pp. 94–6.
128. Orlova-Savina, *Avtobiografiia*, p. 69.
129. *Ibid.*, p. 79.
130. *Ibid.*, p. 82.

8
Peter the Great's St Petersburg in the Works of Pavel Svin'in (1787–1839)

Lindsey Hughes

> Rumours of the extraordinary beauty of the iron railings of the Summer Palace persuaded a certain Englishman, a great connoisseur of the arts, to travel to St Petersburg in order to verify this claim with his own eyes. Having inspected the railings and confirmed that he had not been deceived about their fine qualities, he immediately returned to his homeland.[1]

This passage about an eccentric Englishman comes from *The Sights of St Petersburg and its Environs* (*Dostopamiatnosti Sanktpeterburga i ego okrestnostei*), a pioneering guide that appeared in a dual Russian–French text in five volumes between 1816 and 1828. Each volume contains several chapters on individual monuments or architectural ensembles, each section illustrated with an engraving based on sketches by the guide's author, Pavel Petrovich Svin'in (1787–1839). The subject of this essay is St Petersburg as presented in the pages of Svin'in's guide and other works by him and his contemporaries, which allow us a glimpse of the city viewed through the prism of early nineteenth-century, post-Napoleonic, pre-Pushkin and (mostly) pre-Decembrist sensibility and national self-awareness.

The Sights of St Petersburg and its Environs examines buildings, gardens and other monuments constructed throughout the hundred or so years of St Petersburg's existence, but our focus will be on several sites associated with Peter I (1682–1725), who in the early nineteenth century, for Russians and foreigners alike, remained a looming presence in the city that he had created. In Svin'in's words: 'Like some Genius, [Peter] appeared on the Russian horizon and illuminated it with rays of glory.'² *The Sights of St Petersburg* celebrated Peter's creation as the equal of other great European cities. At the same time, as the opening quotation suggests, Svin'in and fellow writers cared about what foreigners thought. It was possible to mock the Englishman for his eccentricity and extravagance, while desperately craving his approval. The anecdote would hardly have been included in the guide if the visitor had been disappointed by the renowned railings.

Pavel Svin'in has generally been regarded as an enthusiastic dilettante, who tried his hand with mixed success at poetry, journalism, criticism and painting.³ He studied for a time in the Imperial Academy of Arts in St Petersburg, which in 1811 awarded him the status of Academician for a painting on the theme of General Suvorov resting after a battle. (His own portrait was painted by Vasilii Tropinin.) His most solid contribution to the literary scene was the journal *Notes of the Fatherland* (*Otechestvennye zapiski*), which he founded in 1818 and edited until 1830, writing many contributions himself. He soaked up influences, to the point, some critics would claim, of plagiarism. His memoir of a sea voyage, written in 1818, for example, imitated the style of Nikolai Karamzin's *Letters of a Russian Traveller* (*Pis'ma russkogo puteshestvennika*, 1789–90; 1797).⁴ He was an acquaintance of Pushkin, who was rude about him, calling him the 'Russian bug' (*Rossiiskii zhuk*), among other things, and served as a prototype for Khlestakov in Gogol's play *The Government Inspector* (*Revizor*, 1836), not a very flattering comparison.

Although Svin'in apparently ignored the jibes of contemporaries by remaining devoted to literature and art, for a number of years he earned his living as a civil servant on the payroll of the Ministry of Foreign Affairs, a post that turned him into a seasoned traveller. In 1807–08 he served as secretary to Vice-Admiral Dmitrii Siniavin with a Russian squadron in the Mediterranean, during a spell abroad that took him as far as Portugal, Spain and England. When Russia withdrew its forces following the peace of Tilsit with France in 1809, he returned home to spend some time sketching Russian views before being posted to North America as secretary to N. Ia. Kozlov, Russia's Consul-General in the USA, where in 1811–13 – far removed from momentous events unfolding in Russia – he made sketches and water-colours of North American scenes.⁵ In the USA he published *Sketches of Moscow and St Petersburg* (Philadelphia, 1813), a version of which appeared in London in 1814 as *Sketches of Russia Illustrated with Fifteen Engravings*. As he wrote at the beginning of the latter:

> I flatter myself that these little Sketches will be favourably accepted by the Public on account of the new interest and glory, which my countrymen have recently acquired, in co-operation with the noble efforts of the British nation, for the establishment of general peace and independence.[6]

These earlier books provided material for *The Sights of St Petersburg*, including the anecdote about the Englishman.[7] In both the USA and England (which he particularly admired), Svin'in had observed attitudes towards tradition and the preservation of the past that he was anxious to inculcate at home in what seemed to be a favourable climate for national heritage. He mentions his earlier books in the Foreword to *The Sights of St Petersburg* as evidence of 'the pleasure with which people everywhere read descriptions of Russia'. The enthusiastic reception apparently 'exceeded his expectations'.[8] As the publisher of Svin'in's last published work later wrote, this was a time when everyone 'thirsted to have the closest acquaintance with a country that had overthrown the colossus that was crushing Europe'.[9]

Thus the publication of *Sketches of Russia* and *The Sights of St Petersburg* was prompted by a combination of Svin'in's experience abroad and events in Russia: the burning of Moscow in 1812, Napoleon's retreat and the disintegration of the Grande Armée, and the entry of Russian troops into Paris in 1814 under Emperor Alexander I's command. These events aroused Russian national feelings in a number of ways, not least by inspiring a sense of protectiveness towards national culture and equality with, even superiority to France. Members of the elite took to speaking Russian, wearing Russian-style dress and taking pride in Russia's past. For example, the first volume of Karamzin's *History of the Russian State* (*Istoriia Gosudarstva Rossiiskogo*) appeared to great acclaim in 1818. Svin'in was one of several men of his generation who promoted the idea of St Petersburg as the equal of Paris, as a symbol of Russia's full membership, even leadership of Europe and a proof of Russia's ability to achieve the miraculous by conjuring up a city from nothing.

A key work in giving voice to some of these ideas was undoubtedly the poet Konstantin Batiushkov's 'A Walk to the Academy of Arts'

('Progulka v Akademiiu khudozhestv'), published in 1814 in the form of a letter to a friend who had lost his art collection in the great fire of Moscow.[10] The letter begins with the poet in his St Petersburg residence falling into a 'sweet reverie' (*sladostnoe mechtanie*), as the sight of the cosmopolitan crowds on the Neva embankment below his window prompts thoughts about how desolate the site must have been before Peter founded the city. He imagines Peter (as Pushkin was to do in his poem *The Bronze Horseman* (*Mednyi vsadnik*) almost twenty years later) surveying the scene: 'He spoke – and Petersburg arose from the wild swamp.' A young artist friend interrupts the writer's daydream with an invitation to view the current exhibition at the Academy of Arts. As they step out, the following sight greets them:

> Magnificent buildings, glittering in the morning sun, were brightly reflected in the clear mirror of the Neva, and we both exclaimed as one 'What a city! What a river!'
>
> 'The only city!' the young man repeated. 'So many subjects for the artist's brush! Take your pick. But what a pity that my fellow artists make so little use of their native riches. Painters of perspective scenes prefer to paint views of Italy and other countries rather than these charming subjects ... You have to get away from St Petersburg for a time and see ancient capitals such as decrepit Paris and smoke-blackened London to appreciate St Petersburg. Just look what unity it has! How all its parts match the whole.'

The artist goes on to enthuse about the lightness and elegance of the already mentioned railings of the Summer Palace, by comparison with which the celebrated ironwork of the Tuilleries in Paris seems ugly. The author agrees with his friend:

> How many wonders we see before us, wonders created in such a short space of time, in a century, just one century! Glory and honour to the great founder of this city! Glory and honour to his successors, who completed what he had barely begun in the midst of wars and domestic and foreign conflicts. Glory and honour to Alexander, who more than anyone during his reign made the capital of the North beautiful![11]

It is worth bearing in mind that in 1814 whole sections of central St Petersburg, including the eastern promontory of Vasil'evskii Island

and the Admiralty district, had been or were being transformed by impressive architectural projects. This fact, coupled with the loss of so much of Moscow and the 'glory' of Alexander's exploits abroad, gave rise to an upsurge of civic pride. Svin'in, as we shall see, drew on the sentiments of Batiushkov's short work to produce the first extensive guide in Russian to 'the only city'.

I have explored elsewhere[12] the extent to which Russians in the eighteenth and early nineteenth centuries visited and appreciated their own native sights and objects of interest. Before Svin'in's time many educated Russians were in most respects alienated from their own cultural monuments, their attitudes shaped by the peculiar development of elite culture following Peter I's reforms, which required the assimilation of Western genres and models, rooted in a universal belief in the virtues of Antiquity.[13] In particular, Russo-Byzantine religious art was marginalized. Modern Russian upper-class 'pilgrims' headed not for the Holy Land, Mount Athos or the great Russian monasteries and shrines, but for Italy, Germany and France. The conservative thinker Prince Mikhail Shcherbatov famously pleaded on Moscow's behalf in a mock petition to Catherine II: 'My ancient ruins can still please and are still useful – they please because they represent my very antiquity and that of your Empire, and they are useful in that they are a reminder of many a service performed for the country.'[14] As it happened, Catherine allocated generous funds to restoring the Kremlin cathedrals. She was well aware of the usefulness of tradition, but personally disliked Moscow and spent as little time there as possible. The Russian town deemed most worthy of the attention of women and men of the Enlightenment was, paradoxically, not the 'most ancient' – Moscow, with its 'Asiatic', 'barbaric' associations – but the most modern, St Petersburg, where Peter I and his successors attempted to implant the virtues of Classical antiquity in a couple of generations.

In the first St Petersburg guide, published in 1779, but based on a work written in 1749–51 by A.I. Bogdanov, the author addressed Empress Elizabeth (1741–61):

> By the energetic efforts of Your Imperial Majesty this City is now so extensive and so adorned with splendid new buildings and so much praised, that it has the advantage over many famous European cities, which are famous for their antiquity, to the great

glory of its Founder, and especially to the glory of Your Imperial Majesty.... Not only people who live here enjoy its beauty but also people from far-distant countries, on hearing about it, are amazed. Many long to visit, to see it for themselves and enjoy its beauty.[15]

The discourse of St Petersburg as an inspiration for emotions of gratitude to its imperial architects was a staple feature of home-produced works. Even before Alexander I's major triumphs, we find Aleksei Pylaev declaring in a pamphlet of 1809 that 'any educated (*prosveshchennyi*) person upon seeing these pleasing wonders of a sagacious and mild Government will experience patriotic gaiety and reverence for their sovereign'.[16] Pylaev recommended that the emperor should erect triumphal gates of marble or granite at the main entrance to the city, topped by a trumpeting Victory and bearing bas-reliefs of military trophies and masons' tools, with one inscription proclaiming that St Petersburg was founded in the year 1703 by Emperor Peter the First and another to show that the gates were built by Alexander the First. 'Thus the first thing in the city that every Russian (*Rossianin*) will behold upon entering brilliant St Petersburg will be dedicated to the glory of Peter the First and created by Alexander and he will feel gratitude.'[17]

Pylaev's praise of the city was conceived in Classical terms, but the late eighteenth–early nineteenth century was also a time when the elite Grand Tour – essentially a journey from north to south, with connotations of self-enlightenment mixed with pleasure, focusing on the appreciation of Classical and Renaissance civilization in a warm southern climate – was giving way to a broader kind of 'sentimental journey', which could include Russia too. 'Tourism' was not far off.[18] By the end of the eighteenth century several guides to the imperial capital catered to foreign visitors and residents, but by and large they were factual compendia, lacking historical or artistic colour. The German Johann Georgi's *Description of the Russian Imperial Capital St Petersburg* (*Opisanie rossiisko-imp. stolichnogo goroda S. Peterburga*) was a characteristic example.[19] The city's centenary in 1803 and the diplomatic activity of the first years of Alexander I's reign attracted further foreign descriptions of the city.[20] but Svin'in spotted a gap in the market for a Russian guide written by a Russian which could appeal to foreigners, too.

Svin'in drew liberally on existing sources, then added his own twists. In both *Sketches of Russia* and *The Sights of St Petersburg*, for example, he cites some 'observations' taken from the *Bagatelles* of a certain M. Fabre, whose *Walks in St Petersburg* first appeared in French in 1811.[21] Fabre/Svin'in ask their readers to imagine a man 'from the most civilized country from the South of Europe, who should be celebrated for his enlightened mind and the experience acquired from travels and accurate observation of the world'. We are to picture this man blindfolded and transported to St Petersburg in summer and asked to guess, first from sounds, then from selected sights, where he is. He is treated to glimpses of 'magnificent spectacles' that fill him with astonishment, to scenes of 'enchantment and fairyland' and to views bringing to mind London, Amsterdam, Venice, Florence, Rome, Berlin and Paris, while others (for example, a peasant market) transfer him 'from the extreme point of civilization to its opposite'.[22] The city 'seems to belong to all nations', but is still itself. Finally he guesses correctly where he is.

This exercise in observing without prejudice – allegorical Justice is shown blindfolded, after all – was, in Svin'in's view, necessitated by previous foreign misrepresentations of Russia in general and St Petersburg in particular. 'If we were to judge [our] country from the accounts of the majority of travellers we should certainly have a very false idea of it. Unfortunately, travels in Russia have generally been the object of speculators who, taking advantage of the remote situation of that country, and desirous of rendering the narrative of their stories interesting, have related ridiculous wonders and strange falsehoods.'[23] Even foreigners who thought they had understood Russia failed to grasp that Russia was 'quite different from all other countries' and that its natives had

> some characteristics, which belong peculiarly to themselves. They must be studied in order to be described. Their constitutional vivacity places them as a people, wholly distinct from other northern nations. Let an Englishman, or a German dress himself in a Russian long wide coat, this alone cannot metamorphose him into a Russian, and the Russian will never mistake him for his countryman.[24]

In the opening lines of *The Sights of St Petersburg* Svin'in hinted that foreigners themselves were now eager for a more balanced picture, for they complained upon arriving in St Petersburg they had no guide – by which he means a fair, reliable one, not written by a foreigner – to acquaint them with the sights. He laments the fact that the capital city of the 'great and strong Russian people', a city which had attracted the attention and respect of the whole world in 1812–14, should languish in oblivion, while in other countries not only capitals but even the smallest towns are described in detail. (The widely travelled Svin'in was well placed to make such an observation.) His love for 'all that belongs to his native country' (*ko vsemu otechestvennomu*) prompts him to publish a guide. Svin'in ended his Foreword by explaining that he was printing the text in Russian and French to acquaint both Russians and foreigners with St Petersburg. In fact, the dual text reflected not only the separate needs of foreign and local readers but also the duality of St Petersburg itself and of Russian educated society. One suspects that many Russian readers, notwithstanding post-Napoleonic enthusiasm for the native tongue, turned to French as their language of choice.

In the eighteenth century homage to St Petersburg had inevitably begun at the feet of the city's founder and in this respect Svin'in is no exception. After a 'Glance at the Capital' and a eulogy to Alexander I (virtually the same text that appears in the earlier *Sketches*), the guide proper begins with Falconet's monument to Peter I.[25] Chronologically and topographically, the 1782 monument is perhaps not the logical opening choice – Pushkin's seminal 'Bronze Horseman' poem was not published until 1833 – but making it the *first* sight of St Petersburg, symbolically, if not chronologically, links the city's recent saviour, Alexander I, with its founder.

As Svin'in writes, only a genius like Peter could have envisaged such a project as St Petersburg. His resourcefulness in founding 'the magnificent capital of the extensive Russian Empire' amidst impenetrable forests and swamps and making it habitable was astounding. Still more amazing was the fact that Peter achieved all this while threatened with invasion by the 'arrogant' Charles XII of Sweden. Readers were no doubt expected to make the connection that the reason why St Petersburg stood free and intact in 1816, ready to be further embellished, was the equally amazing fact that Alexander had repelled the even more arrogant Napoleon. Alexander I personally may have been less devoted to Peter's memory than were some other Romanovs,[26] but no Russian ruler could avoid placing his or her efforts and achievements in the Petrine context, whether they presented themselves as completing his work, protecting it or gaining inspiration from it. Falconet's hero 'seated soundly and firmly on his [metal] steed' was not primarily a warrior but the 'father of his people and a wise lawgiver'. The same could be said of Alexander. By association, Svin'in pays tribute to Alexander by detailing the events that occurred around the monument in May 1803 for the celebration of the city's centenary. Among the participants, guarding Peter's little boat (the Grandfather of the Russian Fleet) were four contemporaries of Peter, including a 107-year-old who had served under the tsar's command in the navy. This detail emphasized direct links with the heroic past. It was made to seem no accident that this important anniversary fell within Alexander's reign. In Svin'in's text one senses none of the growing disillusionment that Russians of a slightly younger generation than Svin'in were beginning to experience in the wake of 1814, which would culminate in the abortive Decembrist revolt of army officers in 1825.

Svin'in does not neglect to supply facts and figures in the manner of Georgi and other foreign writers: that the weight of Falconet's monument was 44,041 Russian *funts*; the cost – 424,610 roubles, and so on. But he strikes a more contemporary note by waxing lyrical over the picturesque and emotional qualities of the statue and its setting. The viewer was invited to admire the view not just with the mind of a patriot (through the evocation of heroic deeds) or of a connoisseur (by appreciating the sculptor's technical skill, for example), but also with the eye of a painter. Here we find echoes of Batiushkov's text and the appeal of his 'young friend' to painters to depict Russian views:

> Let the lover of unique rich views come here towards evening when the purple clouds cover the pedestal of the monument and the rider and horse seem to trample the clouds, to be riding through a world of clouds. What a subject for a painter!

The picturesque qualities of monuments and their settings, which inspire the imagination of a painter, can also stir the heart of a patriot: 'What a sight for every Russian (*Rossianina*)! What Russian can look upon this monument and not be filled with reverence (*blagogovenie*) for and gratitude to the Great Transformer of Russia?'[27]

Buildings constructed in Peter's time arouse especial gratitude and reverence (*blagogovenie*), a key word in Svin'in's work. The Summer Palace (1710–14, by Domenico Trezzini), for example, remained 'in its original state and gives an idea of the noble simplicity and thrift of the immortal monarch'.[28] Relics of Peter's time, especially those made or touched by his own hand, are credited with inspirational qualities. In a tour of the Alexander Nevskii monastery (1710s–1720s, Trezzini), for example, we learn that the treasury contained some interesting Petrine memorabilia, including two of Peter's military batons:

> Who can touch the baton of the Hero of Poltava without experiencing a particular reverent frisson (*blagoveinyi trepet*), that baton in response to a wave of which the young Russian eagles soared from victory to victory and astounded Europe?

Visitors could also see the bed on which the 'immortal' and 'unsleeping' (*sic*!) monarch, who 'devoted every minute of his life to the happiness of his Fatherland', occasionally took a short nap, the same bed on which he died, having uttered the memorable words: 'Friends, see from my example what a wretched creature a man is!'[29]

In Volume 3 Svin'in provided an itinerary for visiting some of the most evocative Petrine places in and near the Peter-Paul fortress, arousing strong associations between the Petrine era and recent 'glories'. Patriotic feelings giving rise to *blagogovenie* are just one of the responses that Svin'in anticipates in his *feeling* traveller, whom he refers to as *strannik* (pilgrim or wanderer). The tour starts with the cathedral of Saints Peter and Paul (Trezzini, 1712–33), the imperial mausoleum, which is characterized initially by some mind-numbing statistics – the height of the cross is 55 *sazhens* or 385 English feet, the roof of the church nave measures 8 $\frac{1}{3}$ *sazhens*, and so on. Whereas the cathedral's religious objects and holy relics – part of the Robe of Our Lord, part of the head of St James, and 'bits of many other saints', the iconostasis 'in the old taste, its high-relief carving amazingly richly gilded' – are routinely described, the visitor is exhorted to approach 'the objects made by the hand of the immortal Founder of this church' with special reverence. These included two ivory chandeliers and a cross.[30]

The mood becomes even more emotionally charged as the *strannik* pauses in front of the tombs of Russia's emperors and empresses.

Here is the place 'where monarchs render account of their deeds to the lowliest of their subjects, where a tear of gratitude and devotion washes the memorial to Titus and blessings for him are sent up to the throne of the King of Kings; and where the groans and reproaches of the innocent assail the bronzes and marbles adorning the obelisks of Neros and Caligulas!' (Despite the Classical distancing, one detects a veiled reference to the fact that the imperial occupants of the tombs were not equally worthy of praise.) As the *strannik* turned his gaze to the 'cold granite holding all that remains of Peter and Catherine II', feelings of gloom about the transience of human existence descended and he would recall the words of Feofan Prokopovich in his funeral oration of 1725: 'What are we doing? Are we really burying Peter the Great?' and cry out with the poet Bobrov: 'Where is the Great Man?...Where is the Immortal Woman?' But the next moment he would recall their deeds (*podvigi*) for the happiness and glory of millions and experience a great rush of love and gratitude, especially when he gazed on the military trophies surrounding the tombs, which made them 'even more precious for a Russian, even more sacred for each foreign pilgrim'. Again, the text seems to conjure up more recent trophies from the war with Napoleon.

Emotions of respect and reverence were sustained as the *strannik* continued his pilgrimage from the cathedral to Peter's first boat (*botik*) in its nearby pavilion, commissioned by Catherine the Great: 'No Russian can see this boat without a particular feeling of respect and reverence and no story teller can remain silent and not recount the tale.' The story of Peter's discovery of the boat in childhood duly follows, 'a testimony to future centuries that he was the author of the fleet in Russia'.[31] Commonplaces about the modesty of truly great men and little acorns growing into great oaks are repeated at the next sight on the route, Peter I's first cabin (*domik*). 'Its very simplicity arouses a sense of reverence [*blagogovenie*], for...nowhere perhaps does this Great Man appear more worthy of respect and admiration than in this humble cabin...From this hut he, the Conqueror of Charles, forced arrogant Europe to respect him', sentiments which again create an underlying association with more recent events in Europe. In Svin'in's view, echoing eighteenth-century rhetoric, the dwellings of truly great men were embellished by their inhabitants' deeds, not by gold and marble. 'In the eyes of him who values true greatness, the diamond and amber thrones of the Great Mogul are less precious than Peter I's wooden bench or Frederick the Great's chair, all stained with ink in his study in Berlin.'³² About another rowing boat of Peter's stored in the cabin, this one made with his own hands, Svin'in wrote: 'Often the monarch would get into this light craft alone and set off down the Neva as far as the galley harbour, turning up in places where no one was expecting him, thereby averting evil and encouraging useful activity. The handiwork on the boat would do credit to the most skilled ship's carpenter.'

In this section in particular Svin'in seems to conduct a dialogue with Batiushkov. In the opening of 'A Walk to the Academy of Arts' Batiushkov looked out across the Neva from the Admiralty and Palace Embankment side, northwards towards the Trinity Bridge and the *domik*. From the *domik* the painter-poet (*zhivopisets-poet*) – here Svin'in himself – takes in at a glance picturesque views of the Summer Garden, Marble Palace, Winter Palace, Admiralty and Stock Exchange, Peter-Paul Fortress and other sights. A pity, he concludes, that there is no visitor's book to hand, for 'the virtues of the object itself and the unparalleled views would give rise to new, happy outpourings of feelings and imagination'. Peter's hut combined the virtues of simplicity with the picturesque qualities of a rustic hovel.

The sensations described here appear to be primarily of a personal, solitary nature. The city could nourish the Romantic soul of the solitary dreamer far from the crowd, providing a rural landscape within the urban one. As Svin'in wrote in his earlier *Sketches*:

> you are here in the middle of an opulent city, yet respire the clear country air; you admire the activity of the population and the magnificence of the capital, and at the same time you enjoy the solitude of the hermit! You behold the beauties of simple nature and the astonishing works of art and human genius... Come here on a night in May or June... plunge your feelings into a melancholy sort of slumber; your imagination flies beyond the limits of this world and seems to hear the celestial music.³³

Equally, St Petersburg was capable also of inspiring communal civic pride in the company of like-minded 'wanderers'. In *The Sights of St Petersburg* and in other works, for example, Svin'in underlines the significance of communal strolling as a mark of civilization:

> We coincide with an observer, that public walks display the progress of fine taste in a capital city and the civilization of its inhabitants. Why, for instance, do not the savage people of Asia

like them? Yet they were the glory of polished Greece, where the inhabitants delighted to assemble in the sweet liberty and mixture of all ranks; where men illustrious by their birth or office, were not ashamed to walk together with the lower class, and enjoy with them the fine summer evening, where was to be found that harmony of minds, which is usually the result of general civilization.[34]

Immediately after the visit to Peter's cabin, Svin'in switches attention to a location situated several miles from the city centre, to the most ambitious but still unfinished of Peter's building projects, the palace at Strel'na, modelled on the palace of Versailles near Paris, which he visited in 1717. Again the experience combines admiration for Peter's bold project with a strong sense of his presence, in this case from some pine trees grown from seed that Peter collected in Germany and planted with his own hand on a man-made island formed by the canals opposite the palace's main façade. The visit to the dense grove growing on 'this sacred place' (*sviatilishche*) becomes a personal, almost religious experience for the lone traveller.[35] Not far from the main building stood a wooden palace, built by Peter after the pattern established at nearby Peterhof of having a grand palace for show and a more modest residence for comfort. Svin'in mentions the tsar's bed and a dresser containing his Dutch teacups, but the highlight of the visit was apparently an old lime tree in which Peter once had a tree house, from which he could look out to sea and entertain his friends.[36] The tsar's palpable presence is a key feature throughout this section.

The final volume of *The Sights of St Petersburg* was published in 1828, already three years into the reign of Nicholas I and three years after the disastrous Decembrist uprising had shattered some of the elite's hopes and illusions. The grand finale is the description of the palace and parks at Peterhof, on which Peter lavished funds and attention during the last two decades of his reign. Here Svin'in makes a conventional apology for his inadequacies as a writer, admitting that to describe Peterhof fully one would require 'the pen of the immortal bard of *Felitsa* and *Waterfall* [Gavrila Derzhavin] or the pen of the most eloquent of our prose-writers, the historiographer of the Russian Empire [Nikolai Karamzin]'.[37] He ends on a subdued note: 'One cannot leave Peterhof without feeling a desire to see the ruins of Menshikov's house and the oak not far from it planted by Peter himself' – two versts from Peterhof on the Strel'na road. Of Menshikov's house, now entirely disappeared, only one wall remained and that was about to collapse, while the oak was just a pathetic stump, crumbling from decay. Only ten years earlier the oak had amazed people with its girth. The hollow trunk had even accommodated a small summer house with benches, where Catherine II entertained Emperor Joseph II to tea.[38]

It is tempting to see post-Alexander, post-Decembrist angst in the references to the transience – *brennost'*, another favourite word – of the works of great men, but in fact Svin'in readily adapted to the tastes and priorities of Russia's new emperor Nicholas (himself a fervent admirer of Peter I) and shared his interest in Russian antiquities. Patriotism had always been in the forefront of Svin'in's writing. In 1814, for example, he proclaimed that the Cathedral of the Icon of our Lady of Kazan on Nevskii Prospect was 'entirely the work of Russian artists… No foreign hand was laid to it, every part of the structure and all that it contains, from the first nail to the admirable pictures, bas-reliefs, and statues are executed by Russian artists'.[39] As Richard Wortman writes, with reference to Svin'in's description of the coronation of Nicholas I in 1826, he gave 'full range to the personal voice of official sentimentalism', which stressed the importance of individual emotional contact either with the person of monarchs or with artefacts associated with them.[40] Such sentiments were wholly in keeping with the new reign.

In the patriotic climate created by Nicholas I and his successors, promoted by the official promulgation of the doctrine of Orthodoxy, Autocracy and National Feeling, Moscow was soon to overtake St Petersburg as a focus for national identity or pride. Svin'in himself caught and contributed to this trend, for example, in a guide to the main exhibits in the Kremlin Armoury. As he wrote, any Russian would not only marvel at the skilled craftsmanship of the objects but would see confirmed the eternal glory and power of his country and be stirred by the thought that every piece of armour had been stained with the blood of his fellow countrymen.[41] He also turned to ethnographic studies. In 1839 his *Pictures of Russia and the Life of its Many Peoples* (*Kartiny Rossii i byt raznoplemennykh eia narodov*) was published posthumously. The publisher's preface sets the work firmly in the context of Official Nationality. Russians of all walks of life were eager to know more about their fatherland, he wrote. The knowledge of various details about one's own past (*rodnoi stariny*) and love for it aroused national pride; such knowledge made people 'ready to achieve feats of courage for the glory of the fatherland... and to raise it to the summit of glory and power'.[42] Towards the end of his life, Svin'in's appreciation of Russian culture manifested itself in a project for a national museum (*Russkii Muzeum*) of art, an idea which pre-empted by a couple of decades the industrialist Pavel Tret'iakov's famous collection of Russian genre painting, historical subjects, portraits and landscapes.[43] Svin'in himself owned works by the Russian painters Anton Losenko, Dmitrii Levitskii, Orest Kiprenskii, Aleksei Venetsianov and Karl Briullov, the sculptor Martos and others, as well as coins and manuscripts.[44]

In turning away from the theme of St Petersburg in the final decade of his life, Svin'in was following a trend. For the rest of the nineteenth century more publications were devoted to Moscow and its monuments than to the imperial capital, as Classicism gave way to the Neo- or Pseudo-Russian architectural style. Various anniversaries, notably the bicentenary of Peter I's birth in 1872, periodically stimulated interest in Peter's city, but it was not until the early twentieth century that writers and painters, especially those associated with the World of Art group, once again turned their attention to the poetic and lyrical qualities of the 'capital of the North' that Pavel Svin'in tried to capture in his works.

Notes

1. P.P. Svin'in, *Dostopamiatnosti Sanktpeterburga i ego okrestnostei*, 5 vols (St Petersburg, 1816–28), I, 66. Volume 2 appeared in 1817, vol. 3 in 1818, and vol. 4 in 1821. A modern edition under the same title (in Russian only) was published in St Petersburg in one volume in 1997. All quotations are taken from the original, unless otherwise stated.
2. Svin'in, *Dostopamiatnosti Sanktpeterburga*, I, 38. Towards the end of his life Svin'in was working on a biography of Peter I, none of which appeared in print.
3. See *Russkii Biograficheskii Slovar'*, XX (St Petersburg, 1904), 218–21; *Dostopamiatnosti Sanktpeterburga* (1997), pp. 408–11.
4. *Vospominaniia na flote Pavla Svin'ina*, 3 parts (St Petersburg, 1818–19).
5. *Traveling across North America, 1812–1813; Watercolors by the Russian Diplomat Pavel Svinin*, transl. Kathleen Carroll (New York, 1992); P.P. Svin'in, *Opyt zhivopisnogo puteshestviia po Severnoi Amerike* (St Petersburg, 1815).

6. *Sketches of Russia Illustrated with Fifteen Engravings* (London, 1814), p. iii. Dedication to Her Imperial Highness the Grand Duchess of Oldenburg.
7. *Sketches*, p. 106.
8. Svin'in, *Dostopamiatnosti Sanktpeterburga*, I, 1.
9. *Kartiny Rossii i byt raznoplemennykh eia narodov* (Moscow, 1839), p. iv.
10. K.N. Batiushkov, 'Progulka v Akademiiu khudozhestv. Pis'mo starogo moskovskogo zhitelia k priateliu v derevniu N.', *Sochineniia* (Moscow, 1955), pp. 327–44. First published in *Syn otechestva* (December 1814).
11. Batiushkov, 'Progulka', pp. 330–1.
12. Lindsey Hughes, 'Monuments and Identity', in S. Franklin and E. Widdis (eds), *'All the Russias.' An Introduction to the Theme of National Identity in Russian Culture* (Cambridge, 2003). See also unpublished papers: 'Accidental Tourists: Seeing the Sights in 18th–early 19th-Century Russia' (BASEES Conference, Cambridge, 7 April 2001); '*Dostopamiatnosti* and *dostoprimechetal'nosti*: Russian "tourists" in 18th-c. Russia' (Workshop on 18th-Century Russia, Gargnano, Italy, 12–15 September 2001).
13. On related matters, see Lindsey Hughes, *Russia in the Age of Peter the Great* (New Haven and London, 1998), especially chapter 7.
14. M.M. Shcherbatov, 'Petition of the City of Moscow on Being Relegated to Oblivion' (1780s), in M. Raeff (ed.), *Russian Intellectual History: An Anthology* (New York, 1966), p. 53. The work remained unpublished.
15. A.I. Bogdanov, *Opisanie Sanktpeterburga* (St Petersburg, 1997), pp. 99, 371.
16. A. Pylaev, *Mysli kasatel'no monumenta Ekaterine Velikoi i pamiatnika Petru Velikomu kak osnovateliu Sanktpeterburga* (St Petersburg, 1809), p. 18.
17. *Ibid.*, pp. 82–3.
18. See Chloe Chard, *Pleasure and Guilt on the Grand Tour. Travel Writing and Imaginative Geography, 1600–1830* (Manchester, 1999). Also Bruce Redford, *Venice and the Grand Tour* (London and New Haven, 1996); Barbara Benedict, 'The "Curious Attitude" in Eighteenth-Century Britain: Observing and Owning', *Eighteenth-Century Life*, XIV (1990) 59–98; Dean MacCannell, *The Tourist: A New Theory of the Leisure Class* (New York, 1976). P. Ia. Chernykh, *Istoriko-etimologicheskii slovar' sovremennogo russkogo iazyka*, II (Moscow, 1993), 272, dates the first dictionary citation of *turist* from 1837, adding that the 'motherland (*rodina*) of these words is England'. *The Shorter Oxford English Dictionary* dates the first use of the English word 'tourist' to 1800: 'One who makes a tour or tours; especially one who does this for recreation; one who travels for pleasure or culture, visiting a number of places for their objects of interest, scenery or the like'.
19. *Opisanie rossiisko-imp. stolichnogo goroda S. Peterburga*, 3 vols (St Petersburg, 1794). See also H.F. Storch, *Gemälde von St. Peterburg* (Riga, 1793). O.S. Ostroi, 'S chego nachinalas' peterburgina? Opisanie putevoditelei po gorodu s momenta ikh vozniknoveniia do serediny XIX stoletiia', *Nevskii arkhiv*, III (1997) 481–91.
20. See, for example, Heinrich Christoph von Reimers, *St. Petersburg am Ende seines ersten Jahrhunderts. Mit Rückblicken auf Entstehung und Wachsthum dieser Residenz unter den verschiedenen Regierungen während dieses Zeitraums*

(St Petersburg, 1805); Johann Gustaf Richter, *Ansichten von St. Petersburg und Moskwa und einigen merkwurdigen Oertern der umliegenden Gegenden* (Leipzig, 1810). For a useful listing, *Istoriia Sankt-Peterburga-Petrograda. 1703–1917. Putevoditel' po istochnikam*, I, part 1 (St Petersburg, 2000).
21. G.F. de Fabre, *Bagatelles. Promenades d'un désoeuvré dans la ville de St. Pétersbourg* (St Petersburg, 1811). Other editions: Paris, 1812; in Dutch, 1813; in German, 1814.
22. *Sketches of Russia*, p. viii.
23. *Ibid.*, p. ii
24. *Ibid.*, p. iii.
25. Svin'in, *Dostopamiatnosti Sanktpeterburga*, I, 25–39. There is an extensive literature on this monument. For a useful summary, see A.L. Kaganovich, *Mednyi vsadnik. Istoriia sozdaniia monumenta* (Leningrad, 1982).
26. See, for example, Richard Wortman, *Scenarios of Power. Myth and Ceremony in Russian Monarchy*, I (Princeton, 1995), 160.
27. Svin'in, *Dostopamiatnosti Sanktpeterburga*, I, 36.
28. *Ibid.*, I, 68.
29. *Ibid.*, II, 18. The source of the quotation is Feofan Prokopovich's *O smerti Petra Velikogo. Kratkaia Povest'*, first published 1726.
30. Svin'in, *Dostopamiatnosti Sanktpeterburga*, III, 16.
31. *Ibid.*, pp. 23–4.
32. *Ibid.*, pp. 44–51. On the *domik*, see Lindsey Hughes, ' "Nothing is Too Small for a Great Man": Peter the Great's Little Houses and the Creation of Some Petrine Myths', *Slavonic and East European Review*, October 2003.
33. Svin'in, *Sketches of Russia*, pp. 107–8.
34. *Ibid.*, p. 37.
35. Svin'in, *Dostopamiatnosti Sanktpeterburga*, III, 53.
36. The wooden palace, which for many years stood derelict, home to a colony of feral cats, was restored and opened to the public in the late 1990s. At the time of writing the grand palace was being renovated as President Vladimir Putin's new presidential residence.
37. Svin'in, *Dostopamiatnosti Sanktpeterburga* (1997), p. 393.
38. *Ibid.*, pp. 406–7.
39. Svin'in, *Sketches of Russia*, p. 58.
40. Wortman, *Scenarios*, I, 282–3.
41. *Ukazatel' glavneishikh dostopamiatnostei, sokhraniaiushchikhsia v masterskoi oruzheinoi palaty* (St Petersburg, 1826), p. 1.
42. Svin'in, *Kartiny Rossii i byt raznoplemennykh eia narodov*, p. ii.
43. On collectors of Russian genre before Tret'iakov, see Rosalind P. Gray, *Russian Genre Painting in the Nineteenth Century* (Oxford, 2000).
44. When in 1834 debts forced Svin'in to sell most of his collection he felt confident of Nicholas I's support. 'Perhaps it will be the desire of His Imperial Majesty to order these things to remain in Russia?' he wrote, but Nicholas's response was to allow the collection to be sold abroad (*Traveling across North America*, p. 36).

9
Vreden sever: The Decembrists' Memories of the Peter-Paul Fortress
Patrick O'Meara

Although the Decembrist movement was by no means confined to St Petersburg, the northern capital was unquestionably its epicentre. Here from 1814 there were formed the first secret societies from which the movement grew; the initiating committee (*korennaia duma*) held its meetings in Petersburg; the Northern Society was based here, and the negotiations between the Northern and Southern Societies from 1823 were conducted in Petersburg. Similarly, it was here the publications which reflected Decembrist ideas were published (*Son of the Fatherland* [*Syn otechestva*], *Champion of Enlightenment and Philanthropy* [*Sorevnovatel' prosveshcheniia i blagotvoreniia*], *Nevskii Observer* [*Nevskii zritel'*], *Polar Star* [*Poliarnaia zvezda*], and *Mnemosyne* [*Mnemozina*]). Senate Square was the theatre of the uprising of 14 December 1825, and it was across the Neva, in the Peter-Paul Fortress, that the final act of the Decembrist tragedy was played out over seven months until 13 July 1826, when five members of the conspiracy were hanged. And it was from this time that the rest of the convicted Decembrists began their long journey to Siberia from which few would ever return.

Of the total number arrested – the figure is around 700 officers and civilians plus a further 700 soldiers – many either lived in Petersburg, were frequent visitors or were quartered with their regiments in the city's numerous barracks.[1] A recent publication lists some 200 Petersburg addresses associated with the Decembrists, including their homes, schools, barracks and places of detention during the investigation. Of the few buildings which have survived, most have been substantially rebuilt. Only a handful exist today in their original form.[2]

Of these, the best preserved is Domenico Trezzini's Peter-Paul Fortress, the city's first building and its most famous landmark. The fortress had been used as a place of incarceration since Peter's time and by the end of the eighteenth century was 'home' to many of the regime's political opponents. In the words of Aleksandr Murav'ev, a Petersburg-born member of the Northern Society: 'The fortress opposite the palace is a repugnant monument of autocracy, an ominous reminder that the one cannot exist without the other.'[3] Nevertheless, it remains the city's most iconic landmark and was constructed in the form of an elongated hexagon with six constituent bastions in turn linked by six walls or curtains (Figure 10).

This essay seeks through the Decembrists' memoirs to shed light on their experience of the Peter-Paul Fortress following their arrest, during the investigation and up to their sentencing in July 1826. A recent publication of thematically arranged extracts from the 30 or so memoirs available to us provides a very accessible source for doing so.[4] While they add considerably to our knowledge and understanding of the Decembrists and their aims, the memoirs vary considerably in matters of detail, recall and fact. Some are clearly more reliable and objective than others, though none of them is dispassionate. However, although they comprise the main source for this article, they are not *per se* its main theme. Rather, the essay focuses on memories of arrest, first interrogations, the prisoners' surroundings, their conditions (including solitary confinement and diet), how they communicated, prison chaplains and religious observance, their dealings with the Investigating Committee, and their reactions to the sentences handed down by the Supreme Criminal Court. Equally, the memoirs afford us insight into the challenges faced by the authorities of the Peter-Paul Fortress as they struggled to accommodate, feed and regulate a prison population which caused it uniquely in its history to burst at the seams.

Following the uprising on Senate Square on Monday, 14 December 1825, the authorities had little difficulty in identifying and rounding up those who had been involved. Some indeed gave themselves up. The conspiracy unravelled at such speed that within hours the first prisoners found themselves in the Winter Palace, subjected to a preliminary interrogation, in many cases by Nicholas I himself, and to the humiliating procedures of arrest and detention. They had little or no idea of what to expect from such a peripeteia and, not surprisingly,

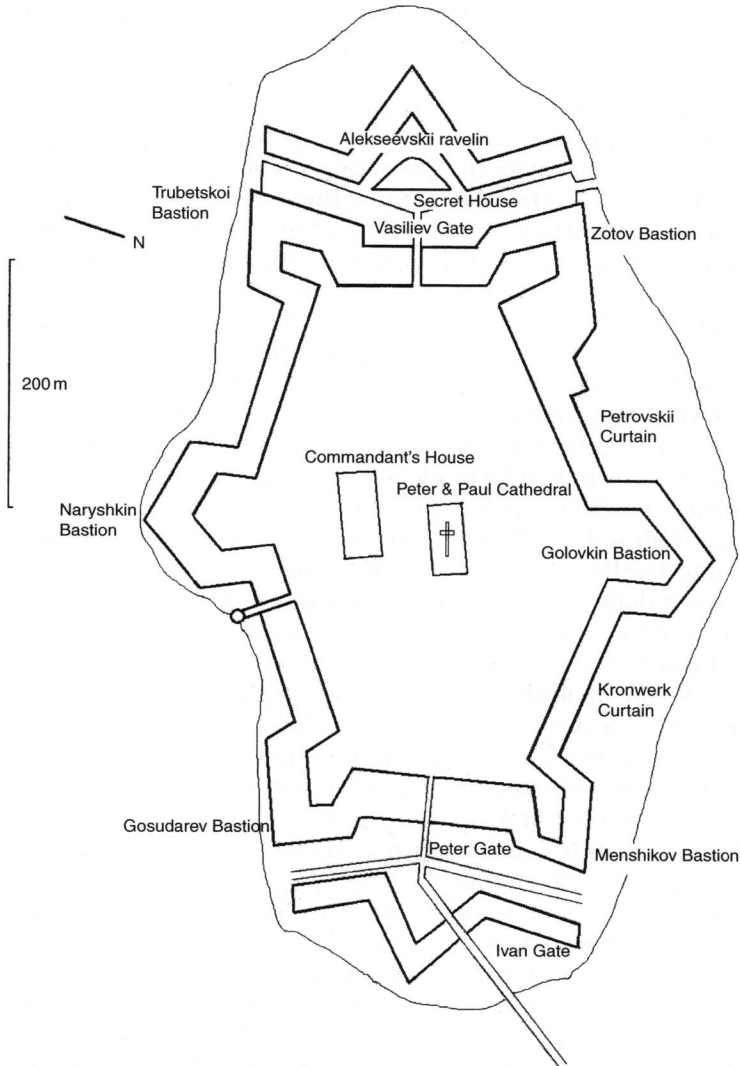

Figure 10 Plan of the Peter-Paul Fortress. (Drawn by Adam Jan Sadowski.)

many of them felt vulnerable and feared torture. This apprehension finds frequent reflection in the memoir literature.

Indeed, one member of the Investigating Committee, General V.V. Levashov, made apparently routine threats of torture when conducting preliminary interrogations in the Winter Palace. Among those he threatened with the use of 'ways of making him talk' was Mikhail Mit'kov. Mit'kov retorted that they were living in the nineteenth century and that torture in Russia had been abolished by law.[5] Similarly, Nikolai Lorer in his response to the same comment from Levashov, observed that in the nineteenth century torture 'does not exist in civilized states and I do not think that Nicholas I will begin his reign with what Elizabeth and Catherine II have abolished'. Nevertheless, Lorer still found himself reciting Luther's comforting words 'Gott ist mein fester Burg'.[6] While Ivan Iakushkin did not dispute General Levashov's bald assertion that 'there is torture in Russia', he insisted that he would not be naming any names; even so he admitted to being troubled by the threat of it, especially as he was being led off to his cell in the fortress after his preliminary interrogation by the tsar.[7] On his arrest, Aleksandr Beliaev and others were taken to a dimly lit room in the prison governor's house where he was certain they were to be tortured for 'such is the lot of autocracy that the most awful and cruel things are rightly or wrongly ascribed to it'. When another member of the Investigating Committee, General A.I. Chernyshev, also threatened Beliaev with coercive measures, the Decembrist assured him that his threats were idle since he knew very well the risk he had taken in joining the conspiracy: he would confirm only what the Investigating Committee already knew and no more. This defiant response, according to Beliaev himself, deeply impressed Chernyshev.[8]

More generally, Andrei Rozen claims that there were those who testified 'under coercion to what they themselves did not know only to rid themselves of the torment'. Specifically, he cites the use made of manacles and shackles, as well as deliberate deprivation of light, food and drink.[9] Mikhail Lunin recalled similarly that members of the Committee would resort to threats and abuse to extract confessions and denunciations, and that those who refused to co-operate were chained, and deprived of light and food.[10] His claim is supported by reference to the minutes of the Investigating Committee's meeting of 15 February, where the tsar's permission is sought to clap a recalcitrant prisoner (Iakov Andreevich) in irons. The measure had its effect: the minute of 25 April records the Committee's recommendation to Nicholas that Andreevich be released from his chains in view of his complete co-operation. On the other hand, Nicholas turned down the Committee's request to put Iosif Podzhio in chains.[11] Andrei Rozen recalls a remark about his neighbour, Mikhail Bestuzhev-Riumin, made to him by his guard to the effect that he had been manacled in order to extract a full confession from him. Bestuzhev-Riumin was indeed manacled from 11 February to 30 April.[12] It is safe to conclude, however, that torture, as broadly understood, was not used. The shock of incarceration and the miserable conditions endured in solitary confinement, including the use of chains, were such that there was no need for any additional torture chamber. And as we have seen, the threat of its use was enough to unsettle many.

The memoirists give a vivid impression of what they experienced in the first hours of arrest. Mikhail Bestuzhev was among those who voluntarily presented themselves at the Winter Palace. Quixotically, he demanded to see the tsar, but instead he was taken to the guardhouse where he was stripped of his uniform. It was burned at the entrance to the palace, a 'miniature *auto-da-fé*', as Bestuzhev put it, which was a foretaste of the 'farcical mass-burning' of uniforms which would follow the sentences in July 1826. His wrists were then bound so tightly with wire that pride alone prevented him from crying out. At that moment all he longed for was to die.[13] Nikolai Lorer was arrested in Tulchin on 23 December and brought to the main guardhouse of the Winter Palace on 3 January. There he had only just emptied his pockets prior to being searched when he was summoned to the presence of the tsar. But still standing on his dignity, he absolutely refused to be marched before him under escort on the grounds that he was still a major of the Russian army and not a convicted criminal. Confused, General Levashov relented and allowed Lorer to proceed to the Hermitage without the customary eight-man escort.[14] When, following his arrest on 14 December, Iakushkin declared to the tsar that he would name no names, Nicholas promptly ordered him to be chained so tightly that he could not move. The instruction was duly implemented and Iakushkin was put in manacles and shackles. He later discovered that they weighed 22 pounds (*funty*). On Palm Sunday (14 April 1826) the tsar at last ordered the removal of Iakushkin's shackles. After four months he had become so used to wearing them that he was now unbalanced by the weight of his manacles which pitched him forward. But these too were removed five days later, on Good Friday, 19 April.[15]

Aleksandr Murav'ev recalled how, on 10 December 1826, after almost a year of solitary confinement in the fortress, chains were placed on him, his brother Nikita, Ivan Annenkov and Konstantin Torson for their journey to Siberia. He points out that this was in breach of the existing law which proscribed the chaining of convicted nobles since this was tantamount to corporal punishment from which they were exempt.[16] Lorer describes how he was strip-searched, with apologies from the embarrassed major of the palace guard, E.M. Podushkin. He noticed tears welling in the eyes of the NCO as he replaced Lorer's uniform with its gold epaulettes with a 'motley, foul-smelling gown'.[17] Nikolai Basargin records the same humiliating process which involved the removal even of his wedding ring. He was left with two shirts, a jacket, a pair of trousers and a hospital gown.[18] By way of contrast, Vasilii Zubkov was told by his arresting officer that although he was supposed to strip-search him, he would just go through his pockets. Even this was done so perfunctorily that he missed a 100 rouble note which Zubkov had in a waistcoat pocket.[19] Writing about these events 30 years later, Petr Falenberg still recalled the 'grief and despair' produced by the 'destructive and unbearable operation' as he called the strip-search.[20]

Sergei Trubetskoi, however, makes no reference to being searched or manacled, though he is among many to recount the furious verbal onslaught the tsar subjected him to, threatening to have him summarily shot. Something of Nicholas's anger at Trubetskoi's betrayal can be felt in the instruction the tsar gave to General Aleksandr Sukin, commandant of the fortress: 'Trubetskoi is to be placed in the Alekseevskii ravelin and treated more severely than the others. In particular he is not to be allowed out of his cell and is to have no contact with anyone.'[21] As is well known, Nicholas was very shaken by 14 December and because he lacked a clear idea of how widespread the conspiracy was, he sometimes behaved in a quite paranoid way, according to some memoirists. One of the most bizarre instances of this is recorded by Mikhail Pushchin who had written a note to the main guardhouse, addressed to 'Peter-Paul Square'. It was returned to him with the instruction written in pencil in the emperor's own hand: 'Ask Pushchin why he calls the fortress a square'! Pushchin protested to Sukin that it was a completely innocent mistake and nothing more sinister than that.[22] Lorer describes how the furious tsar assured him that he was going to die and as he said this, drew his hand across his throat 'as though my head should become detached from my body then and there'.[23]

Many of those arrested were no strangers to the places of their initial detention either in the Winter Palace or the Peter-Paul Fortress: they found themselves in familiar surroundings, albeit in very unfamiliar circumstances. Lorer, for example, held initially in the main guardhouse of the Winter Palace, mused in his memoirs on the frequency of his guard duty there with his company, commenting on the 'same old green walls and the same armchair'. Indeed, from the memoirs it is possible to identify the very room in the Winter Palace where the first interrogations took place. Vasilii Zubkov clearly recalled the room where he was detained: it contained a clock decorated with a copy of Martos's statue of Minin and Pozharskii which had been erected on Red Square in 1818. From the next room Zubkov could hear Empress Aleksandra Fedorovna talking with her children including, presumably, the future Alexander II, then aged 7.[24] Following his arrest, Iakushkin, evidently a connoisseur of fine art, was surprised to find himself in the Hermitage, where he was taken to a large room in which hung a portrait of Pope Clement IX. During his first interrogation with General Levashov, he remembered admiring a painting of the Holy Family and afterwards passing through a room containing one of the Prodigal Son. The room Zubkov and Iakushkin referred to is located on the first floor of the Hermitage where pictures by Leonardo da Vinci are now displayed (room 214).[25] Beliaev describes in detail taking a walk prescribed by the fortress doctor along the ramparts, which afforded him an unexpected glimpse of 'long-forgotten' Petersburg. An immense wave of emotion swept over him when he saw carriages rushing along the familiar embankment, and the distant sight of Prince Dolgorukov's house triggered off happy memories of a distant childhood which contrasted so markedly with his present predicament. It was a sight too painful for him to have any wish to repeat.[26]

There are numerous references in the Decembrists' memoirs to the Alekseevskii ravelin and to the infamous 'secret house' (demolished in 1895) within it. The Alekseevskii ravelin, effectively a gaol within the gaol, which was situated at the extreme west end of the fortress, was separated from the main fortress complex by a moat and connected with it by a bridge through the Vasil'ev gate. The ravelin, dating from the reign of Anna Ivanovna, is a triangle-shaped reinforcement for the defence of the curtain and its gate is located between the Trubetskoi and Zotov bastions. According to the detailed account of the Alekseevskii ravelin left by Dmitrii Zavalishin, the bridge was guarded day and night at both ends. As he crossed it, Ivan Iakushkin recalled the words of Dante, 'Lasciate ogni speranza voi ch'entrate', just as Petr Falenberg did on approaching the Peter-Paul Fortress. The commandant of the ravelin, with its 20 single cells and complement of twelve guards, was an elderly Swede named Mikhail Lilienanker who was rumoured to be about 90 but was probably closer to the 78 or 70 years ascribed to him by Lorer and Iakushkin respectively.[27]

The 'secret house' was originally a wooden gaol added to the ravelin in the second half of the eighteenth-century and replaced during Paul's reign by a one-storey stone building containing 26 cells, 20 of which were used for solitary confinement.[28] It was here that Pavel Pestel' and Kondratii Ryleev were incarcerated in cells 13 and 17 respectively. Next to Pestel in No. 14 was Mikhail Bestuzhev, whose neighbour in No. 15 was his brother Nikolai. Between Nikolai Bestuzhev and Ryleev was Prince Aleksandr Odoevskii. Sergei Trubetskoi was placed in cell No. 7.[29]

The routine in the Alekseevskii ravelin as described by a number of its occupants would have been replicated in other parts of the fortress. The prisoners were referred to not by name but by cell number. They were taken out separately twice a week for walks in the little garden. According to Zavalishin's account, they could get up when they wished and within ten minutes they would be visited by the commandant and a detachment of guards. They brought in tea and hot water for washing, and while they cleaned out the cell, the commandant would enquire about the prisoner's health, but avoid any mention of current topics or even the weather. During the day the prisoners were served their meals on request up until 9 p.m. The cells were lit all night.[30]

The memoirs make frequent reference to the shortage of cells. With so many arrested – it was the first time in the Fortress's history that such a large number had been sent there for complicity in the same event – there was unprecedented pressure on the cell accommodation available. Even though 140 new cells were hastily constructed to house the Decembrist prisoners, there was still not enough room for all those detained. Instead, in early January 1826, almost all the lower ranks were sent to the inhospitable northern fortresses at Vyborg (300 men) and Keksholm (400 men), leaving only the 14 most actively involved to be accommodated in the Peter-Paul Fortress along with their arrested officers. In spite of this, on 19 February Sukin reported to the tsar that he did not have a single empty cell available.[31] The Investigating Committee was aware of Sukin's difficulty: four days earlier it had recommended to Nicholas the release of two prisoners, servants respectively of Pestel' and Vil'gel'm Kiukhel'beker, who were 'needlessly occupying cells'.[32] We learn from Mikhail Pushchin's memoirs that he was among the first to be housed in one of the temporary cells made from still wet pinewood which reeked of pitch. They were built on both sides of the corridor in the Kronwerk curtain, which is located on the north side of the Fortress, and were filled by new occupants as soon as they were ready. Other measures taken to meet the accommodation shortage included the conversion of the Fortress's garrison barracks to prison use by dividing up the dormitories into individual cells to ensure the prisoners' isolation rather than their privacy.[33]

We find numerous references to the conditions the Decembrists endured, in which diet and the psychological torment of solitary confinement figure prominently, as well as a wealth of information relating to the prison's regime and routine. Those who were kept busiest by the Investigating Committee, being required to attend interrogations, to confront other prisoners in support of their own testimony (*ochnye stavki*), and to provide written answers in their cells to lists of detailed questions, were actually among the most fortunate. They, at least, had some relief from the enforced solitude and boredom.

A common complaint was that, as prisoners on remand, the Decembrists were not allowed books. Nikolai Basargin movingly describes the mental anguish of his solitary confinement unalleviated by books, ink, pen or paper. Andrei Rozen points out that although in December it got dark early he was not given candles but that since he had nothing to read there was little point in having light anyway. He implies, however, that this was an initial ban only. This is borne out by the experience of Mikhail Pushchin, who relates how by the tsar's personal permission he had books brought to him. In addition, his sister was allowed to bring him a Bible for his spiritual comfort which meant, as he said, he did not languish in the Fortress. Aleksandr Gangeblov mentions having in his cell the latest volume of Pushkin's poems, published on 30 December 1825, a source for him 'of the greatest delight'. Mikhail Bestuzhev-Riumin amused himself by translating Thomas Moore's 'Irish Melodies'. Beliaev read French translations of the novels of Walter Scott and Cooper (presumably James Fennimore whose first novels *The Spy* and *The Pioneers* were published in 1821 and 1823 respectively). Incidentally, it was the novels of Walter Scott that Andrei Rozen particularly relished when, after he had been sentenced in July 1826, he was permitted to have books brought to him from his own library. Zavalishin claims to have had access to Greek and Latin books from his library to which he devoted up to 18 hours a day, determined under imminent threat of execution to pack in as much study as possible in the time left to him. Zavalishin need not have worried. He lived until 1892, dying just four months short of his 88th birthday![34] Smoking, like reading, was also controlled: while generally forbidden, especially in the weeks immediately following arrest, it was permitted to others as a special favour. Beliaev had his pipe and tobacco restored to him after five months' deprivation.[35]

Solitary confinement, by the tsar's express command the common experience of all Decembrist prisoners, is a leitmotiv of their memoirs. The strict segregation of the prisoners and their total isolation was, in Nikolai Lorer's view, calculated to weaken their resolve and their 'mental faculties'. As he recalled, writing in 1862, no one who has not experienced solitary confinement without books, tobacco, light and the sound of conversation can imagine its full horror. He was still trying to establish the identity of his neighbours in May when he was taken from his cell in the secret house of the Alekseevskii ravelin to the bath-house for the first time since his arrest (on 3 January). Nikolai Basargin deemed solitary confinement a 'mental torment crueller and more destructive than physical torture'. Even after 30 years of exile he could not think of his first day of imprisonment without a shudder when he was overwhelmed by a sense of hopelessness and despair, totally cut off from the outside world, 'alone before unlimited autocratic power...buried alive'. Although he spent only eight days in the Fortress, Vasilii Zubkov, like

Basargin, found his brief experience of solitary confinement a spiritual anguish worse than any corporal punishment and surely devised by the 'basest scoundrel'. He was tormented by the inactivity of prison routine, deprived of books and his pipe. Similarly, Aleksandr Beliaev, whose solitary confinement dragged on for 13 months, thought it a more terrible fate than capital punishment. He insisted it drove many to attempt suicide. He cites the case of Nikolai Zaikin who, tormented by the weakness he had shown in betraying Pestel' and his *Russkaia pravda*, tried to end his life by beating his head against the wall of his cell. A similar case is that of Aleksandr Bulatov, who had been recruited to the Northern Society only days before the uprising. Overwhelmed by despair, he went on hunger strike before fatally beating his head against the wall of his cell on 19 January. The Investigating Committee was very concerned by his death. The prison chaplain, Fr Myslovskii, told Ivan Iakushkin that every care was being taken to ensure that nobody else perished before the end of the investigation. Aleksandr Gangeblov heard that in June 1826 Petr Svistunov had ground up a glass lampshade in his cell and swallowed it. Andrei Rozen found solace only in positive memories of the past, disagreeing with Byron's contention that such recollections only aggravate present grief, and preferring instead Zhukovskii's line: 'He who has known happiness lived a hundred years.'[36]

The six-month investigation gave the Decembrists their first opportunity to reflect on what they had been involved in. Agonizing thoughts about the fate of Russia, for which they had sacrificed everything, merely made solitary confinement worse. Beliaev's memoirs dwell on the human cost of revolution. He felt they had nothing to be proud of, but should repent and pray for the innocent victims of their undertaking. Writing in the 1870s, it is perhaps likely that he was reacting to more recent developments in the history of Russia's revolutionary movement. Iakushkin recounts a conversation he had about the uprising with the Fortress commandant, A. Ia. Sukin, who insisted that Russia's vast territory could only be governed by an autocratic tsar: had they succeeded in their enterprise the subsequent chaos would not have been brought under control for a decade or more. Iakushkin replied that they had never expected to bring about instant change.[37]

Despite their solitary confinement, the Decembrists had 'companions' in their cells and their memoirs make frequent reference to them. Lorer, for example, writes of enormous water rats crawling over him at night, and Beliaev and Zubkov of black and red cockroaches in such huge quantities that the walls were almost completely covered in them. Zavalishin recalls that observing the crickets, cockroaches, red ants and mice running around their cells was among the prisoners' most common recreations.[38]

It is no surprise to find many references in the Decembrists' memoirs to food. Equally unsurprising is the fact that such references are almost uniformly negative. Complaints are typically about the poor quality of the food provided, rather than its paucity or total absence. However, Mikhail Lunin's claim that the withdrawal of normal rations was used as a punishment finds support in the minutes of the Investigating Committee. On 22 March the Committee 'found it necessary' to ask the tsar's permission to put the stubborn Stepan Semenov in chains and restrict him to bread and water both as a punishment and as a means of securing his co-operation. By 7 April the Committee was able to recommend Semenov's release from his chains and a restoration of the 'normal diet for prisoners of the Peter-Paul Fortress' in recognition of his 'frankness'.[39]

A few days after his arrest, still detained in the guard house, Andrei Rozen was able to persuade a friend, the colonel in charge of the guards that day, to send out for a change of clothes. His wife thoughtfully enclosed a soft leather cushion, but no food. He complained that all he was served over the Christmas holiday was half a bowl of cold soup and a thin piece of bread twice a day. This was a result, in his view, of a lack of concern on the part of the authorities combined with the 'countless number of unexpected guests who had arrived from all corners of Russia', all of whom had to be fed. Vasilii Zubkov fared rather better, at least on the day of his arrest when at 2 p.m he was brought a bowl of 'quite good' cabbage soup, some thinly sliced roast beef and two slices of bread, black and white, but no knife and fork. Cabbage soup features regularly in the recollections of other memoirists. During Lent it was supplemented with fish rather than meat. Otherwise on Sundays the prisoners were given slices of roast beef. Rozen remembers potato soup and huge quantities of bread. He refers to 'simple yet healthy and adequate' food. This view contrasts sharply with Nikolai Tsebrikov's description of 'the most disgusting food imaginable' consisting of buckwheat porridge covered in rancid green oil and soup made from rotting cabbage.

Like Tsebrikov, Lorer and others, Basargin recalled that the food was inedible. He existed almost exclusively on 'excellent' tea and rolls (the ubiquitous, timeless Russian *bulochka*), and on dried black bread and water. However, Nikolai Lorer recorded an extraordinary and welcome addition to the prisoners' diet after a routine inspection several months into the investigation by Adjutant-General Aleksandr Balashov. The very next day, and following Balashov's report to Nicholas, the prisoners noticed some improvements in their conditions. The most striking of these was the offer of a daily glass of vodka with a *zukuska* of spring onions. Lorer found the effect of this so intoxicating in his weakened state that he barely made it back to his bed! Still, it is curious that no other memoirist appears to have thought this improvement in the quality of prison life worth recording.[40]

Even more remarkable than this episode is the claim made by no fewer than three memoirists that sympathetic stallholders in a Petersburg market sent generous gifts of fruit to the Fortress for the imprisoned Decembrists. Thus, Nikolai Lorer's version tells of his guard, Sokolov, who went off in search of some lemons or even a pineapple, only to return an hour later with a large basket of oranges and the following story: 'When I went up to a stallholder I know, your honour, I asked him for some oranges. But once he realised they were for the unfortunate prisoners he filled a whole basket and took nothing for them, and added that I should go back to him for more when I needed them.' Both Nikolai Basargin and Dmitrii Zavalishin give similar accounts of the spontaneous generosity of an assistant in the Miliutin shop or market. While it is impossible to separate fact from myth, it remains curious that three memoirists record the same episode. The recurrent theme of fruit donated by Petersburg tradesmen to the imprisoned Decembrists points at the very least to a certain sympathy among ordinary townsfolk for those languishing inside the Peter-Paul Fortress.[41]

Interestingly, Basargin does not blame the authorities for the prisoners' poor diet, and quotes the sums provided for their upkeep: 5 roubles a day for generals, 3 roubles for staff-officers and 1r. 50 kopeks for junior officers. In his view, it was more likely 'as is usually the case here in Russia' that those charged with feeding the prisoners pocketed more than half the funds made available. This opinion is echoed in his account by Zubkov, who was convinced that the government intended to feed the prisoners properly. Aleksandr

Murav'ev was also sure that the money intended for their upkeep was embezzled by the Fortress personnel. He added that, according to a report of the Investigating Committee, the emperor had personally approved their dietary regime.[42]

The memoirs reveal that though young and fit at the time of their arrest, many Decembrists, physically weakened by the conditions and the poor diet, succumbed to sickness in the Fortress. Mikhail Pushchin, for example, was tormented by a virulent attack of piles for which G.I. El'kan, the Fortress doctor, prescribed frequent baths, an unusual privilege. Contrast this with the lot of Andrei Rozen, who had to wait until the middle of April for his first trip to the bathhouse. However, if anything, Pushchin's condition worsened and on the strength of his chronic ailment the emperor authorized his move to better accommodation in the Petrovskii curtain as well as a daily walk along the Fortress ramparts. Nikolai Basargin was also moved from his tiny, damp cell to a larger one because he suffered from recurrent chest pains and was spitting blood. In addition, he was prescribed a half bottle of beer with his dinner.[43]

Communication is an important theme for the memoir writers. It is clear that for many Decembrists, French was the language of choice. At this time it was still the unofficial language used at court and by the educated elite in preference to Russian. Rozen recalled that Mikhail Bestuzhev-Riumin had a better command of French than of Russian and was given a dictionary to assist him with his written responses to the Investigating Committee, which had to be in Russian. Basargin's memoirs give Mikhail Bestuzhev's words of farewell as he gave them himself – in French. Iakushkin reproduces more than one exchange with Levashov, his interrogator, in French, suggesting that the entire conversation was conducted in the language. However, when he was being transferred from the Fortress to the transit prison at Rochensalm in Finland in August 1826, he was warned by the duty officer that he should under no circumstances speak in French in the hearing of the escort officer. The penalty for doing so was withdrawal of rations. Iakushkin contrasted this ruefully with his childhood recollection of being sent to bed without supper for speaking to his sisters in Russian! As part of the terms of solitary confinement, the guards were strictly forbidden to talk to their charges, though this ban seems to have been only partly observed. Thus, Beliaev confirms that at first the guards were very taciturn, but gradually they revealed 'their Orthodox Russian nature' and often chatted to their prisoners.[44]

On one occasion, Lorer asked Dr El'kan ('the Jewish doctor') in German for some tea. The doctor replied tartly, and presumably in Russian, that foreign languages were not spoken in the Fortress and nor was tea served. Zubkov, who like Aleksandr Murav'ev, wrote his memoirs originally in French, describes how, on 15 January 1826, Iakubovich managed to whisper an introduction through his cell door, urging Zubkov to reply in French. Zubkov went one better by singing his answer lustily in French. Mikhail Pushchin recalled communicating in just this way with his neighbour, Sergei Krivtsov. Similarly, Gangeblov sang arias from Rossini and Weber to loud applause from his neighbour and without any objection from the guards. But when Mikhail Bestuzhev tried to check whether his brother Nikolai was his neighbour by whistling an operatic aria well known to them both, he was told by a guard that if he persisted in whistling he would be taken to a place where he would no longer feel like doing so. Instead, he developed a system of tapping on the wall which Nikolai understood and tried to use to contact Ryleev. But between them was Aleksandr Odoevskii who, despite the best efforts of Nikolai Bestuzhev, was unable to grasp it. Rozen recounts how prisoners passing his cell (No. 13 Kronwerk curtain) would call out greetings in French, such as 'portez vous bien 13'.[45]

Communication with the world outside the Fortress walls was even more strictly controlled. Although prisoners were not immediately denied the right to correspond, within days of the first arrests it became a privilege granted for co-operative behaviour. For example, although Sergei Trubetskoi had been condemned by a furious Nicholas to harsher treatment than the other arrested prisoners, he was granted as early as 28 December the tsar's permission to correspond with his wife on the recommendation of the Investigation Committee in recognition of his 'full and frank testimony regarding the membership and aims of the society'.[46] Nevertheless, by 17 February, the Investigating Committee was seriously concerned by the volume of mail from and to the prisoners which there was not enough time to monitor properly. It therefore proposed that permission to receive and send letters should be granted only to those who by then had been found guilty of relatively minor offences and had shown sufficient remorse. The content of such letters was to be restricted to family matters.[47] When he was given paper, pen and ink to write to General Levashov, Petr Falenberg took the opportunity to write a letter to his wife. It was returned to him sometime later with the comment that he was allowed to write only that he was alive and well: anything else was a state secret. But Dmitrii Zavalishin describes how he was able to bribe one of the soldiers to take letters for him and managed in this way to correspond unchecked with many of his friends in town. Unfortunately, he does not say how he obtained writing materials, nor how he managed to write letters unobserved, unless this was part of the deal he reached. Kondratii Ryleev was permitted to write to his wife just days after his arrest: she received his first letter on Christmas Day and their correspondence continued throughout the investigation right up to the eve of his execution. Early in February, an officer of the Fortress brought Iakushkin a letter from his wife telling him that she had given birth to a son and that they were both well, news which made him 'the happiest man in all Petersburg'. Occasionally, the tsar granted permission for visits from relatives. Andrei Rozen describes such an unexpected visit from his pregnant wife, Anette, on 13 May at 7 o'clock in the morning. It took place in the commandant's house and in his presence and lasted one hour. Similarly, on 15 June, the tsar's birthday, Ryleev was granted a meeting with his wife, which he had originally told her had been promised by the tsar as long ago as 28 December.[48]

The memoirs also record rare, chance encounters among the prisoners themselves. For example, Nikolai Bestuzhev recalls with great emotion a brief reunion with Ryleev who, on returning from a walk in the ravelin garden, passed the open door of Bestuzhev's cell just as his supper was being cleared away by a warder: 'Such an event was epochal in the Alekseevskii ravelin, where secrecy and silence, eavesdropping and spying relentlessly dogged the unfortunate victims buried alive there.'[49]

There is much to be learnt from these records about the role of prison chaplains and the prisoners' religious observance. The Orthodox priest P.N. Myslovskii, deacon of the Kazan Cathedral, is mentioned in a number of accounts. Iakushkin describes him as a government emissary, but one who 'crossed completely to our side'. When on one of his daily visits to his cell, Iakushkin asked him for his advice about the morality of naming his fellow conspirators to the Investigating Committee, Myslovskii told him that to do anything else would delay its work. But yielding to Iakushkin's heated objections, the embarrassed priest told him to act in accordance with his conscience. Mikhail Bestuzhev recalls his outrage at another priest, Stakhii, who urged him to co-operate with the Investigating Committee. Bestuzhev described the priest as an 'accursed weapon of despotism, a detective in a cassock'. While acknowledging the positive view of Myslovskii taken by many Decembrists, Basargin retained his doubts about him and thought his role as their pastor had been decidedly ambiguous. Aleksandr Murav'ev recalled that after interrogation by the Investigating Committee, the prisoners were immediately visited in their cells by a priest. The clear implication was that, given sufficient encouragement, their confessions might continue.[50]

Many of the prisoners found solace in religion, and some were 'born again'. Beliaev claimed that morning prayers, reading and rereading the Bible preserved his sanity; he wept on reading Christ's words 'V temnitse i posetite Mia' ('I was in prison, and ye came unto me', Matthew 25:36). Zubkov wrote that prayer was his only comfort. He would feel 'calmer and happier' after praying and did so frequently. There are numerous references to Easter (which in 1826 fell on 21 April) and to the ways it was marked inside the Fortress. The emperor allowed prisoners to have religious books, as well as pipes and tobacco, and to receive traditional Easter presents of *kulich* and sugar from the town's shopkeepers. But they were not allowed to attend the main event, the Easter eve service. Rozen describes how he had to content himself by exclaiming 'Christ is risen!' when at midnight the Fortress cannon saluted the arrival of Easter Day.[51]

The Decembrists' dealings with the Investigating Committee are referred to less than might be expected, given that this was the main reason for their imprisonment. Even so, their remarks provide useful insight into the procedures involved. Lorer, for example, describes how he was brought a list of 30 questions drawn up by the Committee, given pen and ink, and just an hour to write his answers. He was instructed to make no notes or drafts. Gangeblov was greatly surprised when handing his written testimony to the duty officer to be ordered to surrender all his draft answers as well. As Rozen recalled, it was solely for the purpose of writing answers to the Committee's questions that prisoners were issued with pens and ink. The amount of time prisoners spent helping the Committee with its enquiries varied enormously. Falenberg, for example, was troubled only once with a request to write answers to twelve questions. Expecting to be interrogated, he waited days, weeks and months for the summons but, rather to his regret, the call never came. In contrast, Zavalishin recalls how for five months barely a day went by without a call to the Committee or a request for written testimony.[52]

Many of those called before the Investigating Committee give the same account of how they were led blindfolded from their cell to the commandant's house. Here the blindfold was removed to reveal a brightly lit room with members of the Committee impressively arrayed in full formal dress, presumably, as Zavalishin suggests, 'to create an effect'.[53] The meetings of the Committee, the first of which was held on 17 December 1825, usually began at 6 p.m. and frequently ran until midnight or 1 a.m. so that most of the interrogations were in any case conducted during hours of darkness.

The memoirists give interesting details of the conduct of individual members of the Investigating Committee. Rozen, whose memoirs, along with those of Aleksandr Murav'ev and Aleksandr Beliaev, give the most detailed accounts of the Investigating Committee, considered General Chernyshev to be its most hardworking member, an indefatigable interrogator, with 'famous good looks' and a dandy of considerable charm. Similarly, Lorer refers to Chernyshev as 'le grand faiseur'. Both Rozen and Beliaev report the recurrent comment of the Investigating Committee's chairman, General A.I. Tatishchev, to a number of the accused. He delighted in pointing out to them that, whereas they had been ruined by reading the likes of Destutt de Tracy, Benjamin Constant and Jeremy Bentham, he had only ever read Holy Scripture yet proudly wore three stars. Those interrogated were required to sign a declaration that they had not answered under duress. Lorer complained that the Investigating Committee was biased from start to finish and was convinced that if there had been a proper defence of the accused, half of them would have been acquitted. Interestingly, he thought that A. Kh. Benkendorf conducted himself best of all, sometimes intervening to calm Chernyshev down when he lost his temper. On one occasion he reduced the Investigating Committee to laughter when he scolded them for being provoked by one of Lorer's co-conspirators with the reproof: 'Gentlemen, what are you shouting about? If you were now junior officers yourselves, you would undoubtedly be members of the secret society!' Like Lorer, A. Murav'ev expressed an unequivocally jaundiced view of the 'secret committee', calling it an 'inquisitorial tribunal, without respect or humane consideration, without the slightest trace of justice or impartiality and completely ignorant of the law'. He singled out for special condemnation the behaviour of Chernyshev and Levashov for whom 'all means were justified' and who routinely tricked their prisoners into betraying one another.[54]

A uniformly negative view of the Investigating Committee is to be found also in the historiography of the Decembrist movement, most notably among Soviet historians. An assessment of such views, let alone an evaluation of the Investigating Committee's conduct, is clearly beyond the scope of the present essay. Nevertheless, it seems worth pointing out that of the 1,400 officers, men and civilians originally arrested in connection with the investigation, only 121 were convicted and sentenced, and of these just five were executed. By way of contrast, if the Decembrist conspiracy and uprising were transposed, for example, to Stalin's Soviet Russia we can be certain that its participants would have been dealt with far more summarily and way more harshly. As it is, the actual outcome suggests that the Investigating Committee did not, as is commonly supposed, work hand in glove with the Supreme Criminal Court, but in fact retained a degree of autonomy. For even though the rule of law did not obtain in Russia in any meaningful sense, as the Decembrists themselves had frequently observed, the fact remains that the Investigating Committee did take six months to complete its work. This included 146 lengthy and meticulously documented meetings as well as 175 appended reports. In addition, the Committee's work generated over a million sheets of paper in the course of its investigation. All this suggests that it took its work seriously and did not rush to summary justice. That said, however, it cannot be denied that both the Investigating Committee and the Supreme Criminal Court were, of course, ultimately answerable to Nicholas. They were, therefore, entirely subservient to his vested interests in elucidating fully the Decembrist affair and duly punishing its ringleaders, despite the emperor's assertions to the contrary. Disingenuous to the last, Nicholas always insisted that he had simply allowed the law to take its course, particularly in the matter of the death sentences imposed. In fact, however, as we have seen, in all matters relating to the Decembrist prisoners, no matter how trivial, the tsar's permission or approval was routinely sought. This indeed would remain the position with regard to his 'amis du quatorze' until his death in 1855.

It is, finally, to the sentences which we now turn. The verdicts of the Supreme Criminal Court and the implementation of the sentences are variously detailed in numerous memoirs. Although 12 July 1826 was the day on which the prisoners would at last learn their fate, the prevailing mood as reflected in the Decembrists' memoirs was one of unbridled joy and elation as friends were reunited on being assembled to hear the verdict of the Supreme Criminal Court. In Basargin's words: 'Everyone was thrilled to be meeting if only for a minute after six months' solitary confinement.' When he was awakened early that morning by the duty officer bearing his officer's uniform, Beliaev was still expecting the firing squad. Instead, he was ordered to dress to attend the court for sentencing. Again, there soon followed 'embraces, conversations, explanations'. The mood changed once the full significance of their sentences registered. These ranged typically from ten to twenty years' hard labour in Siberia, followed by exile there for life. And morale plummeted further when news of the executions the following day spread round the Fortress.

After the sentences and in the days leading up to the emperor's departure to Moscow for his coronation, there was some expectation of an amnesty or, at the very least, a reduction in their sentences. However, as Basargin put it, to believe this was to misread the tsar's character. Nicholas had already decided that the convicted Decembrists were to be excluded from society and separated from their loved ones forever as an example to those who might be thinking of following their lead. In another passage, Basargin details a conversation he had with Mikhail Bestuzhev-Riumin on 11 July, who told him that he was surprised how he was suddenly being treated with such great consideration. The duty officer had arranged for him to be shaved for the first time since his arrest, something he had been unable to do for himself because of his manacles, and he had been taken for a walk in the commandant's garden. All he now hoped for was that he would be able to serve his anticipated terms of imprisonment and exile in the company of his closest friend and fellow conspirator, Sergei Murav'ev-Apostol. It clearly never occurred to him that both he and Murav'ev-Apostol were being prepared for the scaffold just two days later, 13 July. Beliaev, on the other hand, had always assumed that the investigation would be short and that its outcome would be death by firing squad for which he was mentally preparing himself.[55]

Sergei Trubetskoi describes how word of the executions spread among the disbelieving prisoners, and relates the account given to him by the priest Myslovskii, who was stunned by what he had witnessed. On 12 July, the day before the executions, Myslovskii had told Iakushkin not to believe any rumours that death sentences were to be carried out. The priest seems to have convinced many others of this too, so their shock was all the greater when it became clear that five of their number had in fact been hanged. Like Trubetskoi, Iakushkin did not believe it until he heard from Myslovskii his account of the terrible events of the early hours of 13 July. Myslovskii seems to have had a compulsive need to talk about them: Basargin reproduces in his memoirs a very detailed description based entirely on the account given to him by the distraught priest at 5 o'clock that same afternoon. The following day, 14 July, seven months to the day after the uprising, a service of purification was held on Senate Square, which was sprinkled with holy water.[56]

Nikolai Lorer, writing in 1862, was still seething with indignation at the decision of the Cavalry Guards regiment to go ahead on the evening of 14 July with the ball on Elagin Island in honour of their commander-in-chief, the Empress Aleksandra Fedorovna. 'They forgot that only the day before many of their comrades had been sentenced to death, and many were still languishing in their cells. Eternal shame on the officers of the Cavalry Guards regiment!' Against this, however, Aleksandr Murav'ev correctly states that the regiment's colonel, Count A.N. Zubov, categorically refused to attend the executions with the simple objection: 'They are my comrades and I will not go.' Two days later, on 15 July, Myslovskii celebrated a requiem mass in the Kazan cathedral for the five dead Decembrists. The sister of Murav'ev-Apostol, Ekaterina Bibikova, was praying in the cathedral and was astonished to hear Myslovskii, arrayed in black vestments, intone the names of her brother Sergei, and those of Pavel (Pestel'), Mikhail (Bestuzhev-Riumin) and Kondratii (Ryleev). By accident or design, the fifth victim's name, Petr Kakhovskii, was omitted from Iakushkin's list.[57] At any rate, the state had not at this early stage muzzled the Church, though all public reference to the executed and exiled Decembrists would soon be totally banned.

Not all those sentenced were transferred immediately from the Peter-Paul Fortress. It is clear from some accounts that it remained home to a number of convicted Decembrists for a year or even longer.[58] Their memoirs, along with those whose sentences of Siberian forced labour and exile were implemented within days, offer – as this essay has sought to show – valuable insights into life in the Fortress, so enlarging our knowledge and understanding of the Decembrists' fate after the uprising. They also shed considerable light on a unique chapter in the history of one of St Petersburg's most famous original buildings, the Peter-Paul Fortress.

Notes

1. A.D. Margolis, *Tiur'ma i ssylka v imperatorskoi Rossii: issledovaniia i arkhivnye nakhodki* (Moscow, 1995), pp. 61–2; G.A. Printseva and L.I. Bastareva, *Dekabristy v Peterburge* (Leningrad, 1975), pp. 228–30.
2. A.D. Margolis, *Peterburg dekabristov* (St Petersburg, 2000), p. 11. See 'Adresnyi ukazatel' ', pp. 457–505.
3. Printseva, Bastareva, *Dekabristy v Peterburge*, pp. 225–6.
4. Margolis, *Peterburg dekabristov*.
5. A.E. Rozen, *Zapiski dekabrista*, quoted in *ibid.*, p. 196.
6. N.I. Lorer, *Zapiski moego vremeni* (Margolis, pp. 205, 232).
7. I.D. Iakushkin, *Zapiski* (Margolis, pp. 208–10).
8. A.P. Beliaev, *Vospominaniia dekabrista o perezhitom i perechuvstvovannom* (Margolis, pp. 247, 252).
9. Rozen, *Zapiski dekabrista* (Margolis, p. 239).
10. Quoted in Printseva, Bastareva, *Dekabristy v Peterburge*, p. 235.
11. M.V. Nechkina (ed.), *Vosstanie dekabristov. Dokumenty. XVI (Zhurnaly i dokladnye zapiski sledstvennogo komiteta)* (Moscow, 1986), 102, 181–2, 106. See also N.Ia. Eidel'man, 'Zhurnaly i dokladnye zapiski Sledstvennogo komiteta po delu dekabristov', *Arkheograficheskii ezhegodnik za 1972* (Moscow, 1974), pp. 159–76.
12. Rozen, *Zapiski dekabrista* (Margolis, p. 238); S.V. Mironenko, *Dekabristy. Biograficheskii spravochnik* (Moscow, 1988), p. 23.
13. M.A. Bestuzhev, *Alekseevskii ravelin* (Margolis, *Peterburg dekabristov*, p. 201).
14. Lorer, *Zapiski moego vremeni* (Margolis, p. 203).
15. Iakushkin, *Zapiski* (Margolis, pp. 210, 226, 422). The manacles worn by the Decembrists weighed 9 kg and the shackles 12 kg.
16. A.M. Murav'ev, *Sibir'* (Margolis, pp. 339, 449).
17. Lorer, *Zapiski moego vremeni* (Margolis, p. 233).
18. N.V. Basargin, *Zapiski* (Margolis, p. 242).
19. V.P. Zubkov, *Rasskaz o moem zakliuchenii v Sankt-Peterburgskoi kreposti* (Margolis, p. 254).
20. P.I. Falenberg, *Zapiski dekabrista* (Margolis, p. 263).

21. S.P. Trubetskoi, *Zapiski* (Margolis, pp. 193, 413).
22. M.I. Pushchin, *Zapiski (1825–26)* (Margolis, p. 231).
23. Lorer, *Zapiski moego vremeni* (Margolis, p. 204).
24. Zubkov, *Rasskaz o moem zakliuchenii v Sankt-Peterburgskoi kreposti* (Margolis, pp. 207, 417).
25. Iakushkin, *Zapiski* (Margolis, pp. 208–9, 417–18). The pictures Iakushkin listed were, respectively, by Carlo Maratti (1625–1713), Domenichino (1581–1641) and Salvatore Rosa (1615–73).
26. Beliaev, *Vospominaniia dekabrista o perezhitom i perechuvstvovannom* (Margolis, pp. 252–3).
27. D.I. Zavalishin, *Zapiski dekabrista* (Margolis, p. 268); Falenberg, *Zapiski dekabrista* (Margolis, p. 263); Lorer, *Zapiski moego vremeni* (Margolis, pp. 344–5, 450); Iakushkin, *Zapiski* (Margolis, pp. 226, 422 n.3).
28. Printseva, Bastareva, *Dekabristy v Peterburge*, pp. 227–8.
29. N.A. Bestuzhev, *Vospominaniia o Ryleeve* (Margolis, *Peterburg dekabristov*, p. 223); Trubetskoi, *Zapiski* (Margolis, p. 219). A recent study of the precise location of the Decembrists' cells within the Fortress is M.V. Vershevskaia, 'Mesta zakliucheniia dekabristov v bastionakh i kurtinakh Petropavlovskoi kreposti', *Kraevedcheskie zapiski*, IV (St Petersburg, 1996) 91–141. For additional detailed information about life in the Fortress, see the memoir of N.P. Kriukov, who was released after three weeks with no charge against him. 'Rasskaz N.P. Kriukova o zakliuchenii v Petropavlovskoi kreposti', in B.L. Modzalevskii (ed.), *Dela i dni*, III (1922).
30. Bestuzhev, *Vospominaniia o Ryleeve* (Margolis, *Peterburg dekabristov*, p. 223); Lorer, *Zapiski moego vremeni* (Margolis, *ibid.*, pp. 344–5); Zavalishin, *Zapiski dekabrista* (Margolis, *ibid.*, p. 269).
31. Vershevskaia, 'Mesta zaklyucheniya dekabristov v bastionakh i kurtinakh Petropavlovskoi kreposti', p. 92; Printseva and Bastareva, *Dekabristy v Peterburge*, pp. 228–30. The Investigating Committee drew up the arrangements for the transfer of prisoners for the tsar's approval at its meeting of 7 January 1826 (*Vosstanie dekabristov. Dokumenty*, XVI, 236).
32. *Vosstanie dekabristov. Dokumenty*. XVI, 102, minutes of 15 February.
33. Pushchin, *Zapiski (1825–26)* (Margolis, p. 231); A.M. Murav'ev *S.-Peterburgskaia krepost'* (Margolis, p. 271).
34. Basargin, *Zapiski* (Margolis, *ibid.*, p. 243); Rozen, *Zapiski dekabrista* (Margolis, pp. 199, 237, 351); Pushchin, *Zapiski* (Margolis, p. 231); A.S. Gangeblov, *Vospominaniia dekabrista* (Margolis, pp. 266, 429 n.6); Basargin, *Zapiski* (Margolis, p. 309); Beliaev, *Vospominaniia dekabrista o perezhitom i perechuvstvovannom* (Margolis, p. 349); D.I. Zavalishin, *Zapiski dekabrista* (Margolis, p. 270).
35. Rozen, *Zapiski dekabrista* (Margolis, p. 201); Basargin, *Zapiski* (Margolis, p. 245); Beliaev, *Vospominaniia dekabrista o perezhitom i perechuvstvovannom* (Margolis, p. 349).
36. Lorer, *Zapiski moego vremeni* (Margolis, pp. 234–45); Basargin, *Zapiski* (Margolis, pp. 242–3); Zubkov, *Rasskaz o moem zakliuchenii v Sankt-Peterburgskoi kreposti* (Margolis, pp. 256–7); Beliaev, *Vospominaniia dekabrista o perezhitom i perechuvstvovannom* (Margolis, pp. 350, 249, 426);

Iakushkin, *Zapiski* (Margolis, p. 229); Gangeblov, *Vospominaniia dekabrista* (Margolis, p. 267); Rozen, *Zapiski dekabrista* (Margolis, pp. 238, 424, n.10).
37. N.R. Tsebrikov, *Vospominaniia o Kronverkskoi kurtine* (Margolis, p. 242); Beliaev, *Vospominaniia dekabrista o perezhitom i perechuvstvovannom* (Margolis, p. 250); Iakushkin, *Zapiski* (Margolis, p. 228).
38. Lorer, *Zapiski moego vremeni* (Margolis, *ibid.*, p. 234); Zubkov, *Rasskaz o moem zakliuchenii v Sankt-Peterburgskoi kreposti* (Margolis, p. 256); Beliaev, *Vospominaniia dekabrista o perezhitom i perechuvstvovannom* (Margolis, p. 247); Zavalishin, *Zapiski dekabrista* (Margolis, p. 269).
39. *Vosstanie dekabristov. Dokumenty*, XVI, 138, minute of meeting 84; 160, minute of meeting 99.
40. Rozen, *Zapiski dekabrista* (Margolis, pp. 200, 237–8); Zubkov, *Rasskaz o moem zakliuchenii v Sankt-Peterburgskoi kreposti* (Margolis, pp. 206, 255–6, 261); Tsebrikov, *Vospominiia o Kronverskskoi kurtine* (Margolis, p. 241); Trubetskoi, *Zapiski* (Margolis, p. 219); Iakushkin, *Zapiski* (Margolis, pp. 226, 228, 229); Lorer, *Zapiski moego vremeni* (Margolis, pp. 234–5); Basargin, *Zapiski* (Margolis, p. 245).
41. Lorer, *Zapiski moego vremeni* (Margolis, p. 236); Basargin, *Zapiski* (Margolis, p. 246); Zavalishin, *Zapiski dekabrista* (Margolis, p. 268).
42. Basargin, *Zapiski* (Margolis, p. 245); Zubkov, *Rasskaz o moem zakliuchenii v Sankt-Peterburgskoi kreposti* (Margolis, pp. 256–7); Murav'ev S.-*Peterburgskaia krepost'* (Margolis, p. 271).
43. Pushchin, *Zapiski (1825–26)* (Margolis, pp. 231–2); Rozen, *Zapiski dekabrista* (Margolis, p. 239); Basargin, *Zapiski* (Margolis, p. 244).
44. Basargin, *Zapiski* (Margolis, p. 309); Rozen, *Zapiski dekabrista* (Margolis, p. 238); Iakushkin, *Zapiski* (Margolis, pp. 208, 228, 338); Lorer, *Zapiski moego vremeni* (Margolis, p. 234); Beliaev, *Vospominaniia dekabrista o perezhitom i perechuvstvovannom* (Margolis, p. 248).
45. Lorer, *Zapiski moego vremeni* (Margolis, p. 234); Zubkov, *Rasskaz o moem zakliuchenii v Sankt-Peterburgskoi kreposti* (Margolis, p. 258); Pushchin, *Zapiski (1825–26)* (Margolis, p. 232); Gangeblov, *Vospominaniia dekabrista* (Margolis, p. 267); Bestuzhev, *Alekseevskii ravelin* (Margolis, p. 225); Bestuzhev, *Vospominaniia o Ryleeve* (Margolis, p. 223); Rozen, *Zapiski dekabrista* (Margolis p. 282).
46. *Vosstanie dekabristov. Dokumenty*, XVI, 38.
47. *Ibid.*, p. 106.
48. Falenberg, *Zapiski dekabrista* (Margolis, p. 264); Zavalishin, *Zapiski dekabrista* (Margolis, p. 270); Patrick O'Meara, *K.F. Ryleev. A Political Biography of the Decembrist Poet* (Princeton, 1984), pp. 255, 290; Iakushkin, *Zapiski* (Margolis, p. 229); Rozen, *Zapiski dekabrista* (Margolis, p. 240).
49. Bestuzhev, *Vospominaniia o Ryleeve* (Margolis, p. 223); O'Meara, *K.F. Ryleev. A Political Biography of the Decembrist Poet*, pp. 293–4.
50. Iakushkin, *Zapiski* (Margolis, p. 229); Bestuzhev, *Alekseevskii ravelin* (Margolis, p. 224); Basargin, *Zapiski* (Margolis, p. 287); Murav'ev, *Sledstvennyi komitet* (Margolis, p. 293).

51. Beliaev, *Vospominaniia dekabrista o perezhitom i perechuvstvovannom* (Margolis, pp. 249–50); Zubkov, *Rasskaz o moem zakliuchenii v Sankt-Peterburgskoi kreposti* (Margolis, p. 257); Rozen, *Zapiski dekabrista* (Margolis, pp. 239–40).
52. Lorer, *Zapiski moego vremeni* (Margolis, p. 234); Gangeblov, *Vospominaniia dekabrista* (Margolis, p. 267); Rozen, *Zapiski dekabrista* (Margolis, p. 241); Falenberg, *Zapiski dekabrista* (Margolis, p. 264); Zavalishin, *Zapiski dekabrista* (Margolis, p. 270).
53. Zavalishin, *Zapiski dekabrista* (Margolis, p. 268); cf. Basargin's account (Margolis, pp. 287–8) which is remarkably similar in its detail and conclusion.
54. Rozen, *Zapiski dekabrista* (Margolis, pp. 281–2); Lorer, *Zapiski moego vremeni* (Margolis, pp. 284–5); Murav'ev, *Sledstvennyi komitet* (Margolis, p. 292).
55. Basargin, *Zapiski* (Margolis, pp. 309, 341, 247–9, 311); Beliaev, *Vospominaniia dekabrista o perezhitom i perechuvstvovannom* (Margolis, p. 318).
56. Trubetskoi, *Zapiski* (Margolis, p. 304); Iakushkin, *Zapiski* (Margolis, pp. 306–7); Basargin, *Zapiski* (Margolis, pp. 309–12).
57. Lorer, *Zapiski moego vremeni* (Margolis, pp. 315–16); Murav'ev, *Prigovor* (Margolis, p. 317); Iakushkin, *Zapiski* (Margolis, p. 308).
58. Beliaev, *Vospominaniia dekabrista o perezhitom i perechuvstvovannom* (Margolis, p. 349); Rozen, *Zapiski dekabrista* (Margolis, p. 351).

Index

Abrosimov, Grigorei (merchant), 93
Academy of Arts, 50, 149, 151
Academy of Sciences, 16, 17, 18, 19, 26, 31, 42
actresses, 4, 119–43
  and audiences, 119–26
  and prostitution, 133–42
  sexual relationships of, 124–37
Admiralty, 2, 3, 11, 16, 36, 39, 43, 51, 56, 72, 96, 159
Admiralty Side (Island), 41, 50, 51, 52, 54, 55, 87, 151
Ador, Jean (goldsmith), 85, 98
Adrian, Patriarch, 13
Afonaseva, Avdotia (naval widow), 95
Aleksandra Fedorovna, Empress, 171, 185
Aleksandrovskaia, O.A. (geographer), 17
Alekseev, Ivan (peasant), 93
Alekseev, Matvei (serf), 93
Alekseev, Vasilei (merchant), 83–4
Alexander I, Emperor, 4, 64, 67, 150, 151, 152, 153, 155
Alexander Nevskii Monastery, 14, 43, 90, 157
Alexandria, 6
Alfieri, Vittorio (author), 74–5, 76
Algarotti, Francesco (author), 4, 72–4, 75, 77, 78
Amburger, Fedor (merchant), 85
America, 149, 150
Amsterdam, 3, 36, 71, 154
Andreeva, Stepanida (craftsman's widow), 95
Andreevich, Iakov (Decembrist), 169
Anglo-Russian Commercial Treaty (1734), 33–5, 66
Anna Ivanovna, Empress, 3, 33, 34, 56, 58, 62, 65, 172

Annenkov, Ivan (Decembrist), 170
Antipeva, Maria (craftsman's widow), 95
Apaishchikov, Ivan (merchant), 92–3, 94
Arapov, P.N. (playwright), 130
Archetti, Cardinal, 76, 78
architecture, 10, 87, 148–62
Asch, Baron Georg (physician), 85, 98
Asenkova, Aleksandra (actress), 130, 133, 134, 142
assemblies, 9
audiences, theatre, 119–24
Avtanomov, Fedor (merchant), 93
Azarevicheva, Mariia (dancer), 130
Azarevicheva, Nadezhda (actress), 130

Baklanov, Fedor (merchant), 93
Balashov, Aleksandr (soldier), 177
Baltimore, Charles Calvert, 5th Lord (traveller), 72
Barmin, Il'ia (merchant), 86
Basargin, Nikolai (Decembrist), 170, 173, 174, 175, 177, 178, 181, 184, 185
Batiushkov, K.N. (poet), 130, 150–1, 152, 155, 159
Baxter, Alexander (merchant), 66
Beliaev, Aleksandr (Decembrist), 168, 171, 174, 175, 176, 178, 181, 182, 184
Bel'o, Agrippina (dancer), 128, 133
Benkendorf, A.Kh. (Investigating Committee for Decembrists), 182
Bentham, Jeremy, 182
Berdiaev, Nikolai (philosopher), 13
Berezin, Aleksandr (merchant), 93
Bergholz, W.F. (diplomat), 52

Bering Strait, 18
Bering, Vitus (explorer), 18
Berlin, 154
Bestuzhev-Riumin, A.P. (statesman), 59, 62
Bestuzhev-Riumin, Mikhail (Decembrist), 169, 172, 174, 178, 179, 181, 184, 185
Bestuzhev-Riumin, Nikolai (Decembrist), 172, 179, 180
Bezborodko, A.A. (statesman), 140
Biron, E.J. (favourite), 33
Blumentrost, L.L. (Academy), 27
Bobrov, Sergei (poet), 158
Boehtlingk, Login (merchant), 85
Bogdanov, A.I. (author), 152–3
Boltenhagen, D.K. (architect), 68
Bonar, Thomas (merchant), 66, 85
Book of City Inhabitants, 80–97
Borisov, Kozma (merchant), 86
Bottom, John (clockmaker), 85
Bragin, Vasilei (merchant), 93
Brianskii, Ia. (actor), 125
bridges
    Blagoveshchenskii (also Lt Schmidt, Nikolaevskii), 50, 52
    Isaakievskii (pontoon), 56, 59
    Kriukov, 62
British in St Petersburg, 19
Briullov, Karl (artist), 162
Brogden, James (merchant), 67
Bronze Horseman (statue), 50, 53, 151, 155
Bulatov, Aleksandr (Decembrist), 175
Byron, Lord George (poet), 175

canals
    Admiralty, 52
    Galley, 52, 56, 57, 62
    Kriukov, 52, 56, 58, 62, 66
Carr, Sir John (traveller), 140
cartography, 3, 15–24, 30–3, 35–45
Casanova, Giacomo, 77
Casti, Giovanna Batista (author), 75, 77

Castle Forbes (Ireland), 31, 35
Catherine I, Empress, 15
Catherine II, the Great, 2, 3, 62, 66, 74, 76, 77, 80, 81, 87, 94, 137, 152, 158, 161, 168
    as legislatress, 80–1, 97, 99–115
Cayley, John (British consul), 65, 66, 67
ceremonies, 14,
Charles XII, 155, 158
Charter to the Nobility, 80, 104, 107
Charter to the Towns, 4, 80, 81, 100–15
Chernyshev, A.I. (Investigating Committee for Decembrists), 168, 182, 183
Chevallier, Mme (actress), 141
Chicherin, I.I. (police chief), 115
churches
    English, 59, 64, 66, 68
    St Isaac of Dalmatia, 50, 53, 56, 59
    Our Lady of Kazan, 161
    Peter and Paul, 157
Clark, Alexander (merchant), 68
Colley, Linda (historian), 15
Commission for the Orderly Development of St Petersburg, 58
conduct books, 137
Constant, Benjamin, 182
Constantinople, 6
Cooper, James Fennimore (novelist), 174
courts, 104, 105, 108–9, 111–12, 114
Coxe, Rev. William (author), 65
Cozens, Richard (shipbuilder), 53, 56, 58, 65
Cracraft, James (historian), 10, 39

D'Alembert, Jean le Rond, 120
Danilova, Mar'ia (dancer), 123
d'Anville, J.B. (geographer), 24
Decembrists, 5, 64, 165–86
    and communication, 178–80
    and food, 176–8
    homes in capital, 165

Decembrists – *continued*
  and illness, 178,
  and Investigating Committee, 182–3
  prison routine, 172–4
  and religion, 180–1
  sentences on, 184–6
  and solitary confinement, 174–6
  threats of torture against, 168–9
Delisle, Guillaume (geographer), 16, 17, 19, 23
Delisle, J.N. (astronomer), 20, 22–3, 24
Demidov, N.N., 56, 58, 59
Denisov, Ivan (merchant), 86
Derzhavin, Gavrila (poet), 160
Devier, Anton (police chief), 9
districts of city, 83–4, 87–8, 90–2, 95–7, 102
Diurova, Liubov' (actress), 130, 131
Dodgshon, Robert (social scientist), 7
duma (town council), 4, 101–2, 103–4, 109, 113–14

educational institutions, 12, 107, 110
Egorov, I.A. (historian), 36, 39, 41
Eletsk, 84
Eliakov, Ivan (engraver), 59
Elizabeth, 139, 152, 168
El'kan, G.I. (doctor), 178, 179
Elliger, Ottomar (artist), 58, 59
England, 150
English Club, 67
English Embankment, 1, 3, 50–70
  in Alexander's reign, 64–5
  in Anna's reign, 56–9
  British occupants on, 65–7
  in Catherine's reign, 62–4
  in Elizabeth's reign, 59–62
  engravings of, 58–9, 62–3
  granite construction of, 62
  naming of, 65
  in Petrine times, 51–6
engravings, 11, 58–9, 62–3,

Euler, Leonhard (mathematician), 17, 20, 23, 24
expeditions, 17–18, 23
Ezhova, Ekaterina (actress), 130, 131, 132, 133

Fabre, M. (author), 154
Falconet, Etienne (sculptor),155–6
Falenberg, Petr (Decembrist), 170, 172, 180, 182
Farquharson, Henry (mathematician), 16, 19, 21,
Felker, Anna-Kunigunda (procuress), 139
Fel'ten, Iurii (architect), 62
fires, 58, 65–6, 87
Florence, 154
Fontanesi, Francesco (artist), 76
Fonvizin, Denis (author), 68
Forbes, George, Lord, 3, 31, 33–5, 45, 46
Forbes/Maas chart, 33, 42–6
foreign specialists, 10, 19, 33, 72, 85
foreigners, 13, 17, 82, 100–1, 119, 138, 154–5
France, 152
Frederick the Great, 158

Gagarin, I.A., 132
Gagarin, S.S. (theatre official), 128
Galley Wharf, 52, 54, 55, 59,
Gangeblov, Aleksandr (Decembrist), 174, 175, 179, 181
geography, 15–26
George I, 34
George II, 33, 34, 45,
Georgi, J. G. (historian), 90, 153, 155
Germany, 160
Giddens, Anthony (social scientist), 9
Glen, William (merchant), 66, 68
Glinka, V.A. (architect), 64
Glushkovskii (ballet-master), 128
Gogol', N.V. (author), 149
Gonzaga, Pietro (artist), 76, 77

Granard, Earls of, 31, 33, 35, 45
Greig, Sara, 66, 70
Griboedov, A.S. (dramatist), 130, 131, 141
guidebooks, 5, 153
Gulf of Finland, 33, 44, 45, 46, 50

Hanway, Jonas (merchant), 66
Hodgkin, Henry (merchant), 65
Homann, J.B. (cartographer), 36, 39, 41–2
Honourable Mirror of Youth, 9

Iakushkin, I.D. (Decembrist), 169, 171, 175, 178, 180, 181, 185
Iaroslavl', 101, 107, 110
impressions of city:
  by Alfieri, 74
  by Algarotti, 73–4
  by Gonzaga, 76
  by de la Motraye, 55
  by Svin'in, 148–62
  by Weber, 54–5
Irkutsk, 140
Isakova, Ekaterina (actress), 120
Istomina, Avdot'ia (dancer), 124, 126, 136
Italians in St Petersburg, 3–4, 71–8
Ivanov, F.F. (author), 120

Jones, Robert E. (historian), 6, 30, 105
Joseph II, 161

Kaganov, Grigorii (historian), 11, 14,
Kaiserling, G.K. (Academy), 23
Kakhovskii, Petr (Decembrist), 185
Kalashnikov, Semen (official), 83, 84, 96
Kaluga, 93, 109, 110
Kamchatka, 18
Kapitonov, Leontii (merchant), 83
Karamzin, N.M. (historian), 149, 150, 160
Karatygin, V.A. (actor), 136
Khar'kov, 101

Khomuninnikov, Aleksandr (landowner), 94
Kiprenskii, Orest (artist), 162
Kirilov, I.K. (administrator), 23–4
Kiukhel'beker, Vil'gel'm (Decembrist), 173
Klausing, Henry (merchant), 66
Knipper, Karl (theatre manager), 135
Kokoshkin, F.F. (theatre director), 127
Kolosova, Aleksandra (actress), 124, 132
Kolyvan, 106
Konovitsyn, P.P. (administrator), 107, 110
Konstantin Pavlovich, Grand Duke, 127, 128
Korobov, Ivan (architect), 1
Kotlin Island, 44
Kozlov, N.Ia. (diplomat), 149
Krivtsov, Sergei (Decembrist), 179
Kronstadt, 31, 33, 44, 45, 46, 73, 83
Krylova, Mariia (dancer), 125, 126
Kulikova, Praskov'ia (actress), 134, 135, 136, 141, 142
Kutaisov, I.P. (favourite), 141

La Motraye, Aubry de (traveller), 55
Lavals, I.S. and A.G., 64
law and order, 103–4
Le Blond, J.-B.A. (architect), 36–7, 39, 40, 41, 42, 47–8, 53
Le Nôtre, André (architect), 36
Lebina, N.B. (historian), 140
Leibniz, G.W. von, 17
Leonardo da Vinci, 171
Lespinasse, Charles (artist), 59
Levashov, V.V. (Investigating Committee for Decembrists), 168, 169, 171, 178, 180, 183
Levitskii, Dmitrii (artist), 162
Lewitter, L.R. (historian), 15
Lilienanker, Mikhail (soldier), 172
Lincoln, W. Bruce (historian), 6, 13
Lisaevich, I. (historian), 36, 41
Lobanov-Rostovskii, Prince, 135

Locatelli, Francesco (author), 72
Lomonosov, M.V. (polymath), 17, 78
London, 154
Lorer, Nikolai (Decembrist), 168, 169, 170, 171, 174, 176, 177, 179, 181, 183, 185
Losenko, Anton (artist), 162
Lotman, Iu.M., 71, 72, 126, 137
Lunin, Mikhail (Decembrist), 168, 175
Luther, Martin, 168

Maas, Abraham (cartographer), 33, 47
magistracy, 84, 105, 113–14
Maikov, A.A. (theatre director), 130, 136
Makhaev, Mikhail (artist), 59, 62
Mansurov, P.B., 125, 126
mapmaking, 18–25, 30–45
Markov, A.V. (official), 115
Marrese, Michelle (historian), 94
Marselius, Christoph (artist), 11, 58
Mattarnovi, G.-J. (architect), 53
Menshikov, Prince Aleksandr, 3, 53, 54, 55, 56, 57, 64, 160–1
Messerschmidt, D.-G. (physician), 17
Miloradovich, M.A. (governor-general), 129, 130, 131, 132, 133, 136
Mit'kov, Mikhail (Decembrist), 168
Moore, Thomas (poet), 174
Moscow, 1, 7, 10, 11, 12, 14, 15, 87, 101, 102, 103, 104, 109, 135, 136, 150, 151, 152, 162
Murav'ev, Aleksandr (Decembrist), 166, 170, 178, 179, 181, 182, 183, 185
Murav'ev, Nikita (Decembrist), 170
Murav'ev-Apostol, Sergei (Decembrist), 184, 185
Musin-Pushkin, V.V., 132
Myslovskii, P.N. (chaplain), 175, 180–1, 185

Napoleon, 150, 155, 158
Naryshkin, A.L. (theatre administrator), 120, 127, 132
Naryshkin, A.L., 56, 58
Naval Academy, 12, 16, 19, 20, 26
naval supplies, 33–4
Navigation School (Moscow), 12, 19, 20
Nerchinsk, 140
Nevskii Prospekt, 14, 58, 67, 161
New Holland (*Novaia Gollandiia*), 52
Nicholas I, 115, 160, 161
and Decembrists, 164, 166, 169–71, 179, 183, 184
as Grand Duke, 134
noble assemblies, 104, 106–7
Novaia Ladoga, 93
Novgorod, 110
Novikov, N.I. (publisher), 137
Novitskaia, Anastasia (dancer), 129
Nye, Joseph (shipbuilder), 53, 58, 65

Odoevskii, Aleksandr (Decembrist), 172, 179
Ogborn, Miles (historian), 15
Oksman, Iu (critic), 130
Olonets, 93, 106
Oranienbaum, 44, 45
Oranienburg, 106
Orlov, Count Volodimer, 93
Orlova-Savina, Praskov'ia (actress), 125
Osipova, Anna (dancer), 129
Osterman, A.I. (chancellor), 33, 58, 59
Ovoshnikova, Avdot'ia (dancer), 126

Palace Embankment, 51, 58, 151, 159
palaces, 55
  Marble, 159
  Menshikov, 43
  Summer, 43, 143, 151, 157
  Winter, 51, 73, 76, 96, 159, 166, 169, 171

Palmyra, 3
Paris, 150, 151, 154, 160
Paterssen, Benjamin (artist), 62
Paul I, 62, 64, 140, 141
Pestel', Pavel (Decembrist), 172, 173, 175, 185
Peter I, 1, 4, 6, 8, 9, 11, 12, 14–16, 19, 39, 40, 51, 52, 53, 54, 55, 56, 58, 69, 71, 73, 88, 139, 151, 152, 153, 155
  in France, 17, 36–7
  and mapmaking, 18–25, 30
  and his reforms in St Petersburg, 8–14
  sites in city connected with, 148, 155, 157–9, 160
Peterhof, 44, 45, 160
Peter-Paul Fortress, 5, 11, 36, 39, 43, 44, 51, 157–8, 159
  and Decembrists, 165–86
Petrozavodsk, 106
Pikart, Pieter (engraver), 11
Plavil'shchikov, P.A. (dramatist), 120
Podushkin, E.M. (soldier), 170
Podzhio, Iosif (Decembrist), 169
Police Statute, 100, 103, 108, 112
police, 9–10, 83, 104, 112–13
Poltava, victory at, 11
population, 99
Porter, William (merchant), 66
Postnikov, A.V. (geographer), 21
Potapov, U.S. (administrator), 107
Potemkin, P.S. (author), 135
Prokopovich, Feofan (cleric), 158
property ownership, 82–3, 85–97
prostitution, 127, 133–6, 138–42
Pushchin, Mikhail (Decembrist), 170, 173, 178, 179
Pushkin, Alexander, 1, 3, 4, 50, 51, 64, 121, 124, 125, 126, 130, 132, 138, 149, 155, 174
Pylaev, Aleksei (author), 153

Quarenghi, Giacomo (architect), 2, 64, 75–6

Raikes, Timothy (merchant), 65
Rastrelli, Bartolomeo (architect), 73
rivers
  Fontanka, 43
  Moika, 51, 52, 87, 96
  Neva, 1, 3, 14, 30, 39, 43, 44, 50, 51, 55, 56, 58, 59, 62, 67, 77, 87, 96, 151, 159, 165
Rogerson, Dr John, 66
Rome, 71, 74, 78, 154
Rondeau, Claudius (diplomat), 66
ropewalk, 52, 54, 55,
Rossi, Carlo (architect), 50, 64
Rousseau, Jean-Jacques, 120, 121
Rozen, Andrei (Decembrist), 168, 173, 174, 175, 176, 178, 179, 180, 181, 182
Rumiantsev, N.P., 64–5
Rusca, L. (architect), 72
Ryleev, Kondratii (Decembrist), 172, 179, 180, 185
Ryleev, N.I. (police chief), 107

Saltykov, V.F., 64
Sanders, Henry (merchant), 66
Sandunova, Elizaveta (actress), 121, 123
Scott, Sir Walter (novelist), 174
seas
  Azov, 16, 30
  Baltic, 30 , 33, 34, 44
  Black, 16
  Caspian, 16, 19
  White, 33
secret societies, 165
Semenov, Stepan (Decembrist), 175
Semenova, Ekaterina (actress), 123, 124, 132
Semenova, Nimfidora (dancer), 132
Senate, 16, 20
serfs, 93–4
settlements (*slobody*), 51
  Tartar, 43
Shakhovskoi, A.A. (dramatist), 120, 123, 124, 126, 130, 131, 133
Shalikov, P.I. (author), 121

Shcherbatov, Prince M.M., 152
Sheremetev, Vasilii (guards officer), 126, 136
Shkarovskii, M.V. (historian), 140
Shlissel'burg, 101
Shnevenets (officer), 52
Siberia, 17, 18, 21, 24, 115, 165, 170, 186
Siniavin, Dmitrii (sailor), 149
slaughterhouse, 43
squares:
  Decembrists' (also Isaakievskaia, Petrovskaia, Senatskaia), 50, 165, 166;
  Work (Truda), 51, 68
St Alexander Nevskii, 14
St Andrew, 14
St Petersburg News, 65, 106
Starov, Ivan (architect), 62
Statute of Provincial Administration, 100, 103–4, 108
Stock Exchange, 159
Stolpianskii, P.N. (historian), 52
Storch, Heinrich (author), 67
streets, 10, 51
  Galley (Galernaia), 53, 54, 58, 62, 64, 67
  Gorokhovaia, 48
  Millionnaia, 58, 97
  Zamiatin pereulok (also Grafskii, Leonova), 58, 66
Strelka, 2, 36
Strel'na, 44, 128, 160, 164
Sukin, Aleksandr (soldier), 170, 171, 173, 175
Sumarokov, A.P. (author), 78
Summer Garden, 51, 151, 159
Sutherland, Richard (merchant), 66
Suvorov, Fieldmarshal A.V., 149
Svin'in, Pavel (author), 4–5, 148–62
Svistunov, Petr (Decembrist), 175

Tambov, 109, 110
Tatishchev, A.I. (Investigating Committee for Decembrists), 182
Tatishchev, V.N. (historian), 24

Telesheva, Ekaterina (dancer), 129, 130, 132, 141
Thomon, Thomas de (architect), 64
Thornton, Godfrey (merchant), 66
'three prongs', 58
Tiufiakin, P.I. (theatre official), 129
Tooke, Rev. William, 67
Torson, Konstantin (Decembrist), 170
Tret'iakov, Pavel (collector), 162
Trezzini, Domenico (architect), 35–6, 37, 39, 40, 41, 47, 53, 72, 157, 166
Tropinin, Vasilii (artist), 149
Trubetskoi, Sergei (Decembrist), 170, 172, 179, 185
Truscott, John (cartographer), 59
Tsebrikov, Nikolai (Decembrist), 176, 177
Tulchin, 169

Uspenskii, B., 71
Ustinov, Vasilei (merchant), 83

Val'berkh, Ivan (ballet-master), 127
Val'berkhova, Mariia (actress), 123, 127
Val'berkhova, Sof'ia (dancer), 127
Vallin de la Mothe, J.B.M. (architect), 52
Van Zigheim plan (1737), 59
Vasil'ev, Iakov (engraver), 59
Vasil'evskii Island, 8, 36, 39, 41, 43, 44, 50, 62, 90, 151
venereal disease, 139–40
Venetsianov, Aleksei (artist), 162
Venice, 3, 71, 73, 77, 78, 154
Venuti, Giambattista (diplomat), 72
Versailles, 160
Verstovskii, A.N. (theatre official), 135
Viazemskii, P.A. (poet), 130
Vigel', F.F. (memoirist), 120, 130, 133
Vigor, William (merchant), 66
Vol'f, A.I. (diarist), 131
Vologda, 106
Voltaire, 72

Voronikhin, A. (architect), 64
Vorontsov, A.R., 110
Vsevolozhskii, Nikita, 124, 125
Vul'f, A.N. (memoirist), 137
Vyborg Side, 89, 90

Warre, Thomas (merchant), 65
Weber, F.C. (diplomat), 3, 41–2, 54
Wilmot, Martha, 114
Wolff, Jacob (merchant/diplomat), 59, 66
women, position of, 9, 82, 89–90, 94–5, 138–40
Wortman, Richard (historian), 161
Wylie, Dr James, 68

Zakharov, Andreian (architect), 2
Zaikin, Nikolai (Decembrist), 175
Zavalishin, Dmitrii (Decembrist), 172, 174, 176, 177, 180, 182
Zhikharev, S.P. (memoirist), 123
Zhukovskii, Vasilii (poet), 130, 175
Zotov, R.M. (official), 121, 123, 129, 131
Zubkov, Vasilii (Decembrist), 170, 171, 174, 176, 177, 179, 181
Zubov, Aleksei (engraver), 11
Zubov, Count A.N., 185
Zubova, Vera (dancer), 130